THE MIDDLE AGES AND THE MOVIES

THE
MIDDLE AGES
AND THE
MOVIES

EIGHT KEY FILMS

ROBERT BARTLETT

REAKTION BOOKS LTD

To my students at the universities of Edinburgh (1980–86),
Chicago (1986–92) and St Andrews (1992–2016)

Published by Reaktion Books Ltd
Unit 32, Waterside
44–48 Wharf Road
London N1 7UX, UK
www.reaktionbooks.co.uk

First published 2022
Copyright © Robert Bartlett 2022

Printed and bound in Great Britain by
TJ Books Ltd, Padstow, Cornwall

A catalogue record for this book is available from the British Library

ISBN 978 1 78914 552 6

CONTENTS

MEDIEVAL HISTORY ON THE SCREEN

Where do we get our picture of the historical past? For many centuries, any detailed knowledge came from reading, or, in an oral world, listening. And what was read or listened to might, by a modern historian, be classified as either fact or fiction, tricky as that distinction is. Still today, words, printed or online, build up an image of the past for us, whether in the specialized form of the history book, or in historical novels, some of which are read (or at least bought) by hundreds of thousands of people, even, in rare cases like *The Name of the Rose*, by millions. So the experience of the page (including the online page), conveying information and imagery both factual and fictional, has been and continues to be a major channel for our picture of the past. Since the 1890s, however, there has been a radically different way of building up images of the past and forming ideas about it: the screen and the moving images it displays. The cinema audience, engaged in a group experience, unlike the more private act of reading, was presented with historical documentaries and historical dramas almost as soon as moving pictures were invented – there were even Joan of Arc films before 1900, for example. The stream of historical film then widened into one of the main subgenres of the motion pictures. A medium so greedy for storylines turned to actual history, and to modern invented stories set in the past, and to stories based on the literature of the past, for its plots and settings.

Leaving aside the many films, especially war films, set in the fairly recent past, popular subjects of historical film have been the ancient world and the so-called early modern period of the sixteenth and seventeenth centuries. Films set in the days of the Roman Empire became so recognizable that they earned their own label, 'sword and sandal films', and could be parodied, as in the Coen brothers' *Hail, Caesar!* of 2016, without further explanation, while the Tudors, particularly Henry VIII (r. 1509–47) and Elizabeth I (r. 1558–1603), have had many screen lives. Films about the Middle Ages, the subject of this book, are less common but still number in the hundreds. And, like other historical films, they are involved in a vigorous interplay between written sources and visual realization, and between fictional and factual stories and scenes. The historical novel *Ivanhoe*, a best-seller by Walter Scott published in 1819 that spawned numerous stage adaptations including nine operas – the first such production, in 1826, with music based on Rossini – offered prime source material for the cinema. A film version of 1952 has Robert Taylor, who starred as Lancelot in *Knights of the Round Table* the following year, as Ivanhoe, while the young Elizabeth Taylor plays the beautiful Rebecca, the Jewish woman who helps him. Later in the same decade, a 39-episode television adaptation of *Ivanhoe* aired, starring in the lead role Roger Moore, who went on to be cast as James Bond, a role he played in seven films in the 1970s and '80s. Such a transition from Romantic novel to opera to film and television has a natural logic, each incarnation with a similar menu of pageantry, exotic costume, violence, swift plot turns and love interest. In some ways, indeed, opera foreshadowed cinema as the great art form of spectacle.

Just as there is a constant to-and-fro between screen and page, so there is between fact and fiction. Historical fact is continually being turned into historical fiction, either in novels or in films. A very successful example is Hilary Mantel's novel *Wolf Hall*, based on the life of the Tudor politician and official Thomas Cromwell and published in 2009, which won the Man Booker Prize, and was adapted for stage and television. The historian Miles Taylor even coined the verb 'to Wolf-Hall', meaning to create historical fiction from factual history, in a 2016 review of a book by Ferdinand Mount featured in *London Review of Books*: 'Mount has written some historical fiction . . . he has Wolf-Halled his way around the French Revolution and the Crimean War.' Hilary Mantel fictionalizes, then the screen adapts her fictionalization, so there is a complex process of multiple adaptation here. The historical novelist reads deeply (we hope!) in the factual literature about a historical person or period and decides how that can be used in a work of imaginative literature, before the screenwriters, directors and actors transform that work into something that can be effective on stage or screen. And it is in the nature of things that the image of the past conveyed in a successful film will have a far wider public than that depicted in any history book or most historical novels.

This book looks in detail at eight films with a medieval setting, chosen from different decades of the twentieth century and from various countries. They exhibit differences of genre, of ideology, of the political and economic system in which they were produced, and these will be discussed, but they all have in common the attempt to represent the medieval world in that entirely modern medium, the motion picture. That medium has certain distinctive features. While one could reasonably say that both historical writing and historical film have a 'point of view' which can be analysed, it is a phrase that can have different senses, for in film the meaning can be literal, in that we see only what the camera sees. A camera has to be pointed at something and someone has to make the decision about where to point it. And, usually, the camera shows one thing at a time. There are ways of showing more than one thing, such as the split screen or the fade, in which one image emerges as another disappears, but these are occasional devices, not the standard. There are two immediate consequences of this that make the screen different from the page.

People and places on the screen have to have a definite appearance, since there is a camera 'looking' at them. Actors will have a certain hair colour, have a beard or not, be a certain age. Such concreteness is not necessary in a book, where authors are free to give as much or as little visual description as they wish, and where readers can flesh out the characters and locations from their own imagination. And, in historical films, the decisions of the film-makers about the visual world that they are depicting can be controversial. Such films are often classified as 'costume dramas', a term that points to their most immediate visual impact – people then wore different clothes to those we wear today. Some film-makers take great care getting the costume right for the period and some are much more casual about it, just as some viewers are driven to distraction by mistakes in clothing (perhaps especially in military or naval uniform) while others are content with a generalized sense of past dress. Historical accuracy of this type is a topic that will be discussed in the chapter on *Braveheart*.

The second consequence, and an important corollary of the definiteness of the film medium, is that, where a book can use abstractions, even a complex one such as 'feudalism', the camera cannot be pointed at 'feudalism'. If film-makers wish to convey such a thing, they must do so by synecdoche or metonymy, using parts for the whole or associated images for the thing itself: knights, castles, serfs, homage or whatever else they decide might work as an instant evocation. These visual constraints (or possibilities) apply in a special way to films that are set in the past, where the assumptions of the distant society are likely to be alien and need to be conveyed somehow by concrete visual imagery. The alternative, to have a character in the film articulating such assumptions, is usually crass, although occasionally droll, as in the scene in *The Lion in Winter* (1968) where Eleanor of Aquitaine (Katharine Hepburn), reacting to the panicked cry of her son John exclaiming that his older brother, Richard the Lionheart, has a knife, responds:

> Of course he has a knife. He always has a knife. We all have knives. It's 1183 and we're barbarians. How clear we make it. Oh, my piglets, we are the origins of war – not history's forces, nor the times, nor justice, nor the lack of it, nor causes, nor religions, nor ideas, nor kinds of government, nor any other thing.

It is a memorable scene but takes us immediately out of the twelfth-century world. John Wayne expressed a profound insight when, describing his breakthrough film *Stagecoach*, he said: 'The story was told with the camera rather than by the mouthing of the leading men.' It would be impolite to describe Katharine Hepburn's words here as 'mouthing' but the story at this point is certainly not being 'told with the camera' (*The Lion in Winter* began life as a stage play).

If dealing with abstraction is a different matter in book and film, the same is true of the interiority of the characters. Authors can use the written word to describe what is going on 'inside the head' of the characters they write about. If they are writing a historical novel, rather than a history book, they can even venture to use the first-person voice – 'I, Claudius'. In a film, since the characters are observed, their inner state has to be conveyed either by what they say, or by facial expression, stance and so on ('acting'), and the first option always risks the danger of over-explicitness, woodenness and implausibility, and the second can be ambiguous – there are indeed often debates among viewers and fans about what a character's action 'means'. This also complicates the question of any identification with the characters. Since we could say that the camera *chooses* where to look for us, are we, the viewers, that observing eye or are we the object viewed? This affects whom we identify with. Logic demands that we are the camera, since, as viewers of the film, we see and therefore cannot be what we see. But logic is not everything; we can identify with figures on the screen and then we, the viewing audience, are identifying with someone we see, the object of our gaze.

But, if abstraction and interiority are two things it is harder to do in film than with the written word, there are things film can do more effectively, since it can *show*, while the written word has to *tell*. The impression of a film image on the eye is instantaneous, and hence perception of an object or a scene in front of the camera takes less than a second, where a book might need a paragraph of written description. This difference is especially pronounced in the case of action scenes. In fact, writers have been known to describe a scene of fast action and then write, 'all this happened faster than it takes to tell', a recognition of an unavoidable limitation of word and page. Some films are labelled 'action films' but they are all in fact action films: 'action!' the director calls, to make the transition from the real world of crew, lighting, set, worries about lunch breaks, to the world of the film – it may be the Wild West, the mean streets of the noir metropolis, the greenwood of Sherwood Forest, where horses gallop, guns fire and outlaws guffaw, but equally 'action' can be love, doubt, belief, if ways can be found to show them on the screen, instantaneously before our eyes.

Both the author writing a historical novel and the screenwriter of a historical film have one great decision to make before all else: how are their characters to speak? Will their speech be archaic, sprinkled with 'thee' and 'thou' and 'gadzooks!', or will it be simply modern colloquial language, or is there some middle neutral ground between these extremes? The book or film has to be comprehensible to a modern audience, so speech cannot be 'too authentic', that is, actually what was spoken at the time (though there have been rare attempts at this, as in Mel Gibson's *The Passion of the Christ* of 2004), but words and phrases that sound too contemporary will be jarring, unless used consciously for comical anachronism. There is a balance to be struck, as in all considerations of the past, between bringing out its genuine difference from the present – 'the past is a foreign country' – and trying to make the people of that time comprehensible, perhaps admirable, at least human, like us. And they, of course, did not know that they were living in the past. If the first thing that strikes us about the world of a book or a film is its 'pastness', then we are already looking at the inhabitants of that past world as if in a display cabinet. This is where archaic language, especially of a stereotyped kind, can lead to the danger of gadzook-sism, of being charmed by the pastness of the past, forgetting the advice of the great medievalist F. W. Maitland, who wrote, 'we should always be aware that what now lies in the past once lay in the future.'

Walter Scott (1771–1832), pioneer of the historical novel, was well aware of these issues and in the Dedicatory Epistle prefaced to *Ivanhoe* he discusses them in some detail. He talks explicitly about the question of the language to be employed:

> He who would imitate an ancient language with success, must attend rather to its grammatical character, turn of expression, and mode of arrangement, than labour to collect extraordinary and antiquated terms . . . His language must not be exclusively obsolete and unintelligible; but he should admit, if possible, no word or turn of phraseology betraying an origin directly modern.

This is counselling a middle ground and drawing particular attention to the undesirability of relying on 'antiquated terms'. Scott also considers other aspects of accuracy and realism, such as the difficulty of actually finding out about 'all those minute circumstances belonging to private life and domestic character, all that gives verisimilitude to a narrative, and individuality to the persons introduced' in the past, and concedes that he cannot attain 'complete accuracy, even in matters of outward costume, much less in the more important points of language and manners'. Yet, he says, it is justifiable to explain 'ancient manners in modern language' as long as the writer introduces 'nothing inconsistent with the manners of the age'. And human beings of all historical epochs have things in common:

> The passions . . . are generally the same in all ranks and conditions, all countries and ages; and it follows, as a matter of course, that the opinions, habits of thinking, and actions,

however influenced by the peculiar state of society, must still, upon the whole, bear a strong resemblance to each other.

Scott's position on the universality of human passions and habits of thinking is far from being universal. Historians of the influential *Annales* school developed the concept of *mentalité*, that is, the thought-world, of the past, with the implication that it was different from the thought-world of the present. Many medievalists today stress the alterity, the otherness of the past. Historical novelists and screenwriters of historical films who set their stories in the Middle Ages do not usually make explicit statements about the subject but their practice reveals their assumptions: do they assume that the medieval world they are depicting was essentially 'other', either in good ways (romantic, chivalrous . . .) or in bad ways (poor, persecuting, repressive . . .), or do they think it was basically like our world (which is also, of course, romantic, chivalrous, poor, persecuting, repressive . . .)?

Alongside these questions of what is displayed on the screen and how, historical films are also shaped, like all films, by the nature of cinema itself, for it is subject to two things more than any other art form: technical changes (often called 'developments') and money. The films discussed here were products of the twentieth century, when cinema was moving rapidly from silent to sound, from black-and-white to colour, from features lasting only minutes to films two hours long or more (sometimes much more). The development of more mobile cameras and later the use of video instead of, or as well as, film, created a faster, less studio-based style, while in the last decades of the century there was the enormous growth in increasingly sophisticated computer-generated images (CGI), including computer animation. Disney's feature-length *The Hunchback of*

Notre Dame of 1996 gave the computer animation treatment to a medieval topic, with a plot based on Victor Hugo's *Notre-Dame de Paris*, a novel which appeared in 1831 and which had already been filmed many times with live actors. In this way fifteenth-century France, as imagined by a Romantic writer of the nineteenth century, was given an incarnation in one of the most complex technologies of the late twentieth-century American film industry. The films discussed in this book varied very much in the technology that produced them. They all had in common, however, the fact that they *were* cinema: the public big screen, the shared experience, the need to know when the show started. Even when television became part of everyday life, from the 1950s, the big screen was still the first home of the feature film. Of course, this gradually changed with the development of domestic videocassette players and recorders from the 1970s onwards, and subsequently other forms of privatization of the viewing experience, but for most of the century 'a night at the movies', 'going to the pictures', was one of the most common collective entertainment experiences.

Partly because it is technologically complex, cinema is expensive, probably the most expensive art form there is. It requires sophisticated technical equipment, specialists with knowledge of filming, recording and processing, actors, writers, sets and costumes, and, of course, the machinery of advertising and distribution. A film cannot even be undertaken until funding is secured. Large numbers of people have to be paid their wages and fed; during filming on location they have to be found accommodation; studios may have to be secured. The first film to cost more than $1 million was Erich von Stroheim's *Foolish Wives* (1922). By the 1990s there were films costing more than $100 million. Even cheap films are not cheap in the usually accepted meaning of the word. Consequently, unlike painting, writing or composing, film-making cannot be done alone in a room with a brush or pen. It is a group effort. So, despite the erstwhile fashion of describing the director as an *auteur*, the 'author' of a film, it is not at all clear who is the author of a film. Its effects come from a combination of directorial decisions, choices in photography, scriptwriting, acting, music, financial limitations and possibilities, and so on. Analysis of a film will therefore differ from analysis of a book or painting, where one can usually assume the work of one mind and one personality.

Moreover, there is another difference that results from the production process behind film-making. Invariably, there will be many takes of the same scene and the director and editor will then have to make a choice of which one to include in the film to be released. Moreover, they may decide to jettison whole sequences of the film, as long as this can be done without incoherence. There is always plenty of leeway in editing, since during filming many hours of film are shot for every hour that is in the final cut. The ratio of film shot to film included in the version for release was around 10:1 in Hollywood films of the mid-twentieth century, although it is now far higher, with the advent of digital media and decline in the use of physical film. This means that, unless the material has been discarded or deleted, there are hours and hours of unused footage that can be reintegrated into the film if there is sufficient incentive for producing a new cut. A powerful director can be one such incentive – hence 'the director's cut'. As a result, there may well circulate more than one version of a film, of varying length and content, none of them more authentic or original than the others. The same is true of early films that have to be reconstructed from partial and diverse sources.

A film is made in the editing, in a much stronger sense than is true of writing. Writers indeed know the pain and pleasure of editing too, but it is rare that they will have a body of discarded material nine times the length of the final published book. Hence, although there can be different versions of a book, especially if the author is given to revision, the existence of variant versions is more characteristic of film. Francis Ford Coppola's *Apocalypse Now* is a well-known (or notorious) example, with an original general release in 1979 at 146 minutes in length, a new release in 2001 (*Apocalypse Now Redux*) with 49 minutes added from material that had not been included in the 1979 version and a version in 2019, the so-called *Final Cut*, at 183 minutes, hence longer than the original and shorter than the *Redux*. Of the films discussed in this book, several show the difficulty of talking of an 'original' or 'authentic' version: *Andrei Rublev* exists in several versions of different length, the two most important being the 205 minute and the 185 minute; *Alexander Nevsky* supposedly reached its present state because a reel of film was overlooked at a crucial moment and *Die Nibelungen I: Siegfried* was reportedly still being edited on the day of its premiere in 1924 and in subsequent years was released in several different forms.

Cinema was a new technology but also – that rarest of things – a new art form. And even new art forms usually continue to bear traces of the old ones (just as some early printed books were designed to resemble manuscripts). Early cinema looked naturally both to theatre and to photography, an ancient and a recent precursor, but sought to free itself from the enclosed scenario of the former and the static nature of the second. Indeed, film critics often have an unfavourable view of films that mimic too closely their theatrical models ('filmed theatre') or are too focused on static composition. Early films do often look like filmed stage plays, but the potential for outdoor action was soon embraced, along with the emphasis of the 'motion' in 'motion pictures'. While most films continued to rely on narrative for their basic structure, the concept of narrative in cinema could be different from that in other art forms, since it relied on its own distinctive language, the juxtaposition of moving images.

The general considerations discussed in this Preface apply to all the films examined in this book. Each film, however, was the product of individual circumstances, meaning both what happened in the production process and the political and social environment of the film-makers' world. The following chapters attempt to describe and analyse that process and those environments.

Wallace and the princess, who have a (historically impossible) sexual relationship.

I

SEX AND NATIONALISM
Braveheart
(1995)

Films can use the medieval world in several ways. Some take medieval legends, such as stories about King Arthur or Siegfried, as their plots. Others have a medieval setting for purely fictional plots created by modern screenwriters. But let us look at a film that is based on dateable historical events and named historical characters, *Braveheart*, an Academy Award winner released in 1995 about William Wallace, leader of the Scottish resistance to English aggression in the late thirteenth century. The opening sequence tells us when and where we are in the most direct way possible, by a caption on the screen and by a voiceover, the caption reading simply 'Scotland: 1280 AD', the voice telling us 'I shall tell you of William Wallace . . . the king of Scotland had died without a son, and the king of England, a cruel pagan known as Edward the Longshanks, claimed the throne of Scotland for himself.' Elements like these, the caption and voiceover, that the cinema audience sees and hears but the characters in the film obviously do not, are referred to by film scholars as non-diegetic, as distinct from the diegetic imagined world of the story, that is, the scenery the characters move in, the dialogue they speak and hear, and so forth. Music can be either diegetic or non-diegetic, depending on whether it has a source in the imagined world of the film or simply emerges from somewhere as background. Such strongly non-diegetic indicators as the caption and voiceover at the opening of *Braveheart* suggest that the audience needs to be told very clearly when and where we are. A film starting with swastikas and goose-stepping German soldiers does not require any further signposting. Presumably someone thought the story of William Wallace might not be so well known to a world audience, especially to the most profitable, the American.

The choice of the date '1280 AD' on the caption has been commented upon by several historians. In historical reality, the king of Scotland did indeed die without a son – but in 1286. Edward I of England did indeed conquer Scotland – but in 1296. Telescoping the complex events of 1286–96 into a sentence or two is completely understandable, but choosing an inaccurate date at random less so. One consideration may have been that the opening scene of the film shows William Wallace as a young boy, encountering his first example of an English atrocity. Since William has to grow up before the main action starts, perhaps there is simply a rough calculation of his age as a boy from his known death date of 1305, though this suggests greater respect for chronology than is shown anywhere else in the film. The assumption must be of a deep ignorance of the period among the audience. Imagine a film about the First World War that started with a caption 'Europe: 1908 AD' and a voiceover describing the assassination of Archduke Franz Ferdinand. This inaccuracy would not have made it to the screen.

Braveheart is a perfect film through which to address the question of historical accuracy and whether it matters in films about the past. One could distinguish three types of accuracy:

Accuracy regarding everyday objects, such as clothes, armour or buildings.

Accuracy about historical events and personages.

Accuracy about motives, beliefs and general outlook.

For the first, it is clear that certain stereotypes about Scotland had a powerful influence on the physical world of the film, especially the equation of Scotland with the highlands, that is, the mountainous and less populous part of the country in the north and west. Scotland is and was a country made up of different component parts, with different languages, cultures and landscapes. In the early Middle Ages at least four languages were spoken in the area of modern Scotland (Gaelic, English, Norse and Brittonic, with Pictish being either a fifth language or a version of Brittonic) and the present political boundaries of Scotland were not established until the second half of the fifteenth century, with the acquisition of Orkney and Shetland and the final loss of Berwick.

A sharp distinction between the Scottish highlands and lowlands was recognized in the Middle Ages, with lowlanders regarding the highlanders as 'wild, untamed and primitive', and this opposition between wild highlanders and civilized lowlanders came to a head in the eighteenth century when support for the exiled Stuart dynasty in the highlands was crushed by the British state after the Battle of Culloden in 1746. Dr Johnson, touring the area less than thirty years later, was quite explicit about what had happened – 'the final conquest of the highlands' – but he was also curious about things that came to be seen as the typical romantic characteristics of the highlands: kilts, bagpipes, the Gaelic language, the martial traditions, even mementoes of the earlier rebellions. Within a few generations this picture of the highlands had become entrenched and had begun to be identified with Scotland as a whole, with the basic choreography provided by Walter Scott, not only in his historical novels such as

Waverley, which is set during the rising of 1745–6, but through his planning of the visit of George IV to Scotland in 1822, when the king wore a tartan kilt, clothing that had been prohibited by law after the rising. National dress was being invented throughout Europe in the nineteenth century, and the championing of highland dress by the lowlander Scott was one of the most successful examples.

There is some debate about where William Wallace was born and grew up. Traditionally he was associated with Elderslie near Paisley (not far from Glasgow) but more recent evidence would suggest he came from a landed family in Ayrshire in the southwest of Scotland. In neither case was he a highlander, and the presentation in *Braveheart* of Wallace's family, who are clothed in tartan and live in thatched huts with a spectacular mountain backdrop, is clearly drawn from the stock tradition of Highlandism rather than any concern for historical accuracy. One French film critic described Wallace as 'coming from a family of poor peasants', which illustrates the impact his portrayal in the film could have when divorced from any other knowledge of historical context. A similar point could be made about the depiction of the Scots nobles. In the later thirteenth century, the Scottish aristocracy would look rather like the English aristocracy, indeed might be the same people. However, we first encounter them, very early in the film, as a slightly bedraggled, plaid-wearing cavalcade. They seem to have no armour and have obviously not combed their hair. This image is consistent throughout the film and serves both to distinguish the Scots from the English and to underline the fact that they are underdogs. It has a visual rationale but no historical justification.

Such Highlandism was, and is, not uncommon in popular representations of Scottish history. In *This Land of Kings*, a history of the medieval kings of England for children, published in 1954

Young William Wallace in front of his Highland croft, suggesting a poor peasant background.

by the successful London publisher Ward, Lock & Co., written by Ida Foulis and illustrated with full-page colour plates by the twin sisters Janet and Anne Grahame Johnstone, there is a picture of the famous single combat between the Scottish king, Robert Bruce, and the English knight Henry de Bohun before the Battle of Bannockburn in 1314. This is described in contemporary sources. Bruce, mounted on 'a little palfrey', that is, an ordinary riding horse not a great warhorse, with an axe in his hand and a crown on his helmet, was organizing his troops when Bohun, well armoured and bearing a lance, saw a chance to capture the king and rode down on him, whereupon Bruce stood up in his stirrups and brought the axe down on Bohun's head, splitting his skull in half. 'This was the first stroke of the fight,' says the medieval Scottish author describing this dramatic event. Ida Foulis's text gives an account of the incident with all these details but the Grahame Johnstone twins seem not to have read it. Their depiction has Bohun in full armour, with a shield bearing the Bohun coat of arms and wielding an improbably long sword, while Bruce is on a dapple-grey pony and wielding an axe, as described, but riding bareback, without the stirrups that are crucial to the story and, tellingly, wearing a long tartan plaid that swirls behind him as he raises his axe. The illustrators of this popular history book for children had no need of original sources to tell them what 'Scottish' meant; they had pictorial assumptions just as strong as the film-makers of *Braveheart*.

If we turn from accuracy about everyday objects to accuracy about historical events and personages, there are two particularly notable divergences from history in the film: the Battle of Stirling Bridge, Wallace's great victory over the English in 1297, has no bridge and William Wallace not only meets but impregnates Isabelle of France, wife of Edward, the son of Edward I. The Battle of Stirling Bridge was determined by the terrain. The English, under the command of Earl Warenne, were on one side of the River Forth, the far smaller Scottish force on the other, between them a narrow bridge. Wallace's tactics were to let a fair number of English troops cross the bridge, then charge down upon them and massacre them, while the larger portion of the English army could only watch this slaughter from the other side of the river. The victory thus depended on the bridge. This was obvious to those who fought that day:

> the earl therefore commanded that they should go up onto the bridge and cross over. It is astonishing to say, and terrible in its outcome, that so many and such discreet men, knowing the enemy to be at hand, went up onto the narrow bridge, which two horsemen could scarcely cross at the same time with difficulty. Some who were in that battle said that, if they had crossed from early morning to the eleventh hour without interruption or impediment, still the rear part of the army

would have largely remained behind. There was no better spot in the kingdom of Scotland to entrap the English in the hands of the Scots and many in the hands of a few.

Explanations of the absence of the bridge from the film vary, but Mel Gibson was clearly happy to stage the battle as a face-to-face confrontation between two forces, one with heavy cavalry, the other consisting mainly of lightly equipped infantry. While it is improbable that the idea of long spears was an inspired conception of William Wallace, as the film suggests, it is true that Stirling Bridge fits well into a series of battles around this time (Courtrai, 1302; Bannockburn, 1314; Morgarten, 1315) in which mounted knights were defeated by commoners on foot. It thus represents a general reality if not the particular circumstances of the encounter. As the film's scriptwriter, Randall Wallace, said, 'you shouldn't let the facts get in the way of the truth.'

This decision allowed Gibson to concentrate on filming a generic medieval battle, following film conventions, without any historical

The Battle of Stirling Bridge, without the bridge.

specificity. As the two sides confront each other, the camera clearly places us on the Scottish side: we pan along their line, we hear what the ordinary Scots soldiers are saying, we look out with them at the massing ranks of English, who are in various types of uniform, unlike the raggle-taggle Scots (many of the English are in red, which would awake in American hearts a vague memory of the redcoats who fought Washington, but is also accurate for Edward I's armies). There is time for Wallace's rousing pre-battle speech, some of it borrowed from that of Shakespeare's Henry V before the Battle of Agincourt. There is no purely computer-generated footage, and the armies were made to look large by carefully chosen camera angles and the use of extras, who were provided by the Irish army, as Scots one day and English the next, with some doubling up of images through technology. There is only one non-naturalistic technique employed, which is slow motion, a device often used when extreme violence is depicted or about to be (Sam Peckinpah made famous use of it in westerns). In *Braveheart*, it is used when showing the English cavalry charge, to give it dramatic suspense. Some of the shots are head on, so we see what the Scots see. Shortly before the English crash into the Scottish lines, the speed returns to normal. It is all very powerful and effective – but there is no bridge.

A far bolder and more shameless manipulation of events than the loss of the bridge is the relationship between Wallace and the French princess Isabelle. Wallace was captured and executed in London in 1305 when Isabelle was only nine years old. She did not marry Edward, son of Edward I, until the year after he became king in 1307, and first came to England after that (their wedding took place in France). The events depicted in the film are therefore completely impossible. Leaving the bridge out of Stirling Bridge is minor stuff in comparison. But presumably there are reasons behind such

Mel Gibson as William Wallace, complete with warpaint.

a divergence from history. It cannot be unmotivated. And it appears that the plot line in this case is closely tied to questions of sexual identity. Wallace is male, masculine, virile and heterosexual; Isabelle is female, feminine, womanly and heterosexual. Early on in the film,

Sophie Marceau as the French princess, wife of King Edward's son.

we have seen Prince Edward's distaste for his new bride and the looks he exchanges with the figure we assume is his male lover (called Philip in the film and inspired by the historical character Piers Gaveston). The voiceover tells us, 'It was widely whispered that, for the princess to conceive, Longshanks would have to do the honours himself.' In fact, Edward I did marry, as his second wife, a twenty-year-old French princess, a relative of Isabelle's, when he himself was sixty, and had three children by her. So, though this may not have been known to the film-makers, his reputation for procreative ability into later life was justified. The portrayal of Prince Edward's homosexuality in *Braveheart* led to understandable protests from gay activists. The film depicts him as a preening effeminate, terrified of his father and cold and unkind to his wife. It is remarkable that this insulting and hackneyed characterization could feature in a major film four years after Derek Jarman's *Edward II* of 1991. Jarman, a gay rights activist, took the play *Edward II* by Christopher Marlowe, a contemporary of Shakespeare, and drastically reshaped it into a radical film, crammed full of even more anachronisms than *Braveheart* and overtly relishing physical sexuality between men. By the time that Jarman's and Gibson's films were made, Edward II's homosexuality had long been established in the popular historical understanding as a given fact. The roots of the idea went back to Edward's lifetime but only in the comments of one of his enemies after the king had been driven from power. It is certainly the case that Edward had a taste for charming young men: Piers Gaveston until he was killed by the king's enemies, later Hugh Despenser. There is no evidence, however, that these relationships were sexual, and great likelihood that they were not, although there is plenty of evidence that they were resented by the aristocracy and by Edward's queen, Isabelle.

Figures like Gaveston and Hugh Despenser appear in the history books with the label 'favourites'. It is a semi-technical term and makes sense only in the world of monarchs and courts, where the 'favour' shown by the ruler determined so much of the distribution of power and wealth. The established nobility and the ruler's family expected that a lot of that favour would shine on them, and if someone from outside that circle became a close companion of the sovereign and received the prestige and the material rewards that flowed from that position, there would be resentment. In fact, the *Oxford English Dictionary* defines 'favourite' as 'one who stands unduly high in the favour of a prince', by the choice of that word 'unduly' rather taking the side of the nobility. Gaveston was resented because he was the king's most intimate friend, because he was promoted from being the younger son of a knight to the peerage – created an earl immediately on Edward II's accession – and because he was given marks of status that were seen as slights both by the barons and by the queen.

The workings of a small and claustrophobic court society explain the dynamics of intimacy and hostility very well, without positing sexual relations between Edward and Gaveston, for which there is no evidence and which would certainly have been used by Gaveston's enemies if there were. The same modern assumptions underlie the film *The Favourite* (2018), which won Olivia Colman the Academy Award for Best Actress for her role as the British Queen Anne (who ruled 1702–14). The position of the Duchess of Marlborough as a 'favourite' of the queen and her replacement by Abigail Masham, as depicted in the film, are well attested historically; their sexual relationships with the queen are not. It is a terrible failure of the historical imagination to think that intense intimacy between a ruler and a member of the same sex can only be interpreted as actively sexual.

Prince Edward's homosexuality in *Braveheart* is contrasted with the ideal of romantic heterosexual love, as experienced by Wallace and his wife Murron in the tender and passionate episodes of the long opening section of the film. It is her brutal killing that transforms Wallace from the man seeking peace and family into the avenger, killer and patriot he becomes. Romantic heterosexual love is something that Princess Isabelle pines for, and finds with Wallace, however improbable the logistics are. As a 'real man', he not only satisfies her but impregnates her, as her husband cannot, and thus wrenches the bloodline of the kings of England away from the ageing Edward I, who is informed of the fact by the princess as he lays dying. Throughout the film, conflicts between men often revolve around possession of women: the English try to rape Wallace's wife and succeed in killing her; Wallace sleeps with and impregnates the wife of the English prince; and, notoriously, Edward I grants the right of *prima nocte*, allowing English lords in Scotland to sleep with the bride of their subjects on her wedding night (a practice also termed *droit de seigneur*).

Mel Gibson himself recognized that *prima nocte* was not actually a contemporary custom and was introduced 'to be cinematically compelling'. Whether it is compelling or not, it makes the clash of English and Scots very clearly about possession of women. In one scene, after an idyllic wedding has been broken up and the wicked English lord has led away the bride, we next see her Scottish husband as one of Wallace's band of guerrilla fighters, who storm the fort commanded by the very lord who took away his bride. They confront each other. 'I never did her any harm,' says the lord. 'It was my right.' 'Your right!' says the husband, 'Well, I'm here to claim the right of a husband.' He then kills the lord. As in the case of Wallace's own wife, the struggle for national independence is here enmeshed with the fight to guard one's women from other men. The *prima nocte* of the film is generally recognized to be entirely mythical, but that does not mean it has not had a very vigorous life in fiction. It is the feudal right by which the count intends to bed Susanna in Mozart's *Marriage of Figaro* and it provides the plot for Charlton Heston's *The War Lord* (1965), which was itself based on an earlier play. *Prima nocte* derives its imaginative power from the concept of 'taking other men's women'. And this is where Wallace balances the account.

33

He may not have personally established Scottish independence and he died at the hands of his enemies, but he takes the wife of the English prince and deprives the English king of his bloodline.

The third kind of accuracy is about motives, beliefs and general outlook. Under the last, one might consider the reality of the film's depiction of medieval nationalism. Wallace wants 'what none of us have ever had – a country of our own'. If this is literally true, it is unclear what 'the king of Scotland' who 'had died without a son', introduced by the voiceover at the very beginning of the film, was ruling. Repeatedly, the film suggests that the English have been oppressing the Scots for generations: Wallace's grandfather as well as his father seems to have died fighting them; the English have inflicted 'a hundred years of theft, rape and murder', as Wallace puts it. In fact, the crisis that sprang up after the sudden death of Alexander III, king of Scots, in 1286, without a son, ended a generally peaceful period of two centuries of good Anglo-Scottish relations. Within ten years of that event a struggle had begun over the very existence of the kingdom of Scotland; for the next 250 years, warfare between the two kingdoms was to be more common than peace. Mel Columcille Gerard Gibson, who is named after two Irish saints and whose mother was Irish, may well be confusing Scotland and Ireland: the mad comic Irishman in the film, who is so enthusiastic about killing Englishmen, and the fraternization scene in the Battle of Falkirk, when Edward I's Irish troops will not fight the Scots, even perhaps the use of Irish rather than Scottish pipes in the soundtrack, might suggest this. To see Ireland as a victim of centuries of English colonial aggression is hardly controversial, but it is not a good description of relations between England and Scotland.

Be that as it may, it is still possible to ask if the rhetoric of nationalism and freedom that pervades the film is credible for the period. It is not uncommon for modern commentators to claim that nationalism had no place in the Middle Ages, but this claim is wrong and in this case the accuracy of the film is actually greater than in matters of tartans, bridges and princesses. The Declaration of Arbroath of 1320 is a letter that was sent to the pope by Scottish nobles in support of their king, Robert Bruce, outlining their case for the independence of the Scots. Some of the arguments they made were historical: 'One hundred and thirteen kings of their royal lineage have reigned in their kingdom, with no intrusion by a foreigner . . . our people lived until now in freedom and peace under their protection.' They blamed Edward 1 for shattering the peace of this happy kingdom: 'that mighty prince Edward, king of England, attacked our kingdom in hostile fashion.' Robert Bruce had freed them from this oppression and they recognized him as their king and lord. But included in the declaration is this significant reservation:

If he should give up what he has begun, seeking to subject us or our kingdom to the king of the English or the English, we would immediately strive to expel him as our enemy and a subverter of his right and ours, and we would make someone else our king, who is capable of seeing to our defence. For, as long as a hundred of us remain alive, we intend never to be subjected to the lordship of the English in any way. For it is not for glory, riches or honours that we fight, but only for freedom, which no good man loses except along with his life.

The last phrase is a neat borrowing from the ancient Roman author Sallust, but that does not mean it is not sincere. The Scots lords are fighting for freedom and will even change their king if he fails to secure that prize. Their words chime well with the answer that

Wallace reportedly gave to mediators seeking a peaceful resolution before the Battle of Stirling (Bridge): 'Report to your side that we have not come here for the sake of peace but we are prepared for war to avenge ourselves and free our kingdom. Let them come up when they wish and they will find us ready to beard them.' Wallace may not have worn tartan or slept with a French princess, but he did fight and die for the freedom of his country.

Of the three kinds of accuracy, about everyday objects, about historical events and personages, and about motives and beliefs, perhaps some types matter more to some people than others. For viewers with a knowledge of music, a discordant note was struck by the use of Irish uillean pipes (played by Eric Rigler) on the soundtrack rather than Scottish bagpipes; for others it was not an issue, or even not noticed. Historians might have been more troubled by the description of a piped lament for Wallace's father: the pipers are, in the words of Wallace's uncle, 'saying goodbye in their own way, playing outlawed tunes on outlawed pipes'. This refers to a supposed prohibition on bagpipes after the defeat of the Jacobite rising of 1745–6, a prohibition which is in fact legendary, so it combines anachronism and inaccuracy in a particularly inspired way. The non-existent bridge at Stirling, the affair with the princess and other imaginary events, such as the attack on York, all these things that do not correspond with historical reality may well annoy some, pass by unnoticed with others, or provoke the reaction, 'So what? It's a film.'

What is clear is that the tiny amount of actual factual knowledge about Wallace would not have been enough to fill a film almost three hours in length. But pure Hollywood-style invention only accounts for some of the new material. A lot of it is drawn from legends dating back hundreds of years. A crucial figure in the development of stories about Wallace is a Scottish writer known as Blind Harry, who composed, in Scots, a violently anti-English poem, about 12,000 lines in length, in the 1470s, almost two hundred years after Wallace's death. Harry's *Wallace*, which was one of the first books to be printed in Scotland and was regularly reprinted throughout the centuries, formed the basis of later tradition and was an inspiration for Randall Wallace, the screenwriter of the film. In particular, the emphasis that Blind Harry places on Wallace's desire to avenge his wife, killed by the English, and the association in his mind of this personal revenge with the redemption of his land can be seen shaping the film script. The single combat between Wallace and Robert Bruce, who is depicted fighting on the English side at Falkirk, also comes from Blind Harry's poem. Harry states too that women were fascinated by Wallace and, more specifically, that the English queen, who is sent to negotiate with him, 'loved Wallace'. Here, perhaps, is the germ of the idea of the love affair between Wallace and the French princess in the film. (The queen of England at the time of Wallace's continued resistance after the Battle of Falkirk was in fact the French princess in her twenties, the young wife of Edward I mentioned above, but it is improbable that anyone associated with the film knew that.) Other incidents that the screenwriter could find in Blind Harry, but not in the historical record, are the treacherous hanging of the Scots lords, the death of Wallace's father and brother fighting the English and the Siege of York. Blind Harry is not, however, responsible for the film's omission of the bridge at the Battle of Stirling Bridge, since not only does he have the bridge in the battle but he gives it an even more dramatic role in the victory, since Wallace has had it booby-trapped, so that it can be collapsed once sufficient numbers of the English have crossed.

There is no doubt that Blind Harry's *Wallace* is anti-English. Almost the first lines of the poem tell how 'Our old enemies come of Saxon blood,/ That never yet to Scotland would do good.' The question naturally arises whether the film, too, is anti-English. Many commentators thought so, labelling it 'xenophobic' and accusing it of 'toxic Anglophobia'. Partly this is a result of the film's simple 'heroes and villains' approach. The villains have to be bad, so bad that the heroes' violence is justified. After we have been shown the treacherous mass hanging of the Scottish nobles, and young Wallace grieving over the dead bodies of his father and brother, we are not expected to feel any pity for the English soldiers who are burned alive. Some traced this Anglophobia back to the director and star, Mel Gibson. Gibson might have acquired an unexamined hostility to the English not only from his Irish Catholic background but as an Australian. Of course, Australians have many and varied attitudes to the English, but the stereotype of them as effete upper-class types and the existence of a standard derogatory term, 'Pommy bastard', suggest one strand of hostility, one that was expressed in a particularly serious and political form in the Australian film *Gallipoli* (1981). Gallipoli was a disastrous battle of the First World War, when allied troops, including around 50,000 Australians, were landed on the shore of Turkey, an enemy belligerent, but were then pinned down and suffered high casualties before being finally withdrawn. It has remained a significant event in Australian history and commemoration, recalled each year on ANZAC day, the anniversary of the landing of the Australian and New Zealand Army Corps on 25 April 1915, and, for some, it represents the fruitless slaughter of young Australian men under the command of blundering and callous upper-class English officers, which was the outlook of the film. The star of the film was Mel Gibson. Some thought a pattern was emerging here. After the release of *The Patriot* in 2000, another film in which he starred and which had cruel English villains, there was a headline in one English newspaper: 'Mel's vendetta against England'.

The portrayal of the English who appear in the film does indeed support the view that *Braveheart* is Anglophobic. We know very few of them as individuals. The English characters who are identified by name in the film number five: King Edward 'Longshanks'; Philip, the lover of his son; Smythe, who attempts to rape Murron, Wallace's wife; Cheltham, who is the English lord leading the army at Stirling, as we learn when one of the Scots lords tells him who William Wallace is (Cheltham is the film's version of Earl Warenne, with the name changed for no discernible reason); Hamilton, who is the princess's adviser during her interview with Wallace, though we only know this because she tells him to leave (he seems to be English despite his Scottish name). With the exception of King Edward, none of them is named more than once and none occurs in more than a short, sometimes very short, part of the film. Of course, we can work out that Edward's son is called Edward from outside sources, but he is not named in the film. Several of the other English characters have names on the cast list but there is nothing in the film itself to tell us this, and the names are probably a mere convenience for the shooting script. The lower-class English are either grinning rapists or completely anonymous, the upper-class English effete, immoral, usually unnamed aristocrats. Contrast this with the Scottish characters: Malcolm Wallace, John Wallace, William Wallace, Campbell, MacClannough, Hamish, Murron, Argyle, Robert the Bruce, Craig, Lochlan and Mornay . . .

Edward I of England is introduced in the film by the opening voiceover as 'a cruel pagan known as Edward the Longshanks', who 'claimed the throne of Scotland for himself'. It is not at all clear what the screenwriters meant by the phrase 'cruel pagan'. Is it conceivable that they thought the king of England in the thirteenth century was not a Christian? Or is the phrase simply a very unusual way of saying 'a villain'? 'Longshanks' is simpler: Edward I was over 6 feet tall, which meant, especially for the period, that he had 'long shanks' (that is, legs), and the nickname 'Edward Longshanks' occurs in Blind Harry's *Wallace* (indeed, all the early uses of the nickname seem to be in Scottish writers). Edward did think that Scotland was his – as he says in the film, 'Scotland. My land' – but the steps that brought him to the military occupation of Scotland that is depicted in the opening scenes of the film are neither shown nor explained. Perhaps they were too complex.

After the death of Alexander III of Scotland in 1286, whose children had all died before him, his heir was his infant grand-daughter, Margaret. She was three or four years old and living in Norway at the court of her father, King Erik, who had married King Alexander's daughter. Negotiations began for a marriage between

Patrick McGoohan as Edward 'Longshanks' (Edward I of England).

Margaret and King Edward's son and heir, also called Edward (the prince in the film), and in 1290 an agreement was reached. Edward promised 'the community of the realm of Scotland' that, if Margaret and Edward married, 'the kingdom of Scotland should remain separate from the kingdom of England, free in itself and without any subjection forever.' The implication was that, if Edward and Margaret married and had a son, that son would be king of England and king of Scotland, but the two realms would remain distinct. All this hypothetical future disappeared in a moment, when the young Margaret died on the voyage from Norway to Scotland.

This event immediately unleashed a flurry of claims from the possible inheritors, who included, as main contenders, John Balliol and Robert Bruce, two powerful Anglo-Scottish nobles. The Balliol–Bruce competition is reflected in the film, where the explanatory voiceover at the beginning tells us, 'Scotland's nobles fought him [Edward I] and fought each other over the Crown.' But at this point, in historical reality, Edward's involvement in Scottish affairs was not a matter of invasion; he was, in fact, invited to be the arbiter in the dispute over who should be king of Scotland. Perhaps this was a mistake on the part of the Scottish ruling class and it is certainly something that the film would not wish to depict, since, as a condition for his involvement, Edward insisted that the claimants to the throne, including Balliol and Bruce, recognize him unequivocally as overlord of Scotland. Hence, when Balliol was finally awarded the crown, he had had to swear homage and fealty to Edward as 'king of England, overlord of the kingdom of Scotland'. This is why Edward can say, 'Scotland. My land.'

Balliol's reign did not last long. Edward scarcely gave him much of a chance, allowing appeals to be made from Scottish courts to English ones and demanding that the Scots supply troops for his wars in France. Eventually reaching breaking point, the Scottish king and his nobles made a military alliance with Edward's great enemy, the king of France. Edward's reaction was swift and decisive. In 1296 he led an army into Scotland, stormed Berwick, the first town north of the border on the eastern coast, defeated a Scots army at Dunbar and received the submission of John Balliol. He went further than simply enforcing his overlordship, however. Balliol had to abdicate and Edward seized the Stone of Destiny, the ancient slab on which the kings of Scotland had been inaugurated since time out of mind, and had it placed in Westminster Abbey, where it remained (except for a brief period in 1950–51 when it was stolen by Scottish students) until its return to Scotland in 1996, the seventh centenary of its looting by Edward. Edward intended that the kingdom of Scotland should cease to exist. This was harsh enough, but it was not the 'hundred years of theft, rape, and murder' that Wallace charges the English with before the Battle of Stirling in the film. In fact, in the hundred years before 1297, the year of that battle, the king of England had led an army into Scotland only once, for ten days in January 1216. But now, eighty years later, in 1296, the English had come to stay. As King Edward handed over the official seal to Earl Warenne, who was to be his governor of Scotland, he reportedly said, 'a man does good business when he rids himself of a turd.'

It is at this point, with Scotland under English occupation, that the action of the film begins. For a long time, we are presented only with the terrible impact of this occupation on the common people, especially its sexual side – *prima nocte* and attempted rape. But Wallace's military success leads him into encounters with the Scottish nobles. We see very little of them in the first hour of the film, apart from in the opening moments and a brief scene introducing 'Robert, the seventeenth earl of Bruce' – a non-existent title but one that could quickly convey to an American audience 'aristocratic, non-American, possibly glamorous but not democratic' (the historical Robert Bruce was earl of Carrick). When we do meet Scottish nobles in the film, they are characterized as relatively spineless and uncommitted. They 'do nothing but talk', complains Robert Bruce to his leprous father. They are tarred with the brush of 'compromise' and 'negotiation', which are not virtues in a heroic epic, however much they may be in real life. A first climax in this story of fearless nationalist resistance versus vacillating aristocratic self-interest occurs on the battlefield of Stirling before the fighting starts. Wallace arrives, along with his band (notoriously painted with Pictish woad), as the assembled Scots begin to desert and he confronts their leaders. He does not salute them deferentially, because 'he gives homage to Scotland', and then launches into a rousing pre-battle speech in which 'freedom' is the key word. The next scene in this particular thread of the story takes place immediately after Wallace has been honoured with knighthood after the victory at Stirling. No sooner has he risen to his feet than the Balliol party and the Bruce party try to enlist him in their cause and begin squabbling and waving the documents that support their right. Wallace leaves in disgust. The nobles' betrayal of their country culminates in their abandonment of Wallace and his foot soldiers at the Battle of Falkirk.

Throughout all this, Robert Bruce is shown wavering. He is inspired by, and rather hero worships, Wallace's courage and his spirit of patriotic defiance, but he is also cautiously concerned about his own position. Like many of the great Scottish nobles, Bruce was of Norman and English descent and held lands in both kingdoms. His ancestors were all buried in England. Later story-makers, whether they were medieval chroniclers and poets or twentieth-century screenwriters, had to find a way to integrate the story of William Wallace – who was certainly not a great noble – and his remarkable, unexpected victory at Stirling Bridge in 1297, his unshakeable resistance to Edward I and his final defeat, betrayal and gruesome execution in 1305, alongside that of Robert Bruce, a great feudal lord and the descendant of kings, who oscillated in his loyalty to Edward, before making a decisive break with the English king in 1306 by claiming the throne of Scotland, and then fighting for years before his spectacular victory at Bannockburn in 1314. It could not be that Bruce was merely Wallace's successor in the struggle to maintain Scottish independence, taking up the baton, since he had been a Scottish leader long before anyone had heard of Wallace. He could not be presented simply as a quisling, a national traitor, either. Although he had paid homage to Edward I after the king's conquest of Scotland in 1296, he had fought against the English in the years 1297–1302 before submitting once more.

The approach taken by writers like Blind Harry in the fifteenth century and Randall Wallace, screenwriter of *Braveheart*, in the twentieth century was to make Bruce's story one of conversion to the national cause with Wallace as a guiding example. Blind Harry has Bruce fighting on the English side at Falkirk, just as the film does, but on that occasion in Harry's version Wallace and Bruce have a conversation in which Wallace calls Bruce 'a renegade devourer of thy blood', meaning his fellow Scots. Bruce is shamed: 'From that day on he did not fight against Scots.' In the film, Wallace educates Bruce more gently and also recognizes him as the rightful claimant to the throne, something the historical Wallace never did. 'Your title gives you claim to the throne of our country,' says Wallace to Bruce, and urges him to lead the people to freedom. Later he calls him 'the rightful leader' and begs him to 'unite the clans'. They clasp hands.

All the greater betrayal then, when next they meet on opposite sides at Falkirk. Contemporary chroniclers were aware of Bruce's dilemma, or, looked at another way, his 'inconstancy'. One English chronicler describes him explaining his decision to join the Scottish resistance in 1297, saying 'I must join my own people and adhere to the nation in which I was born,' although this did not prevent him from submitting to Edward I again in 1302.

Because of William Wallace's resistance, which was taken up soon after Wallace's death by Bruce, the attempt of Edward I to annihilate the kingdom of the Scots failed. In 1328, Edward's grandson, Edward III, acknowledged that he and his predecessors 'had sought to obtain the right of rule, lordship and superiority over the kingdom of Scotland' but that now he, with the consent of the English Parliament, recognized that 'the kingdom of Scotland should remain in the possession of the lord Robert, illustrious king of Scots, separate from the kingdom of England in all things, whole, free and peaceful forever.' The union of England and Scotland was eventually to take place, not by English conquest, but in two peaceful steps: the acquisition of the throne of England by King James VI of Scotland in 1603, through inheritance, and, in 1707, the merger of the two kingdoms under James's great-granddaughter, Queen Anne, to form the United Kingdom.

Not everybody was happy about the Union of 1707, either at the time or subsequently. The Scottish National Party, which was formed in 1934 from the merger of two earlier nationalist parties, had Scottish independence as its ultimate goal. At the time of the release of *Braveheart* in 1995, the Scottish Nationalists had only three Members of Parliament in the UK Parliament, a body consisting of 651 elected representatives, but they were still actively continuing to campaign for their goal. In 1997 a referendum was held in Scotland, not on the issue of independence, but on whether there should be a Scottish Parliament with certain devolved powers; the UK Parliament would continue to control defence, foreign policy, immigration, the welfare system and other matters (Scotland already had its own legal system, educational system and form of Church government, as specified in the Acts of Union of 1707). In the devolution referendum, which was held on 11 September 1997, the 700th anniversary of Wallace's victory at Stirling Bridge, those in favour won by 75 per cent to 25 per cent and in 1999 the Scottish Parliament was established. Some commentators referred to a *Braveheart* effect' in swaying voters. In 2007, by a remarkable turn of fortune, the Scottish Nationalists did well enough in the Scottish election to form a government. It would take a detailed survey through interviews and questionnaires to establish whether the film really had the effect of encouraging or strengthening nationalist feeling in Scotland, but there is no doubt that the Scottish National Party certainly employed the language and imagery of *Braveheart* in their rhetoric and Mel Gibson's picture as Wallace appeared in their campaign literature (without his consent). But in the 1990s nationalism was anyway on the rise throughout Europe (and beyond) and countries were disintegrating into their constituent parts, so it would be wrong to make too much of the impact of one film.

At the Academy Awards in 1996 *Braveheart* won five Oscars – Best Picture, Director, Cinematography, Sound Effects Editing and Makeup – although it did not have even a single nomination in any of the acting categories (Nicolas Cage won Best Actor in a Leading Role that year for *Leaving Las Vegas*, a film of a very different kind from *Braveheart*). It was commercially successful and was reportedly a stimulus to tourism to Scotland, as well as encouraging

Scottish football supporters to be yet more inventive in their use of blue face paint. Its impression has lasted, with a message so strong and flexible that it has attracted people as diverse as Nelson Mandela, Irish Republicans and white supremacists in the American South. Freedom has always meant many things to many people. It is also, for the purposes of this book, an ideal case study when asking whether historical accuracy is necessary (or attainable) in films about the past. Since there is enough basic information about thirteenth-century Scotland to provide the film-makers with named individuals, such as Wallace, Edward the Longshanks and Robert Bruce, and with recorded events, such as the battles of Stirling Bridge and Falkirk, when the film introduces made-up characters, like Lochlan and Mornay, or depicts the Battle of Stirling Bridge without a bridge, it is natural to ask why, and to ponder what should be the boundaries of invention.

F. Murray Abraham as Bernard Gui, the inquisitor and antagonist of William of Baskerville.

2

FROM THE PAGE
TO THE SCREEN
The Name of the Rose
(1986)

U nlike *Braveheart*, which presents itself as a historical narrative,
the film *The Name of the Rose* made no attempt to disguise its
origin in imaginative literature. It is based on the novel of the same
name by the Italian scholar Umberto Eco (1932–2016), a professor
at the University of Bologna whose early work was on medieval
aesthetics and semiology, the study of signs and symbols, and who
came to fame with the novel, which was published in Italian in 1980
and in English translation in 1983. It tells of a series of sudden deaths
in a Benedictine abbey and the attempt by a visiting Franciscan friar,
William of Baskerville, to find out what lies behind them. The story
is completely fictional; aspects of the setting are not. The events
take place in northern Italy in 1327 and many important elements,
including the Dolcinian heresy and the Inquisitor Bernard Gui, are
real. The book is soaked in academic playfulness (not the same thing
as general playfulness) and literary jokes and allusions abound. The
blind monk in the novel, Jorge de Burgos, is a clear reference to
the Argentinian writer Jorge Luis Borges (1899–1986), who was
fashionable at the time Eco was writing. Borges was blind, worked
nevertheless as a librarian and wrote on labyrinths (among many
other things). Both librarians and labyrinths are crucial to the
plot of the Eco's novel. The main character, William of Baskerville

(played by Sean Connery), is a kind of Sherlock Holmes, as hinted at by his name, who uses observation and rational deduction to follow a trail of clues, that is, present signs of past action, in order to recreate that past action. Large chunks of the book are direct translations from medieval authors, especially those writing on aesthetics and semiology.

One big question that arises when considering *The Name of the Rose* is how a novel can be adapted to become a film. Adaptation of this kind is going on all the time in the world of film-making: of the 73 films that won the Academy Award for Best Picture in the twentieth century, 31 (42 per cent) were adapted from novels. Some of the differences between the two media have been mentioned in the Preface. A book is made up of printed words to be read; a film of images seen and words (and other sounds, notably music) heard. The former can be picked up, put down, read and re-read, perhaps finished only after weeks, but a film was originally intended to be grasped at one continuous sitting, perhaps of an hour or two, and often still finds its first release in that form. The visual world of a book is created by the reader from the written word, so a character in a book is pictured by the reader 'in the mind's eye', using all the verbal information and clues in the text. A character in a film, however, is indisputably there, present before the viewer. The image of an actor in a filmed adaptation of a novel may even come to dominate the reader's visualizations. When planning his film *Alexander Nevsky*, about a medieval Russian prince, the director Sergei Eisenstein thought that lack of any detailed knowledge of the man was a good thing, giving him creative freedom: 'if I cast a fat actor, then Nevsky was fat,' he said. And for how many people do the words 'Mr Darcy' conjure up a picture of Colin Firth?

Intriguingly, while planning the novel, Eco made drawings of all the monks, most of them with beards, even though, as he admitted, he was 'not at all sure that at that time Benedictine monks had beards' (something not too difficult to find out). In the book, beards are not mentioned on any of the monks or friars, except in one case (the bearded Franciscan, Jerome, bishop of Kaffa), so the reader can supply them or not. The director of the film, Jean-Jacques Annaud, obviously had no such leeway: the monks would have to be bearded or not, and, after taking expert advice, he decided, quite rightly, that most of them would not have beards (although, since monks were only shaved every two or three weeks, many of them might have advanced stubble).

Another issue in adapting a book for the screen is how much space or time can be given to dialogue. A ninety-minute film composed entirely of dialogue, admittedly an unlikely scenario, would have about 14,000 words; a short novel has 80,000 words, and Eco's book is not short. Generally, the first decision in transferring a novel to the screen is how much can be cut. It is often the case that radical amputation is more effective than a hundred tiny cuts. The excision of the extra-marital affair in *Jaws* (1975), one of the few film adaptations that removed sex rather than dragging it in, is a good example. In the case of *The Name of the Rose*, it is not sex but acres of talk that goes (and, mercifully, the dream sequence). Here the screenwriters – there were four of them, two French, one English and one American – faced difficult decisions. They wanted to trim the theological and philosophical discussions, but not to the point that the denouement of the plot, which in part depended on these prior discussions, became incomprehensible. As it turned out, the weight of dialogue was very much shifted in favour of the detective mystery at the expense of more abstract speculation about the interpretation of scripture, the function of art and so forth.

Omission is always necessary when adapting a book for the cinema, but the introduction of new or substitute material is a different, and sometimes more controversial, matter. In the film version of the final volume in *The Lord of the Rings* trilogy, *The Return of the King* (2003), for example, no one could complain of the surgical excision of the entire long episode towards the end when the hobbits return to the Shire to find that it now has a socialist government, but there are good grounds for disquiet about the scene, introduced into the film and not in the book, when Frodo orders Sam to leave him on the borders of Mordor, something psychologically implausible and completely out of harmony with the book. A film that incorporated all of the dialogue that Eco packs into the book would be impossible, so omission is unavoidable; what is more at issue is what is put into the film that is not in the book.

Very early in the film there is an example of such an intrusion. This is the first demonstration of William's deductive powers, which is entirely different in the film from that depicted in the novel. In the book, as William of Baskerville and his young disciple Adso of Melk approach the abbey, they encounter an agitated group of monks, headed by the cellarer Remigio, who pauses to greet William politely. William thanks him and then says, 'I appreciate your courtesy all the more since, in order to greet me, you have interrupted your search. But don't worry. The horse came this way and took the path to the right. He will not get far because he will have to stop when he reaches the dungheap.' Remigio asks him when he saw the horse and William answers, with a touch of the vanity that Adso recognizes in him, 'We haven't seen him at all, have we Adso?' and then continues to describe the horse exactly and even

Sean Connery as William of Baskerville and Christian Slater as Adso.

give its name, Brunellus. The monks dash off and soon find the horse. Adso eventually has to ask William how he knew all this and receives the classic Sherlock Holmes answers – a horse's hoofprints in the snow, broken twigs, horsehairs in the brambles, a trail of waste from the dungheap, all of them clues or signs. Some features of the horse, William admits, he guessed at, but his guesses were based on what a monk would think a fine horse should look like. And the name Brunellus is a standard horse name, like Fido for a dog (this is admittedly rather weak). Observation, deduction, rationality.

In the film none of this occurs. William and Adso arrive at the monastery, where William notices that Adso needs to visit the toilet and tells him where it is. Adso is confused by this since he knows that William has never visited the place before. 'When we arrived,' explains William, 'I saw a brother making for the spot in some haste. I noticed, however, that he emerged more slowly with an air of contentment.' This is simpler than the episode in the book but also sillier, a thin piece of toilet humour, and it would not have been too complicated to show on film a slimmed-down version of the episode with the horse. It may be significant that, on this issue, the television version of *The Name of the Rose* in 2019 followed the book rather than the film. Eco explicitly distanced himself from Jean-Jacques Annaud's film, saying that it was the product of the work of the director, not his: 'it is Annaud's baby.' It would have been interesting to have heard the discussion between Eco and Annaud that led to the decision to have the credits call the film 'A palimpsest of Umberto Eco's novel', a palimpsest being a manuscript that has been scraped to remove the original writing and then written over but with traces remaining of the first text. The suggestion is that the novelist's creation has a ghostly presence in the film but no more.

One thing that both the book and the film take seriously is Christian monasticism, the commitment to a life in community, under obedience, without private property and without sex. At the period the events are set, this form of religious life had a history going back over a thousand years and had taken many shapes. The unnamed abbey is Benedictine, following the Rule of St Benedict, who lived in Italy in the sixth century. Benedictine abbeys were ancient, numerous and often very wealthy, for, although individual monks could not own anything, the corporate body of the monastery could. In the novel, the abbot tells William his abbey is rich, and that the sixty monks are served by 150 servants. In the film, too, the monks have easier lives than the peasants around them and can give them charity or use bribes to win sexual favours. The backbone of Benedictine life was the endless sequence of religious services, which structured the monk's day and year, and the novel reflects this explicitly, being divided into chapters named after those services:

matins, vespers and so on. The film is also visually punctuated by these assemblies in the abbey church. Apart from short arrival and departure scenes, the whole of the film (following the book) takes place in the enclosed space of the monastery. Within these closed, same-sex communities there would be constant interaction, gossip and rumour, and intense feelings of jealousy or friendship.

There is one straightforward alteration, introduced in the film and not in the book, that is quite understandable. In the book, Adso is a young Benedictine novice, and hence would wear the dark habit of the Benedictines, while William of Baskerville, a Franciscan friar, would wear grey – the Franciscans are colloquially known as Greyfriars in English and *Graue Brüder* in German. For the film, Adso is made a Franciscan too, which has the advantage of simplicity, since there is no need for the book's complex explanation of why a Benedictine novice is travelling with a Franciscan friar, and is also visually useful, colour-coding him identically to William of Baskerville, not to the monks.

But an aspect of Christian religious life that is obscured or perhaps trivialized in the film is something that features rather more prominently in the novel: the fierce debate over poverty that was taking place in the Church at the time of the events depicted. In 1318, nine years before *The Name of the Rose* is set, four Franciscan friars had been burned at the stake because of their radical views on poverty. The issue went back a century, almost to the date of the foundation of the Franciscan Order by Francis of Assisi, the charismatic religious leader who died in 1226. He had embraced absolute poverty, 'Lady Poverty' as he called her, and expected his followers to do the same. The success of the Order, which soon had thousands of members and hundreds of friaries, made it increasingly difficult to maintain this rigorous ideal, and splits arose between those with a more uncompromising position and those who were prepared to make accommodations, allowing the friars the 'use' of property, as long as they did not claim legal 'ownership'. As always in a scriptural religion, arguments were developed on the basis of the holy writ, and it became important to decide whether Christ and his apostles had owned property: if they had, it would be impossible to say that owning property was wrong and absolute poverty the ideal.

It is this controversy that forms an important part of the background to *The Name of the Rose*. The abbey is the venue for a debate between Franciscans, headed by their Minister-General Michael of Cesena, who had adopted the position that Christ owned nothing, and representatives of the pope, John XXII, who had declared that this position was heretical. Eco has a chapter, 'Prime of the Fifth Day', in which this debate is depicted, with tempers rising, arguments becoming ever more ridiculous and William of Baskerville rolling his eyes and muttering in exasperation. In the book enough attention is given to the issue to endow it with some significance – the right to private property is not, after all, so obvious that it has never been questioned – but scarcely any of this comes through in the film, or only as a trivial caricature. Michael of Cesena is shown opening the debate with the words, 'Good people throughout Christendom are directing their gazes at these venerable walls anxiously awaiting our answer to the vexed question: Did Christ, or did He not, own the clothes that He wore?' A superior smile, or snort, must be the expected audience reaction to this.

The portrayal of the Inquisition in the film is hardly more nuanced. This is partly due to the unrestrained, if memorable, performance of F. Murray Abraham as the inquisitor Bernard Gui. The historical figure Bernard Gui, who was a Dominican friar and an official Inquisitor from 1307, wrote an 'Inquisitor's Manual', which was completed in 1324, a few years before the supposed events of Eco's novel, and in this chilling work he explains the different kinds of heretics, the tricks they use to avoid condemnation and the cunning that Inquisitors must employ to unmask them. Lurking in the background of *The Name of the Rose* is one particular group of heretics, the 'Dolcinians' or 'Dolcinites' as they are termed, who called themselves the 'Apostolic Brethren' and were followers of Fra Dolcino, a radical religious leader who launched a fierce attack on the established Church, attracted thousands of followers, and engaged in a kind of guerrilla war in northern Italy for several years. The movement was finally suppressed by the authorities, and Dolcino was executed, slowly and horribly, in 1307, twenty years before the events of *The Name of the Rose*. In his 'Inquisitor's Manual' Bernard Gui recounts some of his experiences interrogating Dolcinians. Two of the monks in the abbey, Remigio the cellarer and Salvatore, are depicted as having a past as Dolcinians, a past that they are trying to live down, although Salvatore is less than discreet in employing the movement's catchphrase *'penitenziagite!'* – 'do penance!'

It is hard to think of the revolutionary past of these monks and not hear an echo of the Italian Red Brigades, the Marxist revolutionary organization which, in the decade when Eco was writing *The Name of the Rose*, engaged in numerous acts of violence, notably the kidnapping and murder of the Christian Democrat politician Aldo Moro in 1978. Some members of the group, just like Remigio and Salvatore, sought to leave it and resume a normal life. Eco said that he understood the movement's hostility to 'the imperialist state of the multinationals' but thought the Red Brigades 'mistaken and delusional'. In the book, the conclusion that William of Baskerville's friend, Ubertino da Casale, draws from the story of the Dolcinians is that 'the love of penance and the desire to purify the world can

Eco visits the filming. The director, Jean-Jacques Annaud, is far right, while the abbot enjoys a cigarette.

produce bloodshed and slaughter.' The story of revolutionary idealism giving birth to brutality and inhumanity has been told many times; here it is a semi-visible presence, both confusing and intriguing to the young Adso.

In both book and film, Adso, the young colleague, is also the narrator, many years later, which thus gives retrospective possibilities. Indeed, both start with Adso's words, 'I prepare to leave on this parchment my testimony as to the wondrous and terrible events I witnessed [or: that I happened to observe] in my youth.' Adso can thus comment upon the characters and events with the wisdom of hindsight. There is, however, a difference between the perspective of the book and that of the film, one that relies on the formal possibilities, and the formal constraints, of the two media. Everything in the novel is in the voice of Adso of Melk. It is a first-person narrative in which we know throughout who the 'I' is, and nothing occurs that Adso does not see personally or hear of. This is, of course,

Umberto Eco's choice, since novels can be in many voices, including that of the so-called omniscient narrator, a figure who does not appear as any one character in the novel but tells us, the readers, everything that is going on, including thoughts in the characters' heads. In a film, that effect is difficult to reproduce, since by its nature a film shows many characters, even if some have more screen time, and there is usually no sense that one character is more real than the others. In the film of *The Name of the Rose* Adso's voice is preserved as a voiceover, a non-diegetic device, heard by the viewers but not by the characters in the film. Just as in the book, Adso's voice introduces and concludes the story, giving a useful orientation at the beginning and tying up a few loose ends after the main action, but the voiceover is otherwise used very sparingly, to give reflections on Adso's reactions to his 'Master', William of Baskerville, and to 'the girl' (as she is always named). Apart from these occasional moments of voiceover, Adso is more of a character in the film than its narrator and we have many scenes in which he does not appear or about which he could not have knowledge.

The narrative thread of the book is provided by that classic detective plot, a series of mysterious deaths investigated by a hyper-rational investigator and his appreciative sidekick. Already, before William and Adso arrive at the monastery, a mysterious death had occurred, when the body of the young monk Adelmo, a famous illuminator of manuscripts, was found at the foot of a cliff below the Aedificium, the giant tower that dominates the monastic buildings. Soon after William's arrival at the monastery, the abbot asks him to investigate the death, since its circumstances apparently make it unlikely it was suicide. William then undertakes his investigation, with Adso serving as his Watson-like foil, straight man and earnest interlocutor. The film underlines William's Sherlock

Holmesian quality by giving him lines such as, 'My dear Adso, it's elementary', and also, since William is played by Sean Connery, adds a dash of James Bond to the laconic one-liners – 'A rather dark end for such a brilliant illuminator', he quips when reflecting on the death of Adelmo. Successively, over the seven days of the action, other monks are found dead: Venantius, Berengar, Severinus, Malachi (some viewers found all these characters, with their strange names, confusing). William tries one theory after another to explain the sequence and meaning of this series of mysterious deaths. At one point the idea is raised that the 'the key to the sequence of crimes lay in the book of Revelation', with the methods of death paralleling the plagues unleashed upon the world in the Last Days, but this leads nowhere.

Feodor Chaliapin Jr as Jorge de Burgos, the blind monk whose hostility to Aristotelian rationalism and to laughter is a main mover of the plot of *The Name of the Rose*.

A theme running alongside the murder mystery is formed by the recurrent verbal duels that take place between William, champion of rational inquiry, and the blind monk Jorge. The first of these occurs when the monks in the scriptorium, the room where the monks write their books, are stirred to laughter – in the novel by the fantastic illustrations that the poor Adelmo depicted in the margins of the books he copied, in the film by the shrieks of alarm from the 'invert' Berengar, who has jumped onto a stool in fear after encountering a mouse. In both cases a fierce voice interrupts and reproves them. This is Jorge. We can understand why the film has Jorge cry out, 'A monk should not laugh. Only the fool lifts up his voice in laughter,' rather than follow the novel, which has him say, 'Verba vana aut risui apta non loqui.' Untranslated, and unascribed, in the novel, as was Eco's common practice, these words are in fact from the Benedictine Rule and mean 'Do not speak trivial and trifling words, nor those that lead to laughter.' To have the austere monk Jorge utter these words is entirely in character (Latin was spoken in the cloister) but does require a reader either to know Latin or to have easy access to a Latin dictionary (there being no Internet in 1980 when the book was published!). After Jorge's outburst, there follows a debate about the value of bizarre and fantastic, that is, fabulous and made-up, images, William arguing that humour can play a part in instructing and edifying, Jorge fiercely decrying the carvings of hybrids, monsters and gargoyles that could be found even in monastic settings – here Eco gives him the exact words of St Bernard, the twelfth-century monastic leader who had launched just such an attack on the fantastical carvings of his own day. The film, very reasonably, telescopes some of the exchanges between William and Jorge, so that we have in this scene in the scriptorium passages that occur later in the book, such as the disagreement about whether Jesus ever laughed, a difference of opinion that makes a good pendant to the argument about whether Christ owned his clothes, in both cases a general question – about the uses of humour or the legitimacy of private property – being referred back to the authority of scripture.

The film version of this scene also introduces, earlier than in the book, the topic of Aristotle's *Poetics*. This is a plot-driver, but it is hard to understand without some background information, and background information is always easier to convey on the page than on the screen. The learned world of *The Name of the Rose* is one in which Latin was the standard language of education, law and religion. Very few scholars knew Greek, so the Greek classics were inaccessible to them unless translated. One of the most important developments of the two centuries before 1327, the year *The Name of the Rose* is set, was a sustained, sometimes obsessional, campaign to translate ancient Greek philosophy, science and medicine into Latin, often by way of Arabic intermediary translations, and, incidentally, without any interest at all in the Athenian dramatists, Homer and other works now regarded as great jewels of ancient Greek literature. Aristotle – 'the Philosopher' as he was known in medieval Europe – was the most important of these Greek philosophers to be translated. He had written about everything, including a famous work of literary theory, the *Poetics*. At the beginning of his discussion of tragedy in the *Poetics*, Aristotle says that he will consider epic poetry and comedy later in the work. He does indeed proceed to discuss epic after tragedy but never does get to comedy, and scholars have assumed that the section in which he did so was lost at some point. It is this missing section of Aristotle, described by William of Baskerville (as by many modern scholars) as the second book of *Poetics*, that is the priceless manuscript in the monastery library.

During his final confrontation with William, as described in the novel, Jorge gives his judgement upon Aristotle: 'every book by that man has destroyed a part of the learning that Christianity has accumulated over the centuries.' He was not alone in this view. In Paris, study of the books of Aristotle on natural philosophy was banned in 1210 and 1215 (though even this did not prevent their becoming the core of the university syllabus by the middle of the thirteenth century). Aristotle's view that the universe had no beginning was naturally not acceptable to Christian theologians and was explicitly condemned in 1277. Jorge's hostility to Aristotle and his thought is related to his hostility to laughter, which he regards as subversive: 'laughter is weakness, corruption, the foolishness of our flesh,' he says in the novel. Jorge sees the danger of Aristotle's second book of *Poetics* in that it elevates laughter, justifies jests and undermines God's established order. All this has, of course, to be compressed in the film, but the heart of it is in the brief exchange between William and Jorge:

WILLIAM: Venerable brother, there are many books that speak of comedy. Why does this one fill you with such fear?

JORGE: Because it's by Aristotle.

WILLIAM: But what is so alarming about laughter?

JORGE: Laughter kills fear and without fear there can be no faith. Because without fear of the Devil there is no more need of God.

WILLIAM: But you will not eliminate laughter by eliminating that book.

JORGE: No, to be sure. Laughter will remain the common man's recreation but what would happen if, because of this book, learned men were to pronounce it permissible to laugh at everything? Can we laugh at God? The world would relapse into chaos.

Perhaps unfortunately, this exchange takes place while William and Adso are pursuing Jorge through the labyrinth and is intercut with scenes of the imminent execution of Remigio, Salvatore and the girl. Jorge's words echo through the stairs and corridors. The nature of an argument is hard to follow if it is hard to hear.

But maybe the argument, in the novel as in the film, is also hard to follow because it is not in fact clear what it is. Is it reason or is it laughter that is the enemy for Jorge? On the one hand, he criticizes 'the cold, lifeless scrutiny of reason' as exemplified by the twelfth-century philosopher and theologian Peter Abelard (who was twice condemned for heresy) and attacks outright the ideal of intellectual inquiry: 'There is no progress . . . in the history of knowledge.' But the plot revolves around his attempt to forbid access to Aristotle's work on comedy, not because Aristotle was the champion of rational analysis but because his name would justify laughter, which in turn would undermine 'fear of the Devil' and consequently the 'need of God'. There is something improbable about this chain of thought. There are theories of comedy that see it as intrinsically subversive but there are also theories that regard it as a kind of safety valve, allowing controlled explosions of absurdity and silliness that do not in any way challenge the foundations of the established order and are hence objectively conservative. Jorge more or less describes this second viewpoint when he says, in the film, 'laughter will remain the common man's recreation', or, more fully in the book, laughter 'is the peasant's entertainment, the drunkard's license; even the church in her wisdom has granted the moment of feast, carnival . . . that releases humors and distracts from other desires and other ambitions'.

Jorge's sparring partner, William, does indeed have a high opinion of human reason. Not only does his respect for rational inquiry underpin the Holmesian deductive method that he brings to his investigation of the murders in the monastery, but it is more than just a fruitful method for him: 'our reason was created by God,' he says. Even William's friends criticize him for an excessive veneration of rationality, as when Ubertino tells him, 'your masters at Oxford have taught you to idolize reason.' William's hero is Roger Bacon, like him an English Franciscan, of the generation before William, a figure famous for the stress he placed on the need for empirical proof. 'All things must be verified by the path of experience,' Bacon wrote, and for him this meant 'experiments with instruments'. William speaks explicitly about Bacon in the novel, although any reference to him has been cut from the film: 'Roger Bacon, whom I venerate as my master, teaches that the divine plan will one day encompass the science of machines, which is natural and healthy magic.' This is part of William's portrayal as 'a man ahead of his time', although when discussing the machines of the future, he does not mention Bacon's plans for weapons of mass destruction. William, with the dry humour and empiricism that Eco takes to be characteristically English, is clearly presented as the most sympathetic character in the book, set in a world full of fanaticism, authoritarianism and cruelty. And he does claim that laughter is a sign of man's rationality, so here, perhaps, he brings together the two characteristics that he and Jorge fight over.

If the debates about reason and laughter do not produce a clear and integrated picture, the same might be said of the way both the novel and the film deal with sexuality. It is no surprise that a story

William inspects Berengar's body. Berengar is depicted in the film as obese, bald and effeminate, unlike the 'pale-faced young man' of the book.

set in a monastery is short on female characters. In this respect the film (but not the 2019 television series) follows the novel. The cast is entirely male, the only exception being the anonymous peasant girl, and the issue of sexual relations between the monks recurs. Adso himself refers to love letters he has received as a young novice in his home monastery, and the first death in the monastery is the result of a homosexual encounter between the beautiful Adelmo and the lustful Berengar, an act that Adelmo regrets to such a degree that he takes his own life. Berengar, described in the book as 'a pale-faced young man', becomes in the film obese, bald and effeminate (hence the leaping onto a stool in terror of a mouse), and his body when found naked is described as white, flabby and hairless. This travesty has, rather surprisingly, stirred up little of the outrage that was stimulated by the portrayal of the homosexuality of Prince Edward in *Braveheart*.

Although it takes up relatively few pages in the book and not five minutes in the film, the encounter between Adso and the peasant girl is clearly significant. It is the only scene of any importance involving a female character and it means that Adso, the narrator, has to make major decisions both as a monk or friar and as a teenage boy. In the film, the girl initiates the sexual contact, as well she might, given the difference between the supposed sexual experience of the two fictional characters, not to mention the actual difference in age between those playing them (Christian Slater was sixteen at the time the film was made, Valentina Vargas was 21). She seems to require no foreplay. There are the usual difficulties in getting clothes off. We see her breasts and buttocks, which affected the certification

Adso and the (unnamed) girl, whom he encounters in the monastery kitchen and with whom he has his first and only sexual experience.

of the film in numerous countries. Apart from a line or two at the beginning of the scene, we do not hear Adso's voiceover commentary and the lovers say nothing to each other. The scene is intercut with others showing William of Baskerville and Salvatore.

In the book, of course, we have Adso's first-person account of his encounter with the girl. His inner words about her beauty are expressed in the language of the Song of Songs, the most erotic book of the Bible, and one invariably interpreted allegorically by Christian theologians. This is the source of such phrases as 'thou art fair, my love ... thy lips are like a thread of scarlet', and also, given both in Latin and English, the description of the girl as 'terrible as an army with banners', *terribilis ut castrorum acies ordinata* (although a misprint in the English translation renders this, rather unfortunately, as *castorum acies*, meaning 'an army of beavers'). When Adso first becomes aware of the girl's presence, she is sobbing in fear. He approaches her gently and tells her not to be afraid. They smile at each other. She tells him he is handsome, as far as he can understand her, and she touches his face. This is where Adso begins recalling the Song of Songs. Then,

> she smiled with great joy, emitted the stifled moan of a pleased she-goat, and undid the strings that closed her dress over her bosom, slipped the dress from her body like a tunic, and stood before me as Eve must have appeared to Adam in the garden of Eden.

The romantic simile of Adam and Eve in the Garden of Eden is perhaps an unexpected conclusion to this sentence presenting a mute she-goat ready for sex. Adso's recollections then move on to a few pages of rapture, in which biblical language and reflections on the nature of ecstasy give little in the way of physical description but do include the important assertion, 'nothing could be more right and good and holy than what I was experiencing.'

The sex scene provides an extreme example of the differences between what a book can do and what a film can do. The film shows what is often labelled 'explicit sex' – 'leaving nothing merely implied or suggested', to use a dictionary definition – although, given the constraints of 1986 and the limitations imposed by marketing considerations, there are no visible genitalia. But we do see, rather than imagine, the girl removing her clothes, we see breasts and buttocks, we see naked bodies on top of each other. We have to imagine what is going through the minds of the participants as we have no dialogue between them to help us, although it is true that the style of the film tends to give the scene a romantic as well as a passionate colouring, with two young and beautiful bodies bathed in firelight (some critics thought that the girl was implausibly clean). The book is almost the opposite, with virtually no pictures conjured up, no 'word-painting', because the repeated quotations from the Song of Songs give no real physical information: we do not know the colour of the girl's eyes or hair, whether she is short or tall. We know her dress is of rough cloth but not what colour it is. We do, however, have a long, intense and highly coloured first-person account of Adso's experience and reactions, a stream of consciousness that is as vivid as the physical description is featureless. Screen and page are doing quite different work here.

One of the biggest changes that the film of *The Name of the Rose* makes to the novel is its ending. In the film the girl is saved and Bernard Gui is killed by a peasant uprising. None of this occurs in the book, where, after the girl is arrested and Adso is tempted to go to her, William restrains him with the words, 'Be still, fool. The girl is lost; she is burnt flesh.' We hear no more about her. The departure of Gui and the condemned prisoners, including the girl, is not even described in the book, but reported in a sentence of William to Adso, who reflects that he 'would not have been able to bear the sight of the condemned being dragged off, far away and forever'. The plot then moves fairly quickly and directly – or at least as far as 'quickly and directly' can be applied to the book – to the final showdown with Jorge and the conflagration that end the novel. The film-makers obviously thought this was insufficiently dramatic as a conclusion. They therefore satisfy the desire of the imagined audience for some kind of justice to be done, by hurling Gui to his death, as well as saving the girl for one last slow, wistful scene with Adso. The desire to have a happy ending is strong and sometimes results in bold rewrites, such as the eighteenth-century version of Shakespeare's *King Lear* in which Cordelia does not die after all. Readers and viewers of *The Name of the Rose* can decide which ending, that of the book or that of the film, is less improbable.

In his short book *Reflections on 'The Name of the Rose'*, written after the amazing international success of the novel, Eco devoted a few pages to discussing 'ways of narrating the past' in fiction, which he classified into three types: the romance, the swashbuckler and the historical novel proper. In the first type, the past is 'scenery', a setting for 'the imagination to rove freely'. In fact, romance does not have to be set in the past, it just has to be '*elsewhere*'. Eco cites Tolkien and science fiction as examples (C. S. Lewis also thought that Arthurian romance and science fiction belonged in the same category). The second type is different. It has real historical figures, as well as made-up characters – Eco gives the example of Cardinal Richelieu (real) and d'Artagnan (made up) from *The Three Musketeers* – but the interest in these books is the dramatic action (the swashbuckling) and the plot and the characters' emotions could come from any period. The third type, the historical novel proper, which is what Eco was attempting in *The Name of the Rose*, does not have to include any real historical characters, although it may, but everything the characters do and say must be characteristic of the period and place in which the novel is set. 'Events and characters are made up, yet they tell us things...that history books have never told us so clearly.'

Being Italian, Eco took the most famous historical novel in the Italian language, Alessandro Manzoni's *I promessi sposi* (The Betrothed), as a classic example of the historical novel proper. This was published in the 1820s (at the same time that Walter Scott was publishing his historical novels, including, curiously, one also called *The Betrothed*) and is set in seventeenth-century Lombardy in northern Italy. In Manzoni's book there are some actual events, such as the plague in Milan in 1630, and a few real historical people, but the main characters are fictional, such as Renzo, Lucia and Fra Cristoforo. Eco writes, 'everything that Renzo, Lucia or Fra Cristoforo does could only be done in Lombardy in the seventeenth century. What the characters do serves to make history, what happened, more comprehensible.' This is an extreme claim, and one wonders where it leaves the idea that certain impulses and situations are in fact universal and that explains their power in fiction, but it sets out its ambition plainly: to recreate a credible world of the past which had its own rules, its own possibilities and its own limitations.

Manzoni not only wrote one of the most famous historical novels in the Italian language, but an essay reflecting on the genre, 'On the Historical Novel' (*Del romanzo storico*). In this he sometimes speaks in the voice of those who criticize the historical novel on various grounds, and, in one such passage, spells out what a historical novel might be expected to do: 'the story that we expect from you is not a chronological narration of mere political and military facts but a more general representation of the state of humanity in a circumscribed time and place.' This imaginary critic compares the difference between a history book and a historical novel to that between a large-scale map showing mountain ranges, rivers, cities and main roads and a detailed topographical map on which are indicated 'lesser heights, small unevennesses of the ground, ditches, millstreams, villages, isolated houses, footpaths'. The task of the historical novelist is to depict 'customs, opinions, the private effects of public events, all that was most characteristic of a given society at a given time'. Put this way, the task of the historical novelist may seem too narrowly defined: what, for instance, of novels that do deal with big historical events (*War and Peace*)? Or those that have a biographical focus on important public figures (*Wolf Hall*)? But the general point is right: the historical novelist, by means of imagination, informed speculation and downright invention, tries to give a close-up picture (even of grand events and personages), to convey intimate detail, physical aspects that history has not passed down to us, tones of voice, points of view, inner thoughts – in a word, to use another metaphor of Manzoni's, to put the flesh back on the bare bones of history. Film-makers do the same thing. Manzoni's novel, which became a revered classic in Italy (Verdi wrote his *Requiem* to commemorate Manzoni), has been adapted for the cinema and for television on numerous occasions, from at least 1908, usually in Italian.

An Academy Award has been given for Best Adapted Screenplay since the awards began in 1929 (sadly, the film *Adaptation*, which was nominated in 2002, did not win). Only two films set in the Middle Ages have ever been nominated for this award and, curiously, both of them won: *Becket* in 1964 and *The Lion in Winter* in 1968, both with Peter O'Toole as Henry II of England and both of them adapted from plays rather than novels – one attraction of plays for film-makers being that you already have a script. *The Name of the Rose* won several European awards but did not receive any Academy Award nominations. It may be relevant that *The Name of the Rose* was a German-Italian-French co-production, while the producers of *Becket* and *The Lion in Winter* were American. Members of the Academy of Motion Picture Arts and Sciences, whose votes decide the Oscars, are no less susceptible to advertising and promotion than anyone else. The organization is based in Beverly Hills, California.

The lack of Academy Award nominations for medieval films in the Best Adapted Screenplay category is not especially surprising. Films based on historical novels set in the Middle Ages are themselves not particularly common, especially when set beside the mountain of cinematic adaptations of the novels of Jane Austen, Charles Dickens and a host of modern bestsellers. Examples of adaptations from nineteenth-century novels with a medieval setting include *Ivanhoe*, which, as mentioned in the Preface to this book, has been very fertile in generating screen versions; another of Scott's novels, *Quentin Durward*, which was filmed in 1912 and 1955, and, in a Russian version, in 1988; and the numerous films called *The Hunchback of Notre Dame*, based on Victor Hugo's *Notre-Dame de Paris*, which has inspired film versions from the silent era to the Disney cartoon incarnation of 1996. Robert Louis Stevenson's *Black Arrow*, set during the Wars of the Roses, was the basis for cinematic films in 1911 and 1948, and, again in a Russian version, in 1985, not to mention numerous adaptations for television.

The twentieth century continued to have rare cases. The Czech medieval classic *Marketa Lazarová* (1967) is based on a novel by

Vladislav Vančura, and there is the rarity, *A Walk with Love and Death* (1969), adapted from a 1961 novel of the same name by Hans Koningsberger, which shows the devastation of France during the Hundred Years War and the great popular uprising of the Jacquerie of 1358, and has Anjelica Huston in her first film role, directed by her father. In the 1990s there was a three-hour film in Norwegian, *Kristin Lavransdatter*, directed by Liv Ullmann and adapted by her from the novels of Sigrid Undset, which were published in the 1920s. This is rarely screened. Films with medieval settings based on novels are thus not common. Interest in the process of adaptation, however, has boomed, and has even resulted in an academic sub-discipline, adaptation theory. A very large number of films are adaptations of books or plays with post-medieval or contemporary settings, and so screenwriters continue the daily task of cutting, rewriting and moving scenes around, introducing new characters and all the other tasks involved in 'adaptation'.

Medieval mystery thrillers are now so numerous that they can rightly be regarded as a genre in their own right. The Brother Cadfael series by Ellis Peters, pen name of Edith Pargeter, consists of twenty novels published between 1977 and 1994, so she launched her monk-detective several years before Eco published *The Name of the Rose*. Eco's book was thus not an absolute pioneer of this kind of novel, but it has been by far the biggest seller of the type and the book can still be bought in railway station bookshops many decades after it was first published. Certainly, the film was not as successful commercially and the responses of critics were mixed. This was not through lack of ambition. The film recruited some big, and some biggish, names from the world of cinema. It has characteristically grand and sweeping music by James Horner, who also wrote the music for *Braveheart* (as well as *Titanic*, for which he won an Academy Award), and stars the instantly recognizable Sean Connery and F. Murray Abraham, who was fresh from an Academy Award-winning role as Salieri in *Amadeus*. The film-makers also made a serious effort to get the physical environment and everyday detail right, enlisting a spectacularly distinguished group of historians as advisers, including, among others, Jacques Le Goff as 'historical adviser', François Avril as 'manuscript adviser', Jean-Claude Schmitt as 'comportment adviser', Danièle Alexandre-Bidon as 'contemporary manners adviser' and Michel Pastoureau as 'heraldry adviser'. It remains for some viewers a 'realistic' picture of the Middle Ages (perhaps especially the bad teeth) in contrast to the traditional romanticization of Hollywood films about knights and castles. Both book and film are entirely fictional tales set in a world that their creators tried to make as real and convincing as possible. Whether the film is as successful, as a film, as the book has been, as a book, is a matter of opinion. Screen and page are judged by different criteria, as they should be.

Graham Chapman as King Arthur, with some of his knights.

3

NOW FOR SOMETHING COMPLETELY DIFFERENT:

Monty Python and the Holy Grail

(1975)

Monty Python, the English comic troupe whose legendary television series, *Monty Python's Flying Circus*, ran from 1969 to 1974, soon moved on to make full-length films for the cinema screen, including *Monty Python and the Holy Grail* (1975), *Life of Brian* (1979) and *The Meaning of Life* (1983). In the first of these films, Monty Python addressed the history of the Middle Ages, through the indirect route of parodying films about the Middle Ages. The main character in their film is King Arthur, played by Graham Chapman, and a loose thread is provided by his quest for the Holy Grail, which in medieval legend was the cup from which Jesus drank at the Last Supper, the night before his crucifixion.

There is no historical core to the film, in the sense that there is to *Braveheart*, although some scholars see in Arthur the shadowy figure of a Dark Age warlord, but the film is a comic version of a type of medieval story, the Arthurian romance. This was created in the twelfth century, when the heroic figure of Arthur first burst upon the world, capturing the European imagination and never losing it since, in Geoffrey of Monmouth's *History of the Kings of Britain* (composed around 1136). In this long and fanciful account of the ancient kings of Britain, Arthur has a central place, as a conqueror and a courtly king. Geoffrey presented his work as genuine history, and he wrote in Latin, the learned language, and in prose. The 'romance' was added to the mix later in the twelfth century by Chrétien de Troyes, who wrote in French (*romance*), the language of the international chivalric class, and in verse. It is Chrétien who introduces the story of the adulterous love of Lancelot and Guinevere, Arthur's queen, and who first mentions the Grail.

Subsequently, Arthurian romance became one of the most important genres of the Middle Ages, with some standard narrative components such as the Knights of the Round Table, the Grail, adulterous romantic love, the quest, Merlin and magic. The long prose romances of the thirteenth century are the first European novels for a thousand years, and versions eventually appeared in all European languages, the *Morte D'Arthur* of Sir Thomas Malory, who died in 1471, being the best-known representative in the English language (despite its French title). The characters and stories remained familiar. Before he embarked on his epic poem *Paradise Lost*, John Milton had intended to write of Arthur and 'the great spirited heroes of the table made invincible by their fellowship' (no specific mention of the table being round!). The Arthurian theme was a staple of nineteenth-century Romantic literature and culture. In England, Alfred, Lord Tennyson's *Idylls of the King* (published in instalments between 1859 and 1885) retells many Arthurian stories, drawn mainly from Malory, and became one of the most popular works of the Victorian and Edwardian era. Its tone can be conveyed by the following passage, which incorporates a poem ('Morte d'Arthur') that Tennyson had written much earlier, in 1842, and describes the great last battle and Arthur's passing:

So all day long the noise of battle rolled
Among the mountains by the winter sea;

Until King Arthur's Table, man by man,
Had fallen in Lyonnesse about their lord,
King Arthur. Then, because his wound was deep,
The bold Sir Bedivere uplifted him,
And bore him to a chapel nigh the field,
A broken chancel with a broken cross,
That stood on a dark strait of barren land:
On one side lay the Ocean, and on one
Lay a great water, and the moon was full.

Then spake King Arthur to Sir Bedivere:
'The sequel of today unsolders all
The goodliest fellowship of famous knights
Whereof this world holds record. Such a sleep
They sleep – the men I loved. I think that we
Shall never more, at any future time,
Delight our souls with talk of knightly deeds,
Walking about the gardens and the halls
Of Camelot, as in the days that were.'

It is easy to imagine the attraction of such grand and solemn verse, with its archaism and its elegiac qualities, and also to imagine a reaction against it, the urge to burst its bubble and dismiss it as ponderous, humourless and facile.

The two attitudes, the reverent and the critical, are expressed in a short exchange between schoolboys in James Joyce's *Portrait of the Artist as a Young Man* (1916):

And who is the best poet, Heron? asked Boland.
    Lord Tennyson, of course, answered Heron.

O, yes, Lord Tennyson, said Nash. We have all his poetry at home in a book.

At this Stephen forgot the silent vows he had been making and burst out:

Tennyson a poet! Why, he's only a rhymester!

O, get out! said Heron. Everyone knows that Tennyson is the greatest poet.

This exchange would have taken place, given the chronology of the book, in the mid-1890s, soon after Tennyson's death. Heron's view of the poet and the Nash family's possession of 'all his poetry in a book' show how Tennyson had become a standard feature of ordinary middle-class society in Britain and Ireland, his name recognizable to all and his poetry, or at least some of it, familiar, while the dismissive reaction of Stephen (the lightly disguised Joyce figure) indicates the future, Tennyson's fall from favour in the face of new critical attitudes.

The five English members of the Monty Python troupe were born in the years 1939–43, so would have been at school in the 1950s. By then Tennyson had been, for many decades, the subject of dismissal and even contempt (W. H. Auden called him the stupidest of English poets), attacked as sentimental, moralistic and (though this was obviously through no fault of his own) 'Victorian'. Lampooning the high-flown language and romantic medievalism of Tennyson would be natural to flippant English teenagers of the 1950s. Whether this was true of the young Pythons or not, it was certainly a posture they exhibited in their early careers as television satirists mocking authority figures, and also in *Monty Python and the Holy Grail*. An instance is provided by one of the many moments of comic bathos in the film. Bathos, the sudden shift from high tone to low tone, is perfectly exemplified in the exchange between Arthur and the peasant Dennis about the Lady of the Lake:

> ARTHUR: The Lady of the Lake, her arm clad in the purest shimmering samite, held Excalibur aloft from the bosom of the water to signify by Divine Providence . . . that I, Arthur, was to carry Excalibur . . . That is why I am your king!
>
> DENNIS: Look, strange women lying on their backs in ponds handing out swords . . . that's no basis for a system of government. Supreme executive power derives from a mandate from the masses, not from some farcical aquatic ceremony.
>
> ARTHUR: Be quiet!
>
> DENNIS: You can't expect to wield supreme executive power just because some watery tart threw a sword at you!

To have its effect, bathos presupposes some familiarity with the high tone, which, here, as elsewhere in the film, is as much Victorian as medieval. It is true that Malory describes an encounter with the Lady of the Lake – 'Arthur was ware of an arm clothed in white samite' – but the immediate source of the phrase in the screenplay is more likely Tennyson: 'An arm Clothed in white samite, mystic, wonderful.' The word 'samite' in both cases is meant to indicate something rich and glamorous, since samite was an expensive silk, but for Malory it denoted something rich and expensive in the contemporary world, while for Tennyson, writing when 'samite' was no longer found in the everyday world, it summoned up something lost and romantic, hence 'mystic, wonderful'. The crash from the high tone of 'The Lady of the Lake, her arm clad in the purest shimmering samite' to 'some watery tart' is thus not, in essence, deflating the Middle Ages but deflating the Victorian conception of the Middle Ages.

Bathos is a form of incongruity, the juxtaposition of inappropriate things, and requires knowledge of certain associations for that incongruity to be recognized. For example, the only reason that having a wizard called 'Tim the Enchanter' is supposed to be funny is that the name conjures up someone mild, well-meaning but perhaps not very clever, probably from the English upper or upper-middle class. It is thus quintessentially *not* a suitable name for a medieval magus. Similarly, a shrubbery, an area planted with a collection of bushes, is a feature of English middle-class gardens that became popular in the early nineteenth century. In Jane Austen's *Mansfield Park*, Lady Bertram recommends one: 'if I were you, I would have a very pretty shrubbery. One likes to get out into a shrubbery in fine weather.' To have the huge and threatening knights who say 'Ni!' demanding a shrubbery brings the epic and the suburban into jarring contact.

Parody of medieval chivalry and romance has a long history, going back at least as far as Miguel de Cervantes' *Don Quixote* of 1605, which relates the adventures of Don Quixote, whose head has been turned by reading too much medieval romance literature, and Sancho Panza, his down-to-earth squire. Terry Gilliam, the only American-born member of the Monty Python troupe, spent decades trying to make a film based on *Don Quixote* and finally succeeded with *The Man who Killed Don Quixote*, released in 2018. This is set in modern Spain. Gilliam's experience playing King Arthur's squire in *Monty Python and the Holy Grail* perhaps encouraged him to persist in his dream project.

One of the most famous modern parodies of Arthurian chivalry is Mark Twain's *A Connecticut Yankee in King Arthur's Court* (also published under the title *A Yankee at the Court of King Arthur*), which appeared in 1889. As its title suggests, the story is about a time traveller who goes back to King Arthur's court, which is here dated to the sixth century although described in the book with the costumes and customs of many centuries later (H. G. Wells's *The Time Machine* appeared just five years after *Connecticut Yankee*, though there the travel is forward in time from the present, not back). Mark Twain's book is in the form of a framed narrative, introduced and concluded by a narrator, but otherwise consisting of a first-person account by the time traveller. Tellingly, the narrator, in the brief introduction, has been reading Malory's *Morte D'Arthur*, an entire chapter of which is given in the novel, thus ensuring that even readers unfamiliar with Arthurian romance have a taste of it before they encounter Twain's parodic version – parody works best when audiences know the original.

The 'Yankee' of the title is 'a practical Connecticut man', familiar with machines and quite contemptuous of the ignorance and superstition around him. The Holy Grail is dismissed: 'every year expeditions went out holy grailing . . . though no one of them had any idea where the Holy Grail really was . . . or would have known what to do with it if he *had* run across it.' Mark Twain believed that the medievalizing romanticism of Walter Scott had been one of the dangerous illusions which shaped the American 'Old South', leading it to the confrontation and disaster of the Civil War. In *Life on the Mississippi*, he wrote: 'Sir Walter had so large a hand in making Southern character, as it existed before the war, that he is in great measure responsible for the war.' Conversely, Twain admired Cervantes' satirical undermining of 'chivalry-silliness'. Whereas in *Monty Python and the Holy Grail* the modern intrusions are comic anachronisms, in *Connecticut Yankee* they are plot devices dependent on time travel. The comedy turns on the bewilderment of the Arthurian knights and ladies at the everyday objects of industrial America. C. S. Lewis, an admirer of many aspects of the Middle Ages and an opponent of chronological snobbery – that is, the assumption that our own time is superior to any past time – condemned the 'vulgar ridicule' of the book, but it was enormously influential, and continues to be so. Film-makers loved it and *Connecticut Yankee* was adapted for cinema and television many times in the twentieth century: 1920, 1931, 1949 (with Bing Crosby), 1952, 1954, 1955, 1970 (cartoon), 1978 and 1989 (modernized).

The Monty Python team were attempting something rather different from *Connecticut Yankee* but, nonetheless, frequently base their humour on exaggerated portrayals of the brutality, squalor and superstition of the Middle Ages. There is always something disheartening about a discussion of what makes anything funny, but, in an analysis of *Monty Python and the Holy Grail*, it has to be undertaken. If, to take a concrete example, we ask what is comic in the witchcraft scene, things become quite complicated. The scene opens with a procession of monks, chanting '*Pie Jesu Domine, dona eis requiem*' – 'Good Lord Jesus, give them rest' – a verse from the famous hymn *Dies irae*, which refers to Judgement Day, and these monks then, after each line, ludicrously smash themselves on the head with the wooden boards they carry. This has both a specific and a general reference. The self-punishing procession going through a village and the *Dies irae* verse point fairly unmistakeably to Ingmar Bergman's film *The Seventh Seal* (discussed later in this book), which opens with the *Dies irae*, and includes a scene with penitents, including monks, beating themselves as they pass through a village while singing this same hymn. This would be a film the Monty Python troupe would know. The more general purpose of the scene is to indicate the irrational, guilt-ridden mentality of the Middle Ages, which saw self-harm as a valuable way of cleansing the soul and averting God's anger. So, there is both a cinematic in-joke and also a broad satirical point about the medieval period.

The procession of monks continues on its way while the villagers are now heard shouting excitedly, 'A witch, a witch! We've found a witch!' They are running through the streets, dragging along the supposed witch, while the camera darts around for sudden close-ups, before we see Sir Bedivere (spelt Bedevere in the film's subtitles) engaged in a scientific test to see if swallows can carry coconuts – a running gag. The villagers coming to the knight to ask permission to burn the witch have the dynamics of schoolboys consulting their schoolmaster, an impression that is deepened by the dialogue between them, in a traditional Socratic style, where the teacher does not give answers but asks questions in order to get the students to answer their own questions. This exchange between the knight/schoolmaster, standing on a higher level, and the villagers/schoolboys below him shows that the scriptwriters had some definite knowledge of the more obscure aspects of medieval beliefs.

Bedivere begins by asking, 'How do you know she is a witch?', a classic Socratic question – 'you assert something; how do you know?' We then go through the rigmarole of the claim that 'she looks like one', deflated by the fact that the villagers have to confess that they dressed her as a witch, followed by the claim 'she has got a wart' and the assertion by the villager played by John Cleese (at the time married to Connie Booth, who played the witch) 'she turned me into a newt'. Neither of these points are regarded as compelling, although in historical reality those accused of witchcraft were often investigated for a 'witch's mark', usually some small lump or bump, distinguished by the fact that it had no feeling – thrusting a pin into it was a way of demonstrating this. Bedivere then helps them out: 'There are ways of telling whether she is a witch.' He does not tell them what these ways are directly, but elicits the answer in good schoolmaster fashion:

Tell me . . . what do you do with witches?
   Burn them.
And what do you burn, apart from witches?
   Wood?
So why do witches burn?
   Because they're made of wood . . .?

Having got to a correct answer, there is now a moment of confusion over how to tell if the accused is made of wood. Wood floats in water and hence a witch would also do so, and one proposal is 'Throw her

The villagers bring the witch they say they have discovered to Sir Bedivere, who explains ways of identifying a witch.

into the pond!' But Bedivere guides the discussion further, asking 'What also floats in water?', whereupon King Arthur, listening on the sidelines, astonishes them all with the wise answer 'A duck', and they then draw the conclusion 'logically', 'If she weighs the same as a duck, she's made of wood.' 'And therefore?', ask Bedivere. 'A witch!', they reply, and proceed to weigh the witch against a duck on a giant pair of scales.

There are three things interwoven here. One is some genuine reference to medieval (and later) witch beliefs: the mention of the wart, with its hint of the witch's mark, and also the suggestion 'Throw her into the pond!' Accused witches were indeed often tried by being tied up and thrown into water: if they sank, they were innocent; if they floated, guilty (they were, of course, meant to be hauled out before they drowned if they sank). It was one form of the ancient trial by ordeal. And the examination of witches by trial by water ('swimming of witches') was a common practice that survived, at least unofficially, down to the nineteenth century. A vivid cinematic depiction of its use in a seventeenth-century witch hunt can be seen in *Witchfinder General* (1968) with Vincent Price in the title role (the film was also released with the title *The Conqueror Worm*). To most people in the modern world, trial by ordeal seems 'irrational', 'superstitious' and a classic example of medieval nonsense.

A second feature of the scene is the role of logic, or apparent logic. The dialogue proceeds step-by-step in a consequential argument of an 'if-then' type. Witches are burned, but wood is also burned, so witches must be made of wood. If they are made of wood, they will float, like a duck. So, if someone weighs the same as a duck, they must be a witch. It is not necessary to spell out the flaws in these deductions, but the point is the style of argument being portrayed. Medieval intellectual endeavour was built on a foundation of logic and its greatest thinkers, like Thomas Aquinas, constructed their works from chains of logical deduction. It is easy enough to parody – later, Bedivere is heard explaining to King Arthur 'how we know the earth to be banana-shaped' – and the harnessing of the supposed ridiculousness of medieval witch beliefs and trial by ordeal with this hyperlogical, step-by-step thinking thus hits two targets in one scene. But the third thing conveyed by the witch scene is the irrational violence, the brutality and cruelty, of the medieval villagers, who are presented as a bloodthirsty mob, intent on burning their victim at all costs.

The Monty Python troupe worked together, usually writing material in pairs (Terry Jones and Michael Palin, Graham Chapman and John Cleese, though Eric Idle wrote alone) but always then reviewing and revising the material as a group, so it is hard to assign any particular line or scene to an individual. Nevertheless, the member of the troupe with the greatest knowledge of the Middle Ages was Terry Jones, the co-director of the film, and it might have been he who was responsible for this informed parody of the persecution of witches. Michael Palin, his writing partner, has said that 'an awful lot of reading went into the *Holy Grail*.' Jones had studied medieval literature at Oxford and later wrote or co-authored two books on the medieval period, *Chaucer's Knight: The Portrait of a Medieval Mercenary* (1980) and, jointly with Alan Ereira, *Crusades* (1994), intended to accompany his television series on the subject (his subsequent television series with historical themes included *Medieval Lives* and *Barbarians*). These two books both stress the brutality of the Middle Ages: the first attempting to argue against the usual romantic interpretation of the knight in Chaucer's *Canterbury Tales* as 'a perfect knight' and suggesting that Chaucer's description is, in fact, an ironic portrait of a brutal,

The Monty Python troupe (left to right): Graham Chapman, Eric Idle, Terry Gilliam (seated), Michael Palin, Terry Jones and John Cleese.

avaricious killer; the second placing a stress on the fanatical and savage side of the crusades (easy to do). The works are widely re-searched and based on a range of scholarly literature, as well as consultation with experts, and they argue their case without flip-pancy, but, nevertheless, they are still exercises in deriding and diminishing their subjects, though in a documentary series for the BBC in 2004, *Terry Jones' Medieval Lives*, he advanced a more nuanced view of the period.

We might also consider the scene with the Holy Hand Grenade. The humour in this case is partly from the concept itself, 'the Holy Hand Grenade', which blends a blatant anachronism with an implied criticism of the well-attested involvement of the Church in pro-moting and encouraging war – the reference to Antioch brings to mind the Crusades, for this city was the site of the decisive military

The Holy Hand Grenade of Antioch, in a scene parodying the medieval cult of relics.

action of the First Crusade. But there is also comic parody in the instructions from *The Book of Armaments* that one of the monks reads out:

and the Lord spake, saying, 'First shalt thou take out the Holy Pin, then shalt thou count to three, no more, no less. Three shall be the number thou shalt count, and the number of the counting shall be three. Four shalt thou not count, neither count thou two, excepting that thou then proceed to three. Five is right out. Once the number three, being the third number, be reached, then lobbest thou thy Holy Hand Grenade of Antioch towards thy foe, who being naughty in my sight, shall snuff it.'

It is hard to imagine a viewer without experience of Church of England services grasping exactly what is being parodied here, namely readings from the King James Bible, particularly those parts that give complex rules about recondite subjects and are found especially in the Books of the Law. The passage in the film is attentive to archaic biblical language, with its 'shalt', 'thou' and 'thy', and its well-observed 'naughty', which in the King James Bible means 'wicked', and does not have its modern sense referring only to the bad behaviour of children or, semi-comically, to sex. 'Lobbest' is a tour-de-force, taking the standard modern verb 'to lob' and giving it a correct Jacobean form. And it is of course an example of the comic linguistic anachronism found also in 'five is right out' and 'snuff it', in which modern colloquial speech suddenly appears in the midst of serious and solemn rhetoric. Not everyone will find all this funny, but the nature of the humour that is being attempted is clear, and its roots lie in the compulsory religious services most of the Pythons will have experienced at school.

One aspect of medieval Arthurian romance that the film represents very well is its narrative structure, the way that stories keep interweaving with other stories, a technique that has been called 'interlace'. In writing, the twists and turns of the medieval romance tale are often marked by clear signposts. In Malory we find such phrases as 'Now turn we unto King Arthur', 'Now leave we these knights prisoner', 'Now leave we there and speak of Sir Lancelot'. The equivalent in film is the cut. But the cuts in *Monty Python* often include a link between one scene and another. The opening shot of the film shows, through the mist, the body of an executed criminal upon an elevated wheel (a well-attested historical practice, which is dramatically depicted in Pieter Bruegel's *Triumph of Death* and also appears in the next film to be discussed, *Andrei Rublev*), as we hear the sound of hoofbeats, before the arrival, on foot, of King Arthur and his squire, who is famously making the sound of the horse's hooves by clapping two halves of a coconut shell together. This is more specific than mere madcap surrealism, since such a method was used to simulate hoofbeats on radio (an example of the Foley effect – the creation of naturalistic sounds throught the manipulation of props), and the Monty Pythons grew up in the radio generation. It also means that one of the most immediately visible aspects of medieval life – travel by horse – is completely absent from the film.

In this opening scene we are thus introduced to the two characters whose travels will provide a connecting thread through what is basically a series of sketches, and we are also given an immediate taste of the nature of the film – a comically ridiculous picture of the Middle Ages. After the first encounter between Arthur and the castle guards who debate the carrying powers of the swallow, there is a cut to a completely different scene, a village of filth where desperate figures moan and grovel in the mud while the weekly collection of the dead takes place ('bring out your dead!'). Only at the end of this scene do Arthur and his squire appear, simply passing through the village. It is a small link, but it does locate these two pieces of action, the debate at the castle and the collection of the dead, in the same filmic world. The next cut takes us to peasants grubbing for filth in the foreground, Arthur and his squire appearing in the background to rousing music, and another execution wheel silhouetted against the sky. After the exchange about 'supreme executive power', the next cut takes us to Arthur and his squire travelling through woodland to the same rousing music. Here they encounter the psychopathic Black Knight. And so on . . .

No one would claim that *Monty Python and the Holy Grail* presents a realistic picture of the Middle Ages, but the film does have this central, if loose, narrative thread in which Arthur and his companions (accompanied in their journeying with their own theme music) travel through a recognizably medieval world, with its castles, peasant villages, knights, monks and minstrels. Armour, dress and buildings are reasonably accurate for the twelfth and thirteenth centuries, which is the period of the birth of Arthurian romance, though not of the opening screen date '932 AD'. The geography of this world is not clearly defined, and this too reflects the tradition of Arthurian romance, which has its own geography, mixing the real and the imaginary (it is possible to travel from Dover to Camelot), and even, it seems, its own measurements of distance: in one of Chrétien's romances, we read 'the castle was not more than half a league away, of the leagues that there are in that country, for measured by ours two leagues are one and four are two'. But the imaginary locations of the film correspond to the medieval narrative stock: Camelot, of course, but also the Bridge of Death, paralleled by many perilous bridges in romance, or the Cave of Caerbannog, with its Celtic flavour. Into this world intrudes from time to time two completely incongruous elements: animation and a television historian.

The animation was the work of Terry Gilliam and had been a regular feature of Monty Python's earlier TV series. In this film it is used sparingly, sometimes to develop the narrative, as in the appearance of God to entrust Arthur with the task of finding the Grail or the scene with the Legendary Black Beast of Arrrghhh, but often it is for decorative or comic effect at the beginning of new sequences, these drawings having a hint of the style of medieval manuscript illumination of just the fantastical type drawn by the young illuminator Adelmo in *The Name of the Rose*. Its effect is to take the film completely out of the world of illusionistic realism. The scenes (one might call them 'skits') with Arthur and his knights usually contain nothing 'unrealistic', in the sense of physical impossibilities, however ludicrous the situation. Arthur in conversation with a cartoon God in the sky is different.

The scene with the historian dispels illusionistic realism in a different way. Although the caption identifies the modern academic who appears commenting on the story only as 'A Famous Historian' (an oxymoron, of course), there is no doubt he is based on A.J.P. Taylor, one of the earliest and most well known of the 'telly dons', academics who turned their hand to presenting television documentaries. A specialist in European history of the nineteenth and twentieth century, Taylor gave lectures on television from the late 1950s, standing and addressing the camera directly and speaking without notes. His manner, and his trademark bow-tie and glasses, were those of the TV historian in the Monty Python film. The Monty Python troupe had already parodied Taylor in 1969 in an episode of *Monty Python's Flying Circus*, in which a woman in erotic underwear lying on a bed discusses 'Eighteenth Century Social Legislation' in John Cleese's overdubbed male voice; a caption on the screen identifies this figure as 'A.J.P. Taylor'. The identification of the 'Famous Historian' with Taylor is made certain by the cast list in the booklet that accompanied the film of *Monty Python and the Holy Grail*, which identifies John Young as 'The historian who isn't A.J.P. Taylor at all' (John Young was a Scottish actor who had a TV career that lasted from 1950 to 1992 and who played Matthias in *Life of Brian*). The effect of the scene with the TV historian is to create a twofold breach with even the slightest appearance of realistic narrative. On the one hand, we are transported abruptly from the world of Arthur and his knights to a recognizably modern scene, a television commentary on what we have just been viewing ('the ferocity of the French taunting'); on the other, that medieval world immediately comes crashing back into the picture, with lethal consequences for the TV historian. This is a stage beyond the anachronisms that occur throughout the story of Arthur and his knights, it is a collision of two worlds. The police hunt for the historian's killer then recurs in short scenes throughout the rest of the film, and culminates in the finale, when the modern world catches up with, and arrests, the Arthurian world.

As mentioned, *Monty Python and the Holy Grail* is parodying films about the Middle Ages as much as the Middle Ages itself, as is especially clear in the music, which follows the conventions of traditional films about knights or merrie men. Indeed, one reason for the film's wide appeal is that it was not particularly aimed at the small group of people with detailed knowledge of the Middle Ages, but at the much larger group of people who are only familiar with the screen Middle Ages. Anyone who had watched *Knights of the Round Table*, or a version of *Ivanhoe* in the cinema or on television, or a Robin Hood film would be familiar with the tropes and conventions that were being parodied in *Monty Python and the Holy Grail*. These echoes of other films begin with the credits, where the Swedish subtitles and the ominous music must, like the monks' self-punishing procession, be intended to bring to mind the popular art-house film *The Seventh Seal*. That film's seriousness, which some might see as pretentiousness, and its popularity with student audiences in the years when the Pythons were at Oxford or Cambridge, made it a natural target for them.

Once the opening credits have finished, we then proceed to a parodic non-diegetic opening with a caption giving the random date of 'England 932 AD' (it seems, from various versions of the screenplay, that it might originally have been the equally random 'England AD 787'). There is no link between this date and any aspect of the story of Arthur. It is there simply to mark the film as a parody

Ava Gardner and Mel Ferrer in *Knights of the Round Table* (1953, dir. Richard Thorpe), typical of the serious Hollywood Arthuriana that the Monty Python troupe were parodying.

of a historical film, just as *Braveheart*'s opening caption of 'Scotland 1280 AD' showed it was a historical film, with serious intent.

Two scenes in the film which draw strongly on the conventions of the medieval historical film are the wedding and the battle. We know there is to be a wedding at Swamp Castle from the exchange between the reluctant bridegroom, Prince Herbert, and his domi-neering father, a scene which is followed by Lancelot's receipt of Herbert's plea for help. We cut to an extreme close-up of the bride's face, and then pull back to show her having her hair braided by her bridesmaids, as they engage in twittering girlish conversation. They are all dressed in white with floral patterns and have chaplets of flowers on their heads. It is a classic image of the solidarity of young women as one of them prepares to launch into a different, adult world. The camera next moves to explore the scene around them, as quintessentially 'medieval' music is heard. We see all that we would expect to see at a medieval wedding: a priest, a feast with food piled high, a whole sheep roasting on a spit, before moving outside for a shot from above of the castle courtyard, where we see piles of barrels, girls dancing in a ring, and a group of musicians with fiddle, flute, lute and bagpipes producing the music we have been hearing. There is nothing in this that is comic, anachronistic or parodic (unless the fact that the bride is rather overweight is intended to be comic).

Preparations for the wedding of the daughter of the king of Swamp Castle before Sir Lancelot's homicidal intrusion on the scene.

It is simply composed of a closely observed set of conventions of how to portray a medieval wedding in film. Although the wedding scene in *Braveheart*, with its 'test of manhood' between William Wallace and Hamish and the disruption of the celebration by the English lord claiming his right of *prima nocta* (as he terms it), is dramatically a world away from that in *Monty Python and the Holy Grail*, it presents us with the same components.

Equally indebted to the conventions of cinema is the battle scene at the end of the film. Like the wedding scene, a battle scene is a familiar sight in more serious cinema, and in *Monty Python and the Holy Grail* there is at first no attempt to inject the comic or preposterous into it. Just as in dozens of other battle scenes, Arthur's army first appears in line, facing the viewer and advancing over a ridge (although there is no explanation in the plot of who they are or where they have come from). As drums roll, they come closer and closer. There are then shots from the side showing figures marching with spears, and quick cuts to throwing-machines being prepared, hands sharpening blades, helmets being donned, before sudden silence as the drumrolls stop. The camera then pans along the line in silence, broken only by the whistling of the wind and an intermittent drum beat. There are shots of upraised spears, extreme close-ups of hands grasping weapons and of faces looking out off-screen, then a full view of the line facing us with the huge sky behind. After Arthur's rousing speech, the army charges with a great shout, and quick cutting and a hand-held camera shows a jostling advance, but at the moment when we might expect combat to begin, the police cars turn up to bring the whole thing to an anticlimax, and end the film. Until that moment, the cinematic techniques and conventions for depicting pre-modern warfare have been employed with great skill and imagination. *Braveheart* would again provide a comparison, as would the battle in *Alexander Nevsky*, discussed in a later chapter.

Although the film includes several aspects of medieval Arthurian romance – Arthur himself, the quest for the Grail, the adventures of the individual knights, Lancelot, Galahad and so forth – one thing it notably does not have is a love triangle, so important in medieval tales of Arthur, Guinevere and Lancelot, or Mark, Isolde and Tristan, where the plot is driven by adulterous passion. The female characters who appear in the film, apart from the bride in the wedding scene and the famous historian's wife, are two old women, one, played by Terry Jones, scrabbling in the mud, the other 'a crone'; the witch (with four lines of speech); and 'eight score young blondes, all between sixteen and nineteen and a half', very excited at the prospect of oral sex – crones and witches on the one hand, erotic fantasies on the other. Most of the Monty Python troupe went to single-sex schools before going to single-sex colleges at Oxford and Cambridge, where women at that time made up well under a fifth of the student body, so perhaps, for them, women were rare and strange (according to his own account John Cleese was 24 when he lost his virginity, although Michael Palin was happily married by that age).

A traditional account of 'the rise of romance', as it has been termed, would see the new literature of the twelfth century, the songs of the troubadours and Arthurian romance, as presenting a new conception of love: passionate, romantic, heterosexual love, with the lover totally devoted to his lady, obedient, suffering, imbued with courtliness. This ideal – 'noble love, fount of all goodness' – is clearly not concerned with the realities of relations between the sexes or the practicalities of marriage and family. It has indeed been argued that it is an idealization of women that, in practice, worsened their position, or at least made no practical difference to the balance of power, putting women on a pedestal the more effectively to ignore them, an attitude, as it has been well and wittily described, of men who are willing to admit that women are superior to men as long as they do not seek to be equal. Romance women are unreal women. Perhaps the makers of *Monty Python and the Holy Grail* were wise to completely omit any consideration of romantic love. It would probably not have worked in a film dedicated to parody and pastiche. Romance is actually carefully avoided at points when it might be expected, as when one of the tropes of the knightly quest, the rescue of a maiden in a tower, is introduced with a difference, in that the 'maiden' is in fact a man – a man whom his father initially addresses as 'Alice', and who has a taste for musical theatre.

But, if romantic love is absent, class is not. In some ways it is surprising that a comedy which was so dependent on the complex markers of English class society was popular on the international market. In 1966, three years before Monty Python first appeared on British television, John Cleese had participated in a celebrated comedy skit satirizing the class system. In the skit, at 6 foot 4 inches, and wearing a bowler hat and suit, Cleese represented the upper class, while Ronnie Barker (5 foot 8 inches) represented the middle class and Ronnie Corbett (5 foot), in cloth cap and muffler, the working class. It is significant that this simple scenario came to be regarded as a classic piece of comedy. The Pythons would, like everybody else in mid-twentieth-century Britain, be immersed in class consciousness and one of the biggest class distinctions in modern Britain has been between those who went to private schools (known, confusingly, as public schools) and those who attended state schools, all of which, after 1944, were free. Of the

English Pythons, two went to private school but only Michael Palin to an elite public school, as defined by the 1868 Public Schools Act (Shrewsbury in his case), two went to grammar schools, which were academically selective but free at the time, and Eric Idle attended a charity boarding school. Between 1959 and 1964, the years when the Pythons were attending the universities of Oxford or Cambridge, the number of entrants to those universities from state schools rose from 26 per cent to 37 per cent, and it is impossible to deny that this was a move to greater diversity and greater opportunity for those from less wealthy families, but it still meant that in 1964 63 per cent of Oxford and Cambridge entrants were privately educated. This was the world in which the Pythons had their formative student experience. It is also worth noting that the total number of students in the country was far smaller at this time. The expansion of university education was a dramatic feature of the second half of the twentieth century: in 1950, 17,300 students were awarded undergraduate degrees at UK universities; in 2010 the number was 331,000. The Pythons were at college when students were a tiny minority of their age cohort, and their milieu at Oxford and Cambridge would bring them into contact with a large section of the upper and upper-middle class.

One way that class manifests itself in the film is linguistically. Apart from the outrageous Frenchman and the Scottish wizard, it is mostly English class and regional accents (which are closely associated) that mark out the characters in *Monty Python and the Holy Grail*. King Arthur speaks with the poshest accent, the knights with standard middle- or upper-middle-class accents, the peasants and guards with working-class English accents, often in a truculent or uncooperative tone, while the clergymen have the characteristic intonation of the Anglican Church. The king of Swamp Castle has a strong northern accent and is a stereotype of a calculating, down-to-earth businessman, a type associated by many with the industrial towns of the north of England. The fact that his son has no such accent, along with his 'feminine' characterization, highlights the contrast between the two of them, a contrast that is echoed in their very different forms of masculinity (northern English contempt for 'southern softness' is attested as early as the twelfth century).

There is no nostalgia or romanticism in Monty Python's Middle Ages, which is depicted as filthy, with villagers scrabbling in mud and a king identifiable because 'he hasn't got shit all over him'; as extremely violent, exemplified by the Black Knight's insane urge to continue the fight even as he loses his limbs, or the carnage caused by Lancelot (whose arrival at Swamp Castle is shot in an experimental, non-naturalistic style, presumably parodying avant-garde cinema); and as irrational, with its superstitions about witchcraft and cracked logic. Higher aspirations, such as those expressed by King Arthur, are mocked and deflated. There is no countervailing balance, a hint that things of value might have been lost in the transition to the modern world, or a sense that the twentieth century has its own darkness. In this respect, Twain's *Connecticut Yankee* is different, for it has a final scene in which the Yankee uses his mechanical and industrial experience in a pitiless battle to destroy his enemies. The murderous explosions, the lethal electrified wire and the Gatling guns that 'vomit death' of this final battle, in a book published in 1889, have understandably been seen as foreshadowing the First World War. The modern world has its own filth, savage violence and irrationality.

Any clearly defined film genre invites parody and one can easily name several spoof westerns, spoof spy films and spoof horror films. Medieval spoof films are less common but there are examples, such as *Robin Hood: Men in Tights* (1993) and *Erik the Viking* (1989), which was written and directed by Terry Jones and has John Cleese in an important part, but few of these spoofs have *Monty Python and the Holy Grail*'s longevity, nor its appeal to successive generations. In 2005, thirty years after the film was released, Eric Idle's musical spin-off, *Spamalot*, directed by Mike Nichols, won the Tony Award for excellence in live Broadway theatre in the category of Best Musical. In some ways, this success is surprising: *Monty Python and the Holy Grail* was the first experience of directing for its co-directors Terry Jones and Terry Gilliam and the estimated cost of the film was a modest £230,000 (much of it provided by fans from the world of rock music), so it had neither experienced directors nor a big budget.

It was also very much of its time: untouched by feminism, deeply coloured by the English class system, and having its roots in the male undergraduate humour of the 1960s. It can hardly be called a 'political film' except in the most general sense. There are no implied references to contemporary politics, except for the mention of the 'anarcho-syndicalist commune' that figures in the film, which does indeed refer to aspects of the thinking of the European Left of the time, though whether to ridicule it or with some sympathy for it is hard to say (though perhaps the Pythons' portrayal of the People's Front of Judea in *Life of Brian*, with their hatred of the Judean People's Front and the Judean Popular People's Front, might suggest the former). The comic world from which Monty Python emerged was a world of subversive parody and satire, which often targeted 'the Establishment', a loosely defined category that might include generals, bishops and politicians, but it mocked them through parody and pastiche, burlesque and comic incongruities – it did not advocate a programme. There is no doubt, however, that *Monty*

Python and the Holy Grail has transcended the environment in which it was created, as its financial success and its popularity among viewers shows. It has made fifty times what it cost to make and has continued over the decades to find a top place in surveys of readers' or viewers' favourite comedy films. It may well be that it has created a picture of the Middle Ages that is more enduring and more widespread than that of any serious film set in the period, and certainly more enduring and more widespread than that of any history book. Our picture of the past draws on many sources, and spoofs and parodies may well be among them. At the very least, one can say that *Monty Python and the Holy Grail* is more realistic than *Camelot* (1967).

4

THE ARTIST
AND THE STATE
Andrei Rublev
(1966)

*B*raveheart, *The Name of the Rose* and *Monty Python and the Holy Grail* were all made by private companies that aimed at commercial success. There were certain things they could not show for legal reasons and they were given a certification by the state as a guide to viewers, but otherwise they had artistic freedom. Films made in the Soviet Union did not have such freedom and were subject to state supervision of a quite different degree. Mosfilm, which funded and supervised Andrei Tarkovsky's early films, including *Andrei Rublev*, was a state body. In the Soviet Union, films needed political approval both to be made in the first place, and also when completed, and film-makers could get into serious trouble if their work was deemed politically subversive or deviant. Tarkovsky finished *Andrei Rublev* in 1966, at a time when the Soviet Union was led by Leonid Brezhnev, a conservative politician who was opposed to the very mild liberalization that had taken place after the death of Stalin in 1953 and who pursued a policy of repression towards dissident intellectuals and artists. Once Tarkovsky's film was completed, it was then subject to examination by bodies of the Soviet state, and various cuts had to be made. It had still not been released in the Soviet Union when, in 1969, a copy was sent to the Cannes film festival, where it won the International Federation of Film Critics award. It was finally released in the Soviet Union in 1971. This history partly explains why the film exists in more than one version (references in this chapter are to the 185-minute version). It also partly explains why Tarkovsky left the Soviet Union to make his last films in the West.

Since this is the first non-English-language film discussed in this book, it is worth noting at this point that, when foreign films are given subtitles for an English-speaking audience, this does not necessarily create an unchanging standard text: different versions may be made for Britain and for North America, and, if an old classic is reissued, then a new translation may be commissioned. The citations from foreign-language films in this book may therefore differ from those which the reader encounters. The differences are small, however, and never change the general sense.

Tarkovsky (1932–1986) is generally recognized as one of the more important directors in post-war Soviet cinema. His other films include the science-fiction film *Solaris* (1972; remade with George Clooney in 2002) and the dystopian *Stalker* (1979). *Andrei Rublev* is his only film set in the distant past, its title character a historical figure, a monk and Russia's most famous painter of icons, who was active in the early decades of the fifteenth century. Christianity came to Russia from Byzantium and the Russian Church was fully part of the Orthodox world, which had certain differences from the Western (Catholic) Church, such as the intensity of its veneration of icons, those sacred images of Christ and the saints that were the object of devotion and covered the screen between the sanctuary and the nave in Orthodox churches. Orthodox monasticism was also very decentralized in contrast to the monastic Orders that developed in the Western Church (as seen in *The Name of the Rose*). The formative influence that Byzantine culture continued to have upon Russia is embodied in *Andrei Rublev* by the painter Theophanes the Greek, also a historically attested figure, who worked in Russia and was a mentor to Andrei Rublev. Important political features of Russia during Andrei Rublev's lifetime that also appear in the film include the continuing threat of Mongol (Tatar) power and the division of Russia into several principalities – in the film there are two competing princes, the Grand Prince and his younger brother, played by the same actor (which must have made it tricky to film their reconciliation scene).

Tarkovsky conceived of the film as episodic, with the sections clearly marked by a caption and date that appear on the screen, and the link between episodes is often no more than the presence of Andrei Rublev in them or observing them (and sometimes not even that). More remarkable yet, we scarcely see Andrei, the famous icon painter, painting. What we get is a mixture of long, slow scenes, in which deep discussions take place, and vivid and sometimes violent action, including the sacking of the town of Vladimir. Because the Russian state, of whatever constitutional form, has always been highly repressive, its intellectuals and artists have tended to react by becoming either deeply serious or absurdists. The former ponder the meaning of life and may become serious critics of the status quo; the latter presume that life has no meaning and create an avant-garde without a political programme in the usual sense. Tarkovsky clearly belongs to the first group and had an exalted view of the film-maker as an artist with a unique vision that had to be communicated. *Andrei Rublev* is a film unafraid of long reflective dialogues (often with the participants not looking directly at each other), just the kind of thing that was dropped from *The Name of the Rose* when it was turned from a book into a film – one wonders what the result would have been if Tarkovsky had filmed Umberto Eco's novel.

This measured pace is reflected in the length of the film overall (three hours or more, though it was sometimes cut for foreign distribution) and the average length of a shot. In general, the shot or take (a sequence produced by a single continuous period of filming, whether the camera moves or not) has become shorter over time. Before 1960 shots in standard Hollywood films averaged around 10 seconds, by the 1980s about 5 seconds, and in *Braveheart* (1995) the average shot is 2–3 seconds. Long takes are characteristic of Tarkovsky, with the average shot length in *Stalker* being, amazingly, more than a minute. The average shot length in *Andrei Rublev*, calculated by Robert Bird, is 28 seconds. The shot of the naked pagan woman swimming past the monks' boat and escaping across the river lasts 34 seconds, with very gradual and gentle camera movement. Tarkovsky was quite capable of filming fast dramatic action, so this unhurried pace was a choice. Likewise, the use of black-and-white film rather than colour, although influenced by simple financial considerations, was also an aesthetic decision. Rublev's world is stark; this is not an opulent costume drama of the Hollywood type.

Contemporary evidence for Rublev's life is sparse: he was working with Theophanes the Greek in 1405 on frescoes for the church of the Grand Prince in Moscow; working with his companion, Daniel (who appears in the film), in 1408 in the Cathedral of the Dormition in Vladimir; working, again with Daniel, in 1425–7 on the frescoes of the Cathedral of the Trinity in the Monastery of the Trinity of St Sergius; and he also lived and worked in the Andronikov Monastery, where he was buried. His tombstone there, which is now lost, recorded his death on 29 January 1430. Today, apart from his frescoes, or wall paintings, there are in modern Russian collections and galleries several icons (which were painted on wooden panels) that are ascribed to him.

Some of the details of the events depicted in the film are drawn from Russian chronicles, such as the *Nikonian Chronicle*, a compilation of earlier sources put together in the 1520s, which gives an account of the raid on Vladimir. In this case, the film-makers have not followed historical events literally. The nearest actual equivalents of the two rival brothers in the film are Vasili of Moscow (d. 1425) and Yuri of Zvenigorod (d. 1434), sons of the famous Dmitri Donsky. The masons who feature in the film are shown departing for Zvenigorod to work for the younger brother, which identifies him clearly as Yuri. Actual warfare, however, did not break out between the brothers but between Yuri and Vasili's son, Vasili II. Nor was the attack on Vladimir the work of Yuri of Zvenigorod but of Daniel Borisovich, a distant cousin of the brothers with his own ambitions. A minor point here: the raid is dated 1411 in the chronicle, but 1408 in the film; however, the next sequence in the film, in which Andrei takes a vow of silence, is dated 1412, suggesting that 1411 would be the proper dating in the film too; it may be that the date of 1408 is given since the film-makers knew that was when Andrei was working on the cathedral murals in Vladimir.

The following is the passage from the chronicle, as translated by the historian Serge Zenkovsky:

Prince Danilo Borisovich of Nizhnii Novgorod . . . brought thither the Khan's son, Talych; he sent him and his boyar, Semion Karamyshev, with two hundred and fifty Tatars and two hundred and fifty Russians against Vladimir. They mercilessly killed a great number of people, took the city's herds, occupied and burned the suburbs . . . [A] certain priest, Patritius, a reliable and highly virtuous man who was keymaster, locked himself up with other people in the church.

He gathered the golden and silver church vessels and other valuable things and took them up to the choir-loft of the church of the Holy Theotokos [the Virgin Mary], where he preserved them. He . . . descended, removed the ladder and remained alone before the Icon of the Most Pure Theotokos . . . The Tatars were yelling and crying out in Russian to open up the church doors to them; but the keymaster remained immovable before the Icon of the Most Pure Theotokos. These godless ones, however, broke down the church doors, entered, removed all the valuables from the miraculous Icon of the Most Pure Theotokos, as well as from the other icons, and sacked the entire church. They started torturing the presbyter, Patritius, asking where the rest of the church treasury was . . . He endured many tortures but told them nothing . . . They flayed him, cut his legs and then dragged him attached to the tail of a horse. He passed away full of patience in this great pain and for the sake of God he accepted a martyr's crown. The Tatars sacked all the churches, burned them, slaughtered an endless number of people, took others into captivity and stole a vast amount of wealth, gold and silver.

Tarkovsky is renowned as the maker of films that are slow, reflective and sometimes obscure, but the raid on Vladimir shows his brilliance as the director of large-scale action, from the muster of the Tatars and their Russian allies, through their headlong ride to Vladimir, to the killing, rape and burning in the streets of the city. The whole sequence, including two short flashbacks, is over 22 minutes long. There is no comparable cinematic account of the sack of a medieval city. The film follows the chronicle down to small details: the breaking down of the church door, the torture of the keymaster culminating in his being dragged off behind a horse, the icon of the Virgin Mary, even the existence of a ladder to a loft in the church. For narrative effect, it has the prince leading the raid with his Tatar ally, rather than just sending his forces, a move that makes perfect sense. One incident, the Tatars stripping the gold from the roof of the church, is borrowed from another account of the raid, in the *Chronicle of Novgorod*.

On more than one occasion during this episode of the film, the bewildered Russians of Vladimir ask why their fellow Russians are attacking them. The keymaster even accuses the prince of being a Judas. Afterwards, Andrei Rublev relates that one of the Mongols mockingly said to him, 'You'll cut one another's throat even

The torture of the keymaster in the cathedral of Vladimir.

without us.' This idea of betrayal from within was an ever-present fear in the Soviet Union, perhaps because, as the world's first Communist state, it was the target of constant efforts to undermine it, or perhaps just an excuse for repression, and it plays an even bigger role in the film *Alexander Nevsky*, made 28 years earlier than *Andrei Rublev*, and discussed in a later chapter. Characteristically, after this scene of atrocity, violence, movement and bloodshed, the next scene, set in the ruined church, is mainly taken up with a long abstract discussion between Andrei Rublev, who has just killed a human being for the first time, in defence of a mute and mentally deficient woman, and Theophanes the Greek, who had died some years earlier and must therefore be a ghost or a vision. This segment is nine minutes long. Theophanes' hands first appear leafing through a charred book in the rubble. Andrei, shattered by what he has gone through, says he will give up painting, a typically sudden and extreme gesture for him, although he eventually takes a vow of silence instead. Theophanes the Greek, looking at a surviving icon of the Virgin Mary, while admitting that Russia's suffering may go on for ever, exclaims, 'And yet all this is so beautiful!' Brutality and cruelty are real, but so is the urge, and the ability, to create beauty.

The film contains much more talk about painting than actual painting. In the scene where the artist-monk Kirill, so envious of Andrei, encounters Theophanes the Greek in the church that he has just finished painting, we see and hear the two protagonists, and observe them looking up at and discussing the wall paintings, but, save for a fleeting moment, never see an image of these paintings themselves. This is where Theophanes makes a philosophical statement about painting: 'You'll penetrate the crux of every thing if you describe it truthfully.' This sounds like a deep Russian equivalent of the English empirical version by the eighteenth-century painter

Andrei and Theophanes the Greek after the sack of Vladimir (Theophanes is dead by this time, so is a ghost or a vision).

Joshua Reynolds: 'Common observation and a plain understanding is the source of all art.' Andrei has none of Theophanes' serenity about his artistic activity and is shown in anxious internal struggles about its meaning and purpose. After Andrei and Daniel are commissioned to paint a mural of the Last Judgement, Andrei has second thoughts and the project becomes bogged down. When Daniel outlines the wonderful torments and fearsome devils they could depict – 'we could depict the sinners boiling in tar in such a way that it would make one's flesh creep' – Andrei says, 'I can't paint this. It's against me . . . I don't want to scare people.' Several characters in the film express opinions about the function of art. The Grand Prince's lieutenant is explicit that the purpose of art is to glorify the ruler, a view that would have been at home in Stalin's Russia.

If we rarely see anyone painting, there are two other creative activities that we do observe directly and at some length, both of them involving inspired, but difficult, processes: the balloon scene which opens the film and the bell-founding scene which concludes it (except for the epilogue, which has no action). In the first, Andrei Rublev does not appear; in the second he is only an observer. The balloon episode is the most apparently unrealistic section in the film, for here we witness a medieval attempt, partially successful, to build and launch a hot-air balloon. There is, of course, no way of being sure this did not happen in medieval Russia, but it certainly left no record. Other attempts at flight are recorded in the Middle Ages, such as that of Eilmer, monk of Malmesbury in southwest England in the eleventh century, who fastened wings to his hands and feet, jumped from a high tower and covered more than an eighth of a mile before crashing and breaking his legs (he attributed this disappointing outcome to his failure to affix a proper tail-piece). The opening setting of the scene in *Andrei Rublev* is a finely carved but apparently abandoned tower beside a wide river. We see the frenetic activity of a group of friends or colleagues, getting ready for the launch of the balloon, which is made of cloth and hides stitched together, while a clearly hostile crowd on boats draws nearer and nearer (in the original screenplay, in which the pioneer of flight uses wooden wings instead of a balloon, this crowd is described as 'an enraged, motley crowd of peasants, children, women and monks'). There is a desperate rush to release the balloon before these enemies can impede it. The balloonist, precariously strapped under the balloon, manages to sail off just as they arrive. Looking down from his perspective, we see one of the balloonist's assistants having a flaming torch thrust into his face by the attackers, who appear incensed by the whole idea of flight. For a while the balloonist floats high above the landscape, with shots looking down at the river, the fields and the villages that he passes, before the ground begins to come ominously near as the balloon loses buoyancy, finally crashing into the river bank – we see what the balloonist sees as the balloon rushes down. After a trademark shot of a horse rolling on the ground – horse scenes, often with no apparent connection with the plot, are a Tarkovsky speciality – we then cut to the first scene with Andrei Rublev: Andrei, Daniel and Kirill on their way to Moscow to take up a painting commission. The balloon scene is a detachable prologue, but it does bring up the issue of innovative creativity faced with a hostile and brutal world, something that might well serve as a description of the film as a whole.

The bell-founding sequence, which the introductory caption dates to 1423, centres on a young man called Boris, son of a bell-founder. In the Middle Ages (as today) knowledge of bell-founding was limited. It was a specialist skill known only to a few. There is actually a letter from the 1430s, very close to the supposed time of the bell-founding in the film, in which the bishop of the Russian city of Novgorod asks the German settlers in the eastern Baltic to send him 'a master of the bell-making craft', presumably having no resident master of the craft in his own city. When emissaries of the Grand Prince come looking for a bell-founder, Boris tells them that his father has died from the plague, along with his whole family and the other craftsmen too. He claims to have the secret of bell-founding, which his father passed on to him, and eventually convinces them to take him with them. The action then turns to the tasks of finding the right clay, building the mould and casting the bell. This is a long and involved process (the whole bell-founding episode is an astonishing 40 minutes long) and is marked by tension between the young Boris and the craftsmen, not themselves master bell-founders, but experienced in the work. At one point Boris has an uncooperative worker flogged. Finally, the bell is fired, the mould is chipped off and the Grand Prince, his nobles, foreign ambassadors and a great crowd of ordinary people assemble to hear it rung

The bell-founding scene. This takes up forty minutes of the film, and Andrei Rublev appears in it only as an occasional observer.

for the first time. After considerable suspense, the bell rings out. Later Andrei Rublev encounters Boris in a state of collapse. He confesses that his father ('the old beast') did not in fact give him the secret of bell-making. Andrei, finally breaking his vow of silence, comforts him, and says, 'You'll be casting bells and I'll be painting icons.' Tarkovsky's father, Arseni, was a famous Russian poet (one of his poems is about Theophanes the Greek) and the director himself said that he felt he was a poet rather than a cinematographer. Despite the fact that Arseni had abandoned his family when Andrei was only five, Andrei always valued his father's judgement of his work, and was delighted when Arseni expressed the opinion that his son's work was more like literature than film. We do not know if the son ever thought about whether his father had passed on 'a secret' to him.

There are only two women who have substantial screen time in *Andrei Rublev*, and one of them does not even speak. Andrei's first encounter with a woman is with a naked reveller engaged in the pagan rituals in the woods that have drawn a fascinated Rublev too close for his own safety. He is seized by a group of men, insulted, tied up in a crucifix position and left (his reservations about painting the Last Judgement to scare people do not stop him from threatening his captors with hellfire). This is when the woman confronts him and they have a short exchange before she kisses him on the mouth and then unties him. Whether or not they then have sex is left open to interpretation, although his companions certainly think so when he rejoins them, in a bedraggled state, the following morning. The interaction between Rublev and the woman takes only a few minutes of the film, but it contains some important dialogue about the nature of love. The woman asks why he cursed and threatened them; Andrei says what they are doing is a sin; she says that this is a night for love and asks if that is a sin; after further discussion, Andrei insists that love should be brotherly, not bestial, and she replies 'it's all love,' which is when she kisses him. Many of the activities that Andrei observes during this episode are mentioned, and condemned, in the rules drawn up by an important Church Council that met in Moscow in 1551, a century or more after his time. On St John's Day (the old midsummer day, 24 June), people say that men, women and girls gather at night to cry out, to talk shameful talk, to sing devilish songs, to dance and leap, to do all sorts of actions

Daniel, Andrei and Kirill in the peasants' hut, sheltering from rain.

condemned by God, and, as the night draws to an end, they go to the river, shouting out great cries, and bathe in the water. Since in the original screenplay of the film and in the captions of some versions of the film itself this scene is identified as being in spring, it cannot be St John's Day, but otherwise these condemned practices fit what is depicted very closely.

The historical Andrei Rublev was a monk and would have taken a vow of celibacy, since this was a defining feature of Christian monasticism, east and west, at all times. An individual was free to choose celibacy, but it left a question: was celibacy a superior state to marriage, and what was the relationship between monks and the bulk of the – sexually active – population? Andrei has been driven to see what the naked pagans are doing and, while observing them, finds that the hem of his robes has burst into flames when he accidentally stands on a fire, a symbolism so obvious as to be almost comic. His encounter with natural sensuality disturbs him and throws him back into a conventional kind of denunciatory religion. This is the only episode in the film in which the life of the monk and the world of human sexuality is juxtaposed in this way. But there is another scene in which the rift between the monks and the world of the common people is emphasized, on the occasion when the three artist-monks, Andrei, Daniel and Kirill, take refuge from the rain among peasants who are being entertained by a jester. The jester's humour is broad, sexual and irreverent, poking fun at boyars (the nobles) and priests. As soon as the monks arrive, the ebullient mood freezes. Kirill expresses the view that jesters are the devil's work. Time passes. Daniel snoozes. Then a group of armed horsemen turn up, grab the jester, smash him against a tree, destroy his musical instrument and carry off his prone body slung across a horse. At this moment Kirill, whose absence has not been noticed, returns. Clearly the implication is that he has betrayed the jester to the authorities (as is confirmed much later in the film). Kirill, like Jorge in *The Name of the Rose*, fears the disruptive and subversive power of humour. For some, the monastic vow excluded not only sex, but laughter.

The other woman who figures in the film is usually called the Holy Fool. She turns up about 75 minutes into the film, after a scene depicting the blinding of the masons by the Grand Prince's men. She is seeking refuge from the rain (a recurrent theme) in the church where Andrei and Daniel are engaged to be working. She is barefoot,

Andrei and the 'Holy Fool', played by Irma Rausch.

unkempt and carrying a bundle of straw, which she guards carefully. She never speaks, although she sometimes makes inarticulate sounds, and she shows great distress at the splatter that Andrei has cast on the walls (the order of scenes in the film makes it possible to interpret Andrei's act as a horrified response to the news of what has happened to the masons, although in the original screenplay there is no connection at all, the events occurring a year apart). She arrives while the Bible is being read out and – it is hard to believe this is accidental – the passage is St Paul's view on women (1 Corinthians 11), in which he decrees that women should cover their heads in church, a practice still observed in some places, and that man was not created for woman, but woman for man. This passage brings Andrei out of his dark reverie to say that having an uncovered head does not make a woman a sinner.

The next episode is the raid on Vladimir, in which both Andrei and the woman are inside the church when the Tatars break in, and it is in this scene that Andrei defends her from rape. They have rather little screen time during the depiction of the raid, but their stories have clearly become intertwined in some way. The final shot of this episode is the woman's sleeping face as she lies in the ruined church and Andrei looks at her, in seeming affection (she is played by Irma Rausch, who was Tarkovsky's wife at the time). In the episode which follows, Andrei and the woman are back in the monastery – what her status is there is unclear – during a time of famine, and Andrei has taken his vow of silence. A group of Tatars arrive, fascinate the woman with gifts of food and fine cloth and suggest she go with them as one of their wives, a suggestion she accepts, despite Andrei's attempts to drag her away, and she canters out of the film less than an hour after she first appeared in it. Unlike the pagan woman, who clearly stands for the sensuous life, which is an alternative to the one chosen by Andrei Rublev, the Holy Fool is enigmatic, arrives mysteriously and disappears unexpectedly.

In the world of the film, violence, especially the brutality and violence of princes, boyars and their enforcers, of the more powerful against the less powerful, is recurrent. The treatment of the jester, early in the film, shows the fierce repressiveness that can be directed against anything perceived as subversive. On the morning after Andrei Rublev's encounter with the pagan woman, he and his companions witness her and other pagans being hunted down by soldiers and monks, although she manages to escape by swimming across the river, passing by Rublev's boat as she does so. The scene in which the masons are blinded by the Grand Prince's henchmen, because they intend to enter the service of his brother and rival, is both fast and brutal. Naturally, the purpose is to prevent them from working for the brother, or for anyone else, but it is symbolic as well as practical, destroying the very faculty that defines them and makes them creators, their sight. In *The Draughtsman's Contract* (1982), a British film directed by Peter Greenaway, the painter is blinded by his enemies before they kill him, again attacking the core faculty that distinguishes him, and in this case doing so by thrusting a burning torch into his face, just as is done to an accomplice of the balloonist in the opening scene of *Andrei Rublev*. Did Tarkovsky consider that Soviet censorship was blinding him?

Tarkovsky's difficulties with the Soviet authorities did not stem from any overt political action on his part, nor from his political opinions. He was explicit, even in his last years as an émigré, that he was a patriotic Russian ('Russia. Dear Russia,' says Andrei Rublev at one point). As a boy, Tarkovsky had lived through the Second World War, or the Great Patriotic War as it is known in Russia, when more than 26 million inhabitants of the Soviet Union died, and his first film, *Ivan's Childhood* (1962) was set in that war. He did not spend time with Russian dissidents. He was anti-American and often expressed contempt for the commercialism of Hollywood. The reason his films aroused suspicion and distrust among Soviet officials is not clear – and was not entirely clear to Tarkovsky. Perhaps the depiction of the brutality of the Russian princes and boyars in *Andrei Rublev* struck Soviet censors as an implied or allegorical attack on the Soviet state, even though it could be seen as an entirely orthodox Marxist critique of the inequalities and repressive violence of feudalism. And there was the question of the unromantic, unglamourized picture of medieval Russia that the film presents. 'They say the film demeans the dignity of the Russian people,' Tarkovsky reported. There certainly were hostile reactions to the extreme moments of violence in the film, and the blinding scene had to be toned down (there was later to be criticism in the West of the depiction of the death of a horse in the raid on Vladimir, since the poor animal was actually killed during filming).

It is also perfectly obvious that Tarkovsky's work did not fit in well with the officially approved aesthetic doctrine of the Soviet Union, which at this time was Socialist Realism. This, apart from commitment to Socialism and the Soviet Union, required realism, that is, a supposedly objective picture of the world, idealization of workers, hostility to experimental form and style, and an optimistic, or even heroic, message. However incoherent this assemblage was, it had state backing and deviation from it could be criticized, possibly with serious consequences. Tarkovsky's experimental style, which became more extreme with time, involved dream sequences, narratives that were not at all obviously linear, focus on seemingly inconsequential features of landscape and so forth. Tarkovsky saw his kind of cinema as an art form, akin to painting and poetry (both of which figured frequently in his films), and was elitist and romantic in his conception of 'art' and the artist. The following quotations from his *Sculpting in Time: Reflections on Cinema* demonstrate this: 'Art is born and takes hold wherever there is a timeless and insatiable longing for the spiritual'; 'artistic creation . . . is the very form of the artist's existence, his sole means of expression, and his alone'; 'editing . . . is not a question of mastering the technique . . . but of a vital need for your own, distinct individual expression'; 'the twentieth century . . . the time when art has steadily been losing its spirituality'; 'commercial films . . . what have any of these to do with art? They are for the mass consumer.' There is not much here on the proletarian revolution and the socialist state.

And then there was his spirituality. He was not brought up a Christian in this officially atheist state, although his grandmother was a believer, but, at some point, he came to describe himself as a believer too, though exactly what he believed in is far from clear. He stressed the importance of 'faith', and was interested in astrology, clairvoyance, transcendental meditation and other kinds of esoteric knowledge and mysticism. To Communist bureaucrats of the 1960s and '70s this was all superstition, reactionary obfuscation and bourgeois self-indulgence. Marx wrote that religion is the opium of the people. In his films Tarkovsky was willing to refer directly to Christianity and in *Andrei Rublev* it would have been impossible not to. The images of brutality in *Andrei Rublev* even include a crucifixion scene, occurring after, or rather during, a debate between Andrei and Theophanes the Greek, who is advancing a pessimistic view of human beings. 'If Jesus came again, they would crucify him again,' Theophanes says. There is then a cut to a Christ-like figure in the snow, and soon a full Passion scene, clearly taking place in Russia rather than in Palestine. We can identify a Virgin

Mary figure and a Mary Magdalene figure. In the Christian tradition, the crucifixion of Jesus is both a powerful example of brutal power crushing the innocent and a promise of salvation: Jesus comes back to life, and his death allows humans to free themselves from the deathly consequences of sin. You could not say the film does not take religion seriously. Whether the crucifixion scene is meant to be purely in the imagination of Andrei and Theophanes, or a Passion Play, or neither of these, is not certain.

The place of religion in the film is not simple. Although Andrei and other main characters are monks, we never see a religious service, in this respect the film being very unlike *The Name of the Rose*, which is structured around the liturgical cycle. It does, however, show other aspects of monastic life carefully. In the early part, there is an effective depiction of the jealousies and resentments that could arise in a community of monks: Kirill is tormented by the high reputation enjoyed by Andrei; Daniel, Andrei's cell-mate, is offended when Andrei simply assumes that he will accompany him to work for Theophanes, rather than asking him, and sulkily refuses to go. There is then an intense scene of reconciliation between them.

But if there are no communal services, there are several readings and citations from the Bible. Sometimes they are deployed to parallel events in the story. When Kirill is in his cell after Theophanes has summoned Andrei, instead of him, as he had expected, and is pondering his rejection, we hear a (non-diegetic) voice reading from the Book of Ecclesiastes, concluding with the famous words, 'Vanity of vanities, saith the preacher; all is vanity' (echoed later in the film by Theophanes – 'everything is vanity'). Immediately afterwards, Kirill, in his raging feelings of frustration and rejection, leaves the monastery after delivering a ferocious rebuke to the monks, even killing his own dog, which has followed him, in his insensate anger.

In his parting denunciation of the monks, he cites the Gospel scene when Jesus expelled the money-changers from the Temple.

The reading from 1 Corinthians when the Holy Fool arrives in the church has already been mentioned, making the first appearance of one of the two significant women in the film coincide with this very concentrated expression of St Paul's views of women: man was not created for woman, but woman for man. Some versions of the English subtitles, but not all, use the Authorized Version (the King James Bible issued in 1611) for Bible passages in the film, which, while obviously both anachronistic and far removed from the Church Slavonic that Andrei Rublev would know, might convey some of the ritual solemnity of the text. This is the rendering in the Authorized Version of what the spirit of (the dead) Theophanes the Greek says to Andrei in the desecrated and plundered cathedral of Vladimir: 'Learn to do well, seek judgement, relieve the oppressed, judge the fatherless. Come now and let us reason together, says the Lord: though your sins be as scarlet, they shall be as white as snow.' These words, from the Book of Isaiah (1:17–18), are one of the more important texts that convey God's willingness to forgive sinful human beings, something very much on the mind of Andrei Rublev, who has just killed a man.

The three main Bible passages that are cited in the film are thus different in form and function. The non-diegetic (voiceover) reading while Kirill ponders his rejection is from the world-weary Ecclesiastes, the book that gave us 'there is no new thing under the sun' and 'all are of the dust, and all turn to dust again.' The passage from Corinthians regarding the subordination of women both forms a kind of counterpoint to the entry of the Holy Fool, with uncovered head, into the church, and elicits Andrei's contrary remark that she is not a sinner, even if she does not wear a head covering. This is, theologically speaking, an unusual position for a monk to take, since, according to Christian teaching, all are sinners. Theophanes' citation from Isaiah conveys God's willingness to blot out sin. Rather charmingly, Theophanes is pleased with himself for being able to remember these biblical verses (despite being dead?). The film has no citations from the Book of Revelation, with its vision of the end of the world, which is important in the plot of *The Name of the Rose* and actually provides the title of *The Seventh Seal*, as we shall see.

In *Sculpting in Time* Tarkovsky reflected on the problems of making a film set in the fifteenth century, specifically how to create its mise-en-scène, that is, setting, props, costumes and so forth, which give any film its 'look'. He wanted to avoid a simple reconstruction based on the evidence of icons and illustrated books from the period, which, he thought, would result in 'a stylised, conventional ancient Russian world'. 'Therefore,' he continued, 'one of the aims of our work was to reconstruct for a modern audience the real world of the fifteenth century, that is, to present that world in such a way that costume, speech, lifestyle and architecture would not give the audience any feeling of relic, of antiquarian rarity.' Opinions will vary as to whether he and his colleagues succeeded in realizing this aim, but there can be no doubt that he is expressing a coherent and cogent view of how to make a historical film: to forget its 'pastness', to avoid any pictorial cliché about the period, even if from the period. There is little or no chance that Tarkovsky had read the wise words of the medievalist F. W. Maitland quoted earlier, in the Preface to this book, 'we should always be aware that what now lies in the past once lay in the future,' but he would certainly have understood this exhortation to avoid being hypnotized by the fact that what we are trying to understand (if historians) or recreate (if film-makers) took place long ago.

In the last eight minutes of the film, it shifts into colour. The camera pans left from the view of Andrei Rublev comforting Boris, the young bell-founder, to the embers of a nearby fire and focuses upon these for a moment. Then there is a cut to what seems to be a close-up of these (or other) embers, but now in colour. The camera slowly zooms in and then there is a dissolve to what we eventually realize are close-ups of Andrei Rublev's paintings. These close-ups are so close that it is not always clear what we are seeing, other than patterns, textures, fragments of things. It is, however, possible to identify many of them and they include scenes from the life of Christ – the Annunciation, the Nativity, Christ's Baptism, the Transfiguration, the Entry into Jerusalem – and also Christ in Glory (and notably no Last Judgement). These are all familiar subjects for icons. The camera dwells particularly on the most famous icon attributed to Andrei Rublev, the Trinity. This is based upon a biblical passage in the Book of Genesis, when three strangers come to visit the patriarch Abraham. It turns out that they are no ordinary human travellers and they inform him that, although he and his wife Sarah are very old, they will have a son. Depending on which religious tradition one follows, there are different interpretations of the identity of the three strangers: three angels; the God of the Old Testament and two angels; or, after Christians developed the theory of the Trinity, the three persons of the Christian Trinity. The icon painted by Andrei Rublev shows three winged figures with haloes, seated around a table, on which the only item is a chalice. Rublev's painting became a standard by which other icons of the Trinity were to be judged, for the great Church Council held in Moscow in 1551, mentioned above, decreed that such icons should follow the ancient models, naming Andrei Rublev specifically (and uniquely). Though there is much discussion among art historians about the origin and

Andrei Rublev's most famous painting, *The Holy Trinity*, 1425–7, tempera on wood.

dating of the icon, tradition associates it with the Cathedral of the Trinity in the Monastery of the Trinity of St Sergius and a commission to Rublev 'to paint the image of the Holy Trinity to honour the father Sergius', that is, Sergius of Radonezh (d. 1392), who had founded the monastery 'so that the odious divisions of this world could be overcome by contemplating the Trinity'. The film has shown us plenty of 'the odious divisions of this world'; now it shows us the antidote.

Tarkovsky wrote that the Trinity icon 'has gone on living through the centuries; it was alive then, and is so now.' It can, he said, be regarded as a museum piece, epitomizing the style of the period, but it 'can be seen in another way: we can turn to the human, spiritual meaning of the "Trinity" which is alive and understandable for us.' So, we finally get to see what Andrei Rublev was famous for – the creation of icons, religious images, the focus of the devotion of Orthodox Christians, a link with the spiritual world. And we see these in colour, after three hours of black-and-white film. Moreover, we no longer have the task of trying to construct a meaningful narrative from the episodes with which we have been presented, since we now have before our eyes the end result of all we have seen, transmuted into glowing images.

Like all great films, *Andrei Rublev* doesn't have a message. But it does create a world, a world we see vividly. Partly this is physical: the vast open plains of Russia; the great rivers that tied it together through transport and commerce and which are almost like extra characters in the film; the endless birch forests with their rough woodland tracks along which the human protagonists make their way to the sound of the song of a thousand birds. Also, the human constructions, the walled towns, the churches and princely mansions that provided painters and masons with their most prestigious commissions. And the weather: rain in plenty, as well as the pressing sense that anything not finished in the summer would have to wait for next year's spring to be completed, since the winters are so harsh. But we also see that this is a world of repression and violence, where a walk through a city street may well have as a casual background an accused criminal being hideously tortured; a world where your town may suddenly become the target of a savage attack, bringing murder, rape and devastation; a world where a surly worker may be flogged, an irreverent song can get your tongue cut out and where monks and soldiers unite to hunt down those whose beliefs are not orthodox. Yet, despite all this, it is also a world of imagination and artistic creation. That is what we see at the end.

There is always a temptation, when analysing a film that depicts creative artists, to interpret those artists as representative of the director, and to see their art, whatever it may be, as a metaphor for the creation of a film. But sometimes it is wise to give in to temptation. We see very little of Andrei Rublev at work, although we learn a lot about his doubts and disquiet, but both the balloon at the start of the film and the bell at the end of it are examples of creative action set in a hostile or sceptical world. The balloon-maker is doing something quite unknown and faces ignorant and violent resentment. The bell-maker has to deal with the doubts of those around him and even with his own doubt about his capacity to make what he promised others that he can make. Bell-making is a collaborative enterprise, involving the coordination of a number of people with special skills and the search for specific materials to be processed in the creation of a beautiful and arresting object which can then be unveiled for the public – perhaps it is rather like making a film, with the first sounding of the bell being its premiere. Tarkovsky never returned to the Soviet Union after 1979 and died of cancer in Paris in 1986. He had made seven full-length films, of very varied types and subjects, and left these behind for future audiences, who could encounter them in formats he could not have imagined. In this respect, he is like the icon-painter who is the subject of his only film set in the Middle Ages.

5

GOOD AND BAD MUSLIMS
El Cid
(1961)

The film *El Cid*, which was made entirely in Spain at the time of the Franco dictatorship, with Charlton Heston in the title role, interweaves two plots, one focused on war and politics in eleventh-century Spain, the other a love story in which passion and duty clash. The first contains many elements drawn from historical reality; the second is almost entirely a legendary and literary creation, focusing on the relationship between El Cid and his wife. One of the few things known about the wife of the historical warrior is that she was called Jimena or Ximena, although she appears in the film in the French form Chimène, for reasons that we shall see.

El Cid is, in essence, a Hollywood epic, but one with a difference. The Hollywood elements are clear. Its star embodies rugged American masculinity. Its director, Anthony Mann, who, like many of those involved in Hollywood at this time, was from a family of European immigrants and was originally Emil Anton Bundsmann, had made his name especially for his westerns, such as *The Man from Laramie* (1955). Indeed, some of the scenes in *El Cid* could easily be from a western if the costumes were changed. The film is in the tradition of grand spectacle, leavened by love interest, that had characterized the more expensive Hollywood productions for decades. Yet it was not the product of one of the big Hollywood studios. Its producer, Samuel Bronston (1908–1994), born in the Russian empire (reputedly a nephew of Trotsky) and brought up in France, had worked in Hollywood for some years before he conceived the bold plan of setting up an independent film production company in Spain. The Hollywood studios had already been making films in Spain under Franco's dictatorship, drawn by cheap costs, good weather and the support (within limits) of the regime, which saw benefits both economic and political in drawing dollars, stars and hopefully tourists to the country. Also, there were strict controls on the export of currency, so American film companies that earned pesetas, the national currency, would find it a convenient way to spend that money within Spain. Bronston went beyond this to establish a vast permanent studio outside Madrid to make films with American financial backing, technical resources and, frequently, stars, while collaborating with local film companies. He established such good relations with Franco's government that he was allowed to borrow the Spanish army for his battle scenes. Bronston's finances were actually very shaky and in 1964 the whole edifice collapsed, but when *El Cid* was being made he was at the height of his career.

Rodrigo Díaz de Vivar (d. 1099), known as 'El Cid', meaning 'the lord' in Arabic, was a Castilian noble who served Sancho II and Alfonso VI of Castile but also, during a period of exile, the Muslim ruler of Zaragoza, Al-Mu'tamin (r. 1081–5), who appears in the film as Moutamin. El Cid lived at a time when the Iberian peninsula was divided among several competing Christian kingdoms and principalities, and also many small Muslim states (known as '*taifa* kingdoms'), which had emerged from the break-up of the Caliphate of Cordoba and were often tributaries of the Christian powers. The Muslim revivalist movement of the Almoravids, which arose in northwest Africa in the middle of the eleventh century, began campaigns in Spain in 1086 – its leader is the 'Ben Yusuf' of the film. El Cid held the city of Valencia against them, although the Christians evacuated it after his death.

The film opens with dramatic graphic credits and a soundtrack of archetypal 'Spanish' music – composed by Miklós Rózsa, the prolific Hungarian émigré who had recently worked on another Charlton Heston epic, *Ben Hur* – and then fades to a shot of a castle set in a Mediterranean landscape. A voiceover tells us when and where we are:

> This is Spain one thousand and eighty years after the coming of Christ. It is a war-torn, unhappy land, half Christian, half Moor. This is the time and the story of Rodrigo Díaz of Vivar, known to history and to legend as El Cid, 'The Lord'. He was a simple man who became Spain's greatest hero. He rose above religious hatreds and called upon all Spaniards, whether Christian or Moor, to face a common enemy who threatened to destroy their land of Spain. This enemy was gathering his savage forces across the Mediterranean.

We thus have our interpretation of the main character before we even see him. He is a unifier, 'above religious hatreds', a champion of Spain and Spaniards, 'whether Christian or Moor'. In the film the term 'Moor' is often used simply as a synonym for 'Spanish, or Iberian, Muslim', but sometimes means 'Muslims from North Africa'; it is a term some people now see as slightly derogatory.

But, whatever terms are used for Spanish Muslims, the interpretation of medieval Spanish history has been highly contested, and the film *El Cid* takes a position on it. Some scholars have idealized the Spanish Middle Ages as a time of *convivencia*, 'living together', when

Herbert Lom as Ben Yusuf, leader of the Almoravids, a North African Muslim reformist movement.

Iberian society included large numbers of Muslims, Christians and Jews, whose relations were, for the most part, peaceful, and whose traditions intermingled and influenced each other. But an older view held that Spain was essentially Christian and its medieval history was the story of how it had almost been subjugated by the Muslims but had then fought back in the 'Reconquest', finally destroying the last Muslim state in the peninsula, Granada, in 1492, significantly enough the same year that Jews were expelled from Castile and the voyage of Columbus launched Spain's overseas empire.

The film takes elements from both of these views. It has bad Muslims and good Muslims. The chief 'bad Muslim' is Ben Yusuf, leader of the fanatical North African sect, who figures as the main villain in the film. The part was played by Herbert Lom, a Czech of partly Jewish ancestry, later well known as the exasperated Commissioner Charles Dreyfus in the 'Pink Panther' films. It is he who is the first character to appear in the film, black-clad, cantering down from his fortress to confront the Spanish Muslim kings. He needs to get them into line. He gives them a pep talk:

The Prophet has commanded us to rule the world. Where in all your land of Spain is the glory of Allah? When men speak of you, they speak of poets, music makers, doctors, scientists. Where are your warriors? You dare call yourselves sons of the Prophet? You have become women.

No greater insult is possible, and the *taifa* kings obediently go back to Spain to launch attacks against the Christians.

This is when we first meet the hero, introduced by his bloody sword, which is seen on screen before he is, but also encounter again the chief 'good Muslim', the emir Moutamin, played by the English actor Douglas Wilmer in brown face, as was standard practice at the time (Wilmer, who died in March 2016 aged 96, was a much-admired Sherlock Holmes in a TV series for the BBC later in the 1960s). Here

El Cid and the Spanish Muslim king Moutamin, played by Douglas Wilmer.

he plays the reasonable and honourable Muslim, who recognizes Rodrigo's worth and gives him his honorific Arabic title of El Cid. Later they fight side by side and have a memorable scene where their troops are fraternizing, and Moutamin introduces Rodrigo to such civilized Muslim practices as eating with forks and wearing flowing silk robes. 'Our Moorish silks suit well your Christian armour,' says Moutamin, which is a mouthful that may have involved more than one take, before El Cid responds with, 'You'll make a Muslim of me yet, my lord,' which is greeted by the special laugh found only in films about the Middle Ages. Shortly afterwards there is the following exchange:

EL CID: How can anyone say this is wrong?
MOUTAMIN: They will say so, on both sides.
EL CID: We have so much to give to each other and to Spain.

Here is the key: Spain. This is what unites the Christians and the good Muslims. As in an earlier scene, when El Cid's wife, played by Sophia Loren, is desperately asking why he has to leave her and go off to fight, the answer, roared by her husband, is 'FOR SPAIN!' The film thus espouses a particular view of the nature of medieval Spain. Both 'Christian' and 'Moor' have a place in it, but it must be defended against the fanatical brand of Islam.

Since 1961, when the film was released, the rise of militant Islam and a great wave of Muslim immigration into Western Europe have given the issues in the film an even greater topicality. Film historians and scholars writing before 2001 usually interpreted Ben Yusuf's fanatical world-conquering brand of Islam as a symbol of, or reference to, totalitarianism, either of a fascist or communist type. If the former, the film was seen as subversively undercutting the authoritarian regime of General Franco, under which it was filmed, by presenting a critical view of right-wing extremism; if the latter, it could fit in with the Cold War ideology of the United States, offering a critique of Communist aggression. No one saw it as simply fanatical world-conquering Islam. After al-Qaeda's spectacularly successful attack on New York in 2001, the opening scene of the film can be, and perhaps has to be, viewed in the light of that event. Conversely, the fraternization scenes between Christians and Moors were interpreted by American liberal commentators, at the time the film was released, as an indisputable reference to the Civil Rights Movement, but that is a (perhaps understandably) parochial perspective, although Charlton Heston did indeed oppose segregation and marched with Martin Luther King. The explicit 'message' of the film, in the sense that it is spelled out both in voice-over and in dialogue, is that loyalty to one's nation is more important than any difference of religion. This is not a self-evident truth.

One source of this message was an elderly Spanish scholar. Although he was ninety years old, the distinguished historian and man of letters Ramón Menéndez Pidal (1869–1968), a world expert on the history and legend of El Cid, was consulted about the film. Charlton Heston, who was renowned for the careful research he did when playing a historical character, recalled arranging to visit Menéndez Pidal in his Madrid home, where they lunched, talked and explored the library. Pidal later visited the set, and there is footage showing him chatting with the cast and seemingly enjoying himself very much. Some aspects of the film reflect Menéndez Pidal's opinions. He tended to give more credence to the later literary traditions about the hero than other more cautious (or timid) scholars, and the film contains several episodes based on these late traditions (an example would be the Cid forcing King Alfonso to swear that he was innocent of the death of his brother Sancho). Menéndez Pidal also had definite political views. He was in no way a Francoist – although those who had fought against Franco sometimes noted that he had left Spain when the Civil War began in 1936 and returned only after Franco's victory in 1939 – but he was a nationalist, in the sense that he revered the nation and, in particular, was dedicated to national unity. Spain had been put together from various separate states and indeed the monarch only assumed the title 'King of Spain' in the nineteenth century, rather than being titled, as in earlier periods, king of the individual territories (Castile, León, Aragon and so on) or, sometimes, 'King of the Spains'. Menéndez Pidal believed that 'the greatest problem Spain has is that of its unity.' In his conversations with Charlton Heston and perhaps with others working on the film, this would be his interpretation of the significance of El Cid, as a unifier.

Alongside the clashes of Muslim and Christian, the film gives attention to the politics of the kingdom of León-Castile, which is treated with some respect for historical detail. King Ferdinand and his sons Sancho and Alfonso and his daughter Urraca, who are characters in the film, are all real people. Just as shown, Ferdinand did have tributary Moors and there was rivalry between León-Castile and other Christian kingdoms – El Cid is recorded fighting in battle against the Aragonese. García Ordóñez, an opponent of El Cid played by the Italian actor Raf Vallone, was a historical figure. The theme that the film explores throughout this material is what makes a king. Ferdinand is mature, certain of himself, able to make decisions. His two sons are different from him and from each other: Sancho is naturally generous, open-hearted but still youthful and with traces of self-doubt, while Alfonso has elements of petulance, malice and vindictiveness. After their father's death, the two brothers nearly kill each other in their fight for the crown. As a medieval Spanish chronicler perceptively remarked, 'royal funerals have been moistened with the blood of brothers.' Then there is the ambiguous position of Urraca, who is clearly in love with El Cid and plays cat and mouse with Jimena. In one scene, with slightly incestuous undertones, Alfonso dashes into her bedroom and then talks in agitation to her through the diaphanous curtains around her bed before she comforts him.

Everyone in the film has opinions about what makes a king. When Sancho goes on his first expedition, his father Ferdinand says, 'peace, not war, is the real task of a king'; after Ordóñez betrays Sancho and Rodrigo, El Cid dissuades Sancho from killing him with the words, 'Any man can kill. Only a king can give life'; when Sancho is dying, he asks El Cid, 'I was almost a king, wasn't I?', to which El Cid replies, 'You are a king, my lord'; Jimena/Chimène tells Alfonso, 'it takes more than courage to make a king'; as he lies dying, El Cid says 'I have not failed. Spain has a king.' Although El Cid is a vassal, not a king, he is intrinsically more regal than the young kings, and trains them to be kings. Here there is a parallel with *Braveheart*. Neither El Cid nor Wallace aspire to be kings but they do inspire kings, Alfonso and Robert Bruce respectively, who are shown in the last scene of each of the films as having learned to become champions of their nations.

The love story with a twist enters the legend of El Cid late. The most important near-contemporary source for the life of El Cid is the *Historia Roderici*, 'The History of Rodrigo', an account in Latin which seems to be well informed and fairly accurate, but it was not long before more elaborate and fanciful stories were being told of the hero. The *Song of the Cid* or *Poem of the Cid*, the most famous work of medieval Spanish literature, was composed before or in 1207 and tells the story of the clash between the Cid and his aristocratic rivals and culminates in a major court-room drama. Virtually none of this is in the film, although the script steals a few good lines from the *Song*, notably 'What a noble subject, if he had only a noble king', spoken by Moutamin when El Cid rejects the crown of Valencia, echoing a famous line from the *Song*, 'what a good vassal if only he had a good lord!'

It was the legendary and literary tradition of even later times that provided the main substance of the plot of the film. By the 1270s, almost two centuries after his death, the story was being told of how El Cid was placed dead on his horse to ride out from Valencia against the Almoravids, the scene that ends the film. And then, in the fourteenth century, the tale was finally embellished with a love story. Both the *Crónica de Castilla* (Chronicle of Castile) and *Las mocedades de Rodrigo* (The Youthful Deeds of Rodrigo) tell how the young Rodrigo kills 'Don Gomes, lord of Gormaz'. His youngest daughter Jimena appeals to the king, tells how the young Rodrigo killed her father and, in a plot turn that might sound surprising, she begs the king to give her in marriage to Rodrigo! Rodrigo accepts but delays the marriage until he has won five battles. The *Historia Roderici* says that both Rodrigo's father and Jimena's father were called Diego, but this is something that, very sensibly, the literary tradition, followed by cinema, changed. The motive for the killing of the count is not stated in the *Crónica*, but in *Las mocedades* it is a response to the count's attack on Rodrigo's father.

These elements now became part of the legend of the Cid and are found in later versions of his story. Rodrigo's killing of Jimena's father and its consequences were the basis of *Las mocedades del Cid* (The Youthful Deeds of the Cid), a play by Guillén de Castro y Mateo (published in 1618), which in turn was used in one of the more important early modern adaptations of the story, Pierre Corneille's *Le Cid* (published in 1637). Corneille's play had a major part in the genesis of the film. French theatre critics have talked of the 'cinematic vigour' of the play, and it seems that one of the screenwriters of *El Cid*, Ben Barzman, who was working in Europe after having escaped the interrogation of HUAC, the House Un-American Activities Committee, in the United States, also saw this quality. According to his wife's memoirs, he was called in to save the film, which was labouring under the burden of an unsatisfactory script. It was so unsatisfactory, in fact, that Sophia Loren was refusing to sign a contract for the film. Barzman and his wife had seen a performance of Corneille's *Le Cid* in Paris and loved it, and he now began reworking scenes from the play for the screen, beginning with those between Rodrigo and his wife. This explains why El Cid's wife, called Jimena or Ximena in medieval Spanish sources, appears in the film in the French pronunciation Chimène, the form of her name in Corneille's play.

Sophia Loren, who played Chimène, was aged 26 at the time the film was made and a classic example of the type labelled 'Latin beauty', with huge dark eyes, a large mouth, dark hair and a full figure. She was in the midst of a very active and successful period in her cinema life at this time, and was awarded the Academy Award for Best Actress the year after *El Cid* was released, for the Italian-language film *La ciociara* (Two Women) directed by Vittorio De Sica. Her role in the film is as El Cid's love interest, complicated by the fact that her family duty is to avenge her father's death on him. When they are eventually reconciled, she also has to recognize that their life cannot be a private idyll, for he is a man with a public role: 'There is no hidden place for a man like you,' she says. Some critics thought there was a lack of 'chemistry' between her and Charlton

Heston ('not a charismatic couple' was the judgement of the *Chicago Tribune* when the film was re-released in 1993), but that is a matter of opinion. The opinion of Sophia Loren's confidant, the screenwriter, director and producer Basilio Franchina, was that the chemistry between the two stars 'was like cold pasta'.

Just like Corneille's play, the film highlights the clash of love and honour. In both play and film, Rodrigo seeks out Jimena's father after he has wronged Rodrigo's father, but the scene plays out differently. Putting Corneille's version of the encounter alongside that in the film highlights some of the choices the screenwriters and director made. In the play, the youthful Rodrigo comes to pick a fight. He begins by asking the count if he knows Don Diego, Rodrigo's father, a question that is clearly not a request for information but an act of derisive aggression. He then asks if the count knows that Diego, 'this old man', was 'the valour and the honour of his time', to which the count, warming to the confrontational tone, replies 'Perhaps'. Rodrigo turns up the pressure: 'Do you know that the ardour in my eyes is his blood? Do you know that?', winning from the count the openly contemptuous response, 'What's that to me?', whereupon Rodrigo moves to a direct challenge: 'I'll let you know that four paces from here.'

From this point the dialogue becomes a frank discussion of whether they are going to try to kill the other. The count is aware of Rodrigo's youth – 'Presumptuous youth!', he exclaims – but the proud (or arrogant?) young man answers that valour is not measured by the years and that his apprentice strokes will be master strokes. 'Do you know who I am?', asks the count. Rodrigo answers 'yes' and admits that anyone else would be terrified to confront the count, but that 'nothing is impossible to he who avenges his father.' And at this point the count makes quite a long speech. He admires

Charlton Heston as El Cid and Sophia Loren as Chimène, whose love has a rocky road to travel.

Rodrigo's courage, sees in him 'the honour of Castile' and declares that his choice of Rodrigo as a future son-in-law was the right one. But he also pities Rodrigo's youth, says that killing him in this 'unequal combat' would bring him little honour and is clearly suggesting that the young man has shown admirable knightly qualities but does not have to die. Rodrigo will have none of this and makes things irrevocable by bringing in the word 'fear': 'So you, who take my honour, fear to take my life?' Shortly they march off-stage to fight the duel, the count's last words being, 'You are doing your duty. The son who outlives one moment the honour of his father is degenerate.'

Clearly there are echoes of this scene in the encounter of Rodrigo and Chimène's father as depicted in the film. When Rodrigo goes to see the count and is asked gruffly what he wants, he replies, 'You shamed my father. I want his name back. But not the way you left it. I want it clean so he can once more wear it proudly.' In Corneille's play, after Rodrigo has killed the count, Diego says of his son, 'he gave me back honour, he washed away my shame,' with the same idea of restitution and cleansing. And there are also reminders of Corneille when the count in the film, simultaneously admiring and dismissing the young challenger, says 'I see that courage and honour are not dead in Castile. And now I remember why I once thought you were worthy of my Chimène. Go home, Rodrigo. What glory is there for the king's champion in killing someone like you?' His patronizing dismissal, however, makes more sense if Rodrigo is the untested young man of Corneille – 'who has never been seen with weapons in his hands' – rather than the hero we have already encountered in the film defending the kingdom and capturing Muslim kings and who is being played by the imposing masculine presence of Charlton Heston, who was 38 at this time.

The fundamental difference between the scene in Corneille and in the film is that in the former Rodrigo intends to kill the count from the outset, while in the latter he is seeking an apology, and is even prepared to abase himself to get one. He beseeches, he begs. The count both 'cannot' and 'will not' apologize. Both protagonists agree that 'a man cannot live without honour' but for Rodrigo honour is compatible with an apology – 'People will only esteem you the more for it' – while the count has the simple position, 'I cannot apologize.' Interestingly, in the Corneille play, there is a moment after the count has slapped Rodrigo's father, when he confesses in confidence to a fellow noble, 'between ourselves, I admit my blood was a little too hot, too moved by a single word, and carried away,' but then concludes, 'but once it is done, there is no remedy,' so coming, despite his momentary admission of being 'carried away', to a position just as inflexible as the count of the film.

The twentieth-century version thus begins with the search for a peaceable solution and portrays the Cid as a man who values his father's honour but regards an apology from the offending party as a sufficient counterweight to the offence. He is a man of peace, forced into violence against his will, again rather like William Wallace in *Braveheart*. The seventeenth-century version has as its hero a man who goes out to kill the man who has slapped his father. Yet both these forms of the story make honour central. What El Cid demands is 'my father's name back'. A nobleman's 'name' is what some Eastern cultures would call his 'face', that is, his public reputation, and to be publicly insulted is to lose face. Hence the name-calling between the father of El Cid and the father of Chimène: 'traitor! 'liar!' So, on both sides, a father's honour is at stake (just as in *Braveheart*, none of the main characters have mothers in *El Cid*). And name-calling is an attested medieval practice. In the *Historia Roderici* (chapter 39),

El Cid and the Count of Barcelona exchange insults by letter, with El Cid calling the count and his men 'women', the same term that Ben Yusuf uses to taunt the *taifa* kings in the opening scene of the film. The extravagant taunting in *Monty Python and the Holy Grail* may be more realistic, a truer picture of the Middle Ages, than it appears at first sight (as Michael Palin noted in his diary).

This was a world in which relations were conducted publicly both in word and in gesture. In the film, Rodrigo clasps his hands in a gesture of humility and supplication before the count, Chimène's father. He does this in a slow and deliberate fashion. It is not the expression of sudden overpowering emotion but the result of a thoughtful decision to move the exchange onto a new plane, because, while the count may reject a straightforward 'man-to-man' appeal, it is harder to disregard this gesture of self-abasement. It is in fact the count's disregard at this point that moves the exchange into physical assault. An even more spectacular gesture is depicted later in the film when Rodrigo comes to King Alfonso to offer the help of Muslim kings in the battle against Ben Yusuf. He throws himself at full length on the floor before the king. This is no Hollywood-style exaggeration. In the *Poem of the Cid*, which stresses Rodrigo's loyalty to the king, when he meets King Alfonso outside Valencia, he not only goes down on his hands and knees but even plucks a mouthful of grass. Indeed, one way to convey some of the strangeness of the medieval world is through its language of gesture: people used their bodies in different ways then – remember that the film-makers of *The Name of the Rose* employed the distinguished French historian Jean-Claude Schmitt as 'comportment adviser'.

Much of the film is taken up with fighting. The title character first appears in the film with his bloody sword and three hours later ends the tale by riding into battle, though by then deceased, his corpse, in full armour, propped up on his horse. His friends have staged this to honour El Cid's dying wish to ride out against his enemies in a final confrontation. In between, there is the swordfight with Chimène's father, single combat in a tournament, an ambush, a fight of one against thirteen, the siege and capture of Valencia and a full-scale battle on the shore outside the city. The centrality of combat, whether individual or in warfare, corresponds to the reality of El Cid's life. In his own time Rodrigo Díaz de Vivar was known as 'the Campeador', a rare term originally meaning 'one who trained men for war'. In the *Historia Roderici*, the Count of Barcelona refers to 'Rodrigo, whom they call the warrior and the Campeador'. We do not see El Cid in action during his first appearance in the film, for he has already defeated and captured the Muslim kings – there is blood on his sword (shockingly, he sheathes his sword without wiping it clean) – so the first time we see him fighting is in the duel with Chimène's father, who was played by the veteran Shakespearean actor Andrew Cruickshank. This is a classic Hollywood-style sword-fight, a set-piece lasting 3 minutes and 40 seconds, from the time El Cid unsheathes his sword to the moment the count falls to the ground. During the confrontation, the gradually escalating tension is signalled by ominous music that begins when Rodrigo draws his sword, and continues until at the climactic moment, when Rodrigo asks, 'Can a man live without honour?', it suddenly stops completely, to give total prominence to the count's reply, 'No.' The fight is on. During the first half of the fight there is no sound except the breathing of the two opponents and the clash of their swords, but after El Cid draws blood and expresses himself satisfied and the count, insensate, refuses to accept this and attacks him again, dramatic music restarts and continues until ominous thudding chords coincide with the count's downfall. For some of this fight Cruickshank had a double, the champion fencer Enzo Musumeci Greco, who had given the actors combat training. Cruickshank was 52 at this time and very soon went on to the less physically demanding role of the older doctor in the BBC series *Dr Finlay's Casebook*, which ran for 191 episodes between 1962 and 1971. The choreography of the fight involves everything we expect in such a scene – the fencing around pillars, the protagonist flat on his back on the table avoiding a lethal downward blow at the last moment, the face-to-face grapple, all filmed in short takes, averaging four or five seconds.

The fight between El Cid and the count involves only the two of them, alone in a deserted torchlit chamber, with no visible windows. In complete contrast, Rodrigo's next combat, the fight with Don Martin to decide whether Calahorra belongs to Castile or Aragon, is public, outdoors, with hundreds watching. There is the opening jousting, the unhorsing of Rodrigo, the fight between the mounted Don Martin and Rodrigo on foot, the unhorsing of Don Martin, the swordplay and hand-to-hand grappling, the duel with two-handed swords and the sudden finale, all in less than three minutes. It is an impressive piece of cinematic spectacle but also one of the relatively rare scenes in the film where most things are out of period. The imposing castle standing in for Calahorra is Belmonte in the province of Cuenca, which was built in the late fifteenth century, four hundred years after the time of the Cid, and the heraldry and the details of the tournament are also dateable to the later Middle Ages, not to the eleventh century, when the action supposedly takes place. The banners and shields decorated with colourful geometric designs and stylized animals are features of the heraldry that first developed in the twelfth century, not the eleventh. Rodrigo bears the lions and castles of the kingdom of León and Castile, first found in this form in 1230, Don Martin the gold and red bars (vertical stripes) of Aragon, which are not known before 1150. Likewise, the large conical hand-guards of their lances (vamplates) were devised only in the fifteenth century. The decor and detail of the scene are thus generically 'medieval', not specific to the time of the Cid. This choice of costume and design was presumably a decision made because of the greater colour and drama of late medieval chivalry. None of this is outrageously anachronistic, and might well not have been noticed by most viewers of the film.

The big set-piece military encounters that take up most of the last third of the film do not include the standard confrontation found in many historical epics of this type, namely, a pitched battle in the open field with the two armies fully deployed and facing each other, such as the battles in *Braveheart* and, as we shall see, in

Belmonte serving as Calahorra for the tournament scene.

Alexander Nevsky. What takes up the later part of *El Cid* is the hero's siege and capture of Valencia, followed by his defence of the city against Almoravid attack. This corresponds exactly to what did happen in historical fact. In 1094 El Cid conquered Valencia, and then defended it against Almoravid attack. It is a curious coincidence that this exact scenario was repeated three years later, when the armies of the First Crusade besieged and captured the Muslim city of Antioch, only to be in their turn attacked by new Muslim forces, that they then defeated outside the walls of the city (without hand grenades). Although film-makers generally prefer to stage a pitched battle, since it is more dramatic, medieval warfare involved many more sieges than battles. The only major change the film makes to the military events of the time is to have King Alfonso arriving to join Rodrigo and his forces, something that did not happen.

The town that stood in for Valencia in the film is Peñíscola, on the Mediterranean coast about 130 kilometres (80 mi.) north of Valencia. Its fortifications and its medieval castle made it visually attractive and any exterior signs of the twentieth century were concealed by a wall constructed for the film, while a huge horseshoe-shaped arch was added (those responsible for the sets of the film, Veniero Colasanti and John Moore, were nominated for an Academy Award). El Cid and Moutamin have concentrated their forces and surrounded Valencia. We see the siege towers and giant catapults that have been constructed. The actual capture of the city as shown in the film combines considerable simplification of events and a large amount of invention designed to demonstrate El Cid's humanity. In the film the ruler of the city is the *taifa* king al-Kadir (al-Qadir), whom we have met earlier, and seen as treacherous, decadent (he has scantily clad women at his court, and wears off-the-shoulder robes and plays chess) and obsequious to power (Ben Yusuf has left his Black Guard in Valencia to ensure al-Kadir's loyalty). In fact, the historical al-Kadir had been deposed and killed some years before El Cid took Valencia. In the film, the starving citizens of Valencia rise up when El Cid orders bread to be catapulted into the city and they kill both al-Kadir and the Black Guard. In contrast, the *Historia Roderici* describes how 'for a long time Rodrigo attacked Valencia on every side with his usual force and energy and at last conquered it manfully with sword and, when captured, immediately plundered it.' No bread from catapults here.

But as soon as El Cid enters Valencia, he has to defend it against Ben Yusuf and his black-clad jihadis, whose arrival from North Africa is indicated by the sinister sound of their drums. The military kettledrum was indeed a feature of Islamic, not Western, armies at this time, and the original term for it in most European languages is derived from the Arabic (for example, Middle English *nakyre* from Arabic *naqara*). Visually, Colasanti and Moore were careful both to distinguish the Almoravids from the Spanish Muslims and to make it clear that El Cid's army contains both Muslims and Christians: the Almoravids are in black robes and hoods, some with partial face-coverings, bear black banners and pennants and many carry zebra-striped shields; some have large turbans; they march to the sound of their kettledrums; among the Spaniards, the Muslims on the side of El Cid are identifiable by baggy trousers and spiked or pointed helmets, round shields and curved swords, versus the Christians' kite-shaped shields and straight swords; banners with geometrical shapes and images (including the anachronistic heraldry and the cross) indicate Christians, while the Muslims carry calligraphic banners, patterned with Arabic script.

The film presents a world in which issues of male honour, relations between lords and vassals and masculinity itself ('you are women!')

are obviously central. At one point, Chimène regrets that she is her father's daughter and not his son. It is also a world in which nationalism is an inspirational notion ('For Spain!'). Perhaps there is a link between these two things. It is a question that can explored through the changing portrayal of Alfonso. When King Ferdinand and the two princes are debating whether to allow El Cid to fight in single combat for the city of Calahorra, Sancho points out that he has already demonstrated his skill and courage by defeating their own royal champion, to which Alfonso replies, 'How do we know it wasn't from behind and in the dark?' 'That is not Rodrigo's way,' says Sancho. Here Alfonso's mind leaps immediately to the possibility of treachery but Sancho knows that Rodrigo is an honourable man (a stab in the back in the dark is exactly how Sancho is killed during his conflict with his brother for the succession). Then there is Alfonso's unhealthy relationship with Urraca. During the knife fight after the death of their father, Sancho accuses Alfonso directly: 'You and our sister, it was always you and our sister. You held her too close. You covet her!' When Sancho's forces turn up at Calahorra, where Alfonso has taken refuge with his sister, he turns to her in panic and begs, 'Don't let him take me, Urraca.' After the Cid has declined to help them, she caresses Alfonso's face and nuzzles him. Later, after the death of Sancho and the exile of the Cid, there is the scene in Urraca's bedroom, where Alfonso comes and tells her of his bad dream and she comforts him. Much later, when El Cid brings Muslim kings as allies, Alfonso and Urraca, holding joint court, reject them: she says, 'We need no such allies,' and he adds, 'We are a Christian kingdom. We treat only with Christians.' Unlike El Cid, whose warm relationship with Moutamin we have seen, Alfonso and Urraca take a hard line on the question of religious identity. After the defeat at Sagrajas, Alfonso has the unchivalrous idea of

Urraca and King Alfonso, who have spurned El Cid and the Muslim kings he brings as allies.

putting pressure on the Cid by imprisoning Chimène and their young daughters.

The critical turning point in Alfonso's development is the moment that the Cid's loyal servant Fáñez brings the crown of Valencia to Alfonso and Urraca. The king cannot believe this gesture. Urraca rejects Fáñez's plea to bring help to the Cid and, kneeling in front of her brother, holds out the crown to him. 'Look,' she says, 'now you are also king of Valencia.' 'I am king of nothing!', he replies, brutally knocking her to the floor. Dashing out, he cries, 'I will make myself a king!' Urraca is left alone in the empty chamber. The next time we see Alfonso, more than twenty minutes later, he is leading his troops into Valencia to bring help to the dying Cid. In the last minutes of the film, as the Cid's dead body leads the charge out of Valencia, Alfonso is on one side, Moutamin on the other. Alfonso's rejection of dependence on his sister is accompanied by this conversion to multiculturalism. His masculine independence and his status as the nation's leader have both been vindicated. Incidentally, John Fraser, who played Alfonso, gave in his autobiography, *Close Up* (2004), a frank (and very well written) account of what it was like to be a homosexual working in the film industry when open acknowledgement of his sexuality would have meant damage to, perhaps even the end of, his career.

After El Cid has freed Alfonso by defeating thirteen of Sancho's men, who are escorting him to prison, Alfonso looks at him in amazement. 'What kind of man are you?', he asks. Later, when El Cid sends him the crown of Valencia, he again asks, 'What kind of man is this?' This is the question, isn't it? He is the kind of man who will fight for his family's honour, who can love a woman deeply, who is never underhand, who believes that differences of religion are not important when it comes to love of one's country. Writing his autobiography more than thirty years after the film was made, Charlton Heston described El Cid 'driving the Moors out of Spain', which, if by 'Moors' he means Spanish Muslims, was exactly what the film shows him not doing. This formulation, which was only given as a casual aside, probably reflects less the actor's well-known shift to the conservative wing of politics than the natural human tendency to revert to simplistic cliché in preference for complex analysis (the respected film critic David Thomson, writing in 2008, also called El Cid 'the Spanish warrior hero' who 'had cleared the Moors out of Spain in the eleventh century').

In the first minutes of *El Cid* we are told that our hero is a man who 'rose above religious hatreds and called upon all Spaniards, whether Christian or Moor, to face a common enemy'. How differently such a subject could be treated is shown by a film that was made a year or two after *El Cid*, titled *The Castilian* (*El valle de las espadas*), which was shot in Spain and produced in both a Spanish- and an English-language version. Like *El Cid*, its hero is a Castilian warrior, Fernán González (d. 970), whose exploits were recounted in later medieval poems and legends. Like El Cid, he kills the father of the woman he loves. The film depicts rivalry between the Christian kingdoms. But its tone towards the Moors is completely different. Although there are some accurate touches – the Moors use pigeon post, play chess and march to the sound of kettledrums – the overall picture is a grotesque caricature. These Spanish Muslims devote themselves to rape and slaughter, desecrate the crucifix, and are depicted as lascivious drunkards, salivating over the thought of 'the hundred Castilian maidens' who are sent to them as tribute each year. Fernán González has the complex double task of securing Castilian independence from the neighbouring Christian kingdoms and of uniting all the Christians against the 'pagans'. In the final climactic battle, he has the help of two 'Christian cavaliers', St James (Santiago, known as 'the Moor-slayer') and St Millan, a hermit saint of the sixth century (both of them, according to legend, are buried in northern Spain), who turn up on horseback. The Castilians first soften up the Moors by sending a stampede of pigs among them. Then, as they advance to battle, they recite the Lord's Prayer, and, at the last moment (after a little supernatural persuasion by the two saints) the kings of Navarre and León join them. The Christian army moves forward in a cross-shaped formation against the Moorish troops, who are drawn up in a crescent (!) and, after some vigorous fighting, which looks as if it might go either way, the two saints resolve the issue by using their swords as flamethrowers. The people creating the film, and the cast, were a mixture of Spaniards and Americans, the latter including the unforgettable figure of Frankie Avalon, the former teen idol from Philadelphia, who had just had 31 hit singles and went on to appear in films such as *Beach Party* (1963), *Bikini Beach* (1964), *Muscle Beach Party* (1964), *Beach Blanket Bingo* (1965) and so on, none of which were set in the Middle Ages. His role in *The Castilian* is that of a minstrel whose songs comment on the plot.

The crass portrayal of Moors in *The Castilian*, its whole-hearted adoption of the picture of evil Muslim attackers and heroic Christian defenders – the 'Reconquest' scenario – and the direct and literal presentation of supernatural Christian saints fighting on the Castilian side, all highlight one of the main features of *El Cid*: its refusal to make the Christians the heroes and the Muslims the villains. Script and story have not a trace of the militant and triumphalist Christianity of the later film. *El Cid* is insistent: Muslims and Christians can be bound together by loyalty to the nation.

Although the attention paid to creating credible visual environments for the film was immense, there is, however, one unrealistic visual feature that all viewers would have noticed. *El Cid*, which is three hours in length, was first shown in the period when such long films would have an intermission, a break when the lights in the cinema would go on, people could wander about, buy ice cream and make themselves more comfortable (*Monty Python and the Holy Grail* has a short spoof intermission, with Wurlitzer music). Some films made artistic use of this to present a different tone or action in the second half. In *El Cid*, the action of the second half begins many years after the end of the first half, and El Cid appears older, greyer and battle-scarred. Throughout the film up to the last scenes, however, Chimène looks exactly the same, just as young and beautiful, for Sophia Loren had refused to be aged cosmetically.

The contrast between the battered El Cid and the ever-radiant Chimène is particularly acute in the final half hour of the film, when they have several scenes involving close physical contact, such as their embrace as he comforts her on the night before the battle against Ben Yusuf or when she attends his sickbed after he has been shot with an arrow. All the scenes with Sophia Loren were filmed early in the shooting programme, since she was present only for twelve weeks of the six-month shoot. As mentioned, 'lack of chemistry' between her and Charlton Heston caused early concern. They ploughed on nevertheless, since the plot required an intense scene between them at this point. The Cid has been brought back to Valencia, wounded by an arrow in the battle. Moutamin, who clearly has the medical knowledge for which Muslims were famous in the Middle Ages, inspects the wound and gives his prognosis: if the arrow is withdrawn from El Cid's chest, he will lose a lot of blood, but may recover; if it is not, he will be dead within a day or two. Chimène wants him to live, but he is determined to lead the renewed attack on Ben Yusuf's army the next day, whatever the cost. He says to Chimène, 'Even if my strength fails me, I must lead the attack tomorrow . . . alive or dead, I must be on my horse at the head of my soldiers,' and she promises this will happen.

The Cid's need to lead his troops from the front reflects a feature of warfare in the medieval West: it was a style of fighting that emphasized the importance of personal leadership on the battlefield. This was noted by the Byzantines, the heirs of the East Roman Empire, who had inherited a tradition different from that of the warriors of Western Europe. The Byzantine princess Anna Comnena, writing in her *Alexiad*, says of the Westerners, 'whenever battle and war occur, there is a baying in their hearts and they cannot be held back. Not only the soldiers but also their leaders fling themselves irresistibly

Bayeux Tapestry: scene of William the Conqueror raising his helmet to be recognized on the battlefield of Hastings. Eustace II, Count of Boulogne, points to him with his finger.

into the midst of the enemy ranks.' She had noticed that there was little distinction between the behaviour of their ordinary knights and their leaders, but all 'fling themselves' into the thick of the fighting, unlike the Byzantines, whose generals remained detached in order to exercise command. It is this that explains the Cid's need to refute rumours of his death and be at the head of his troops. In the very personal world of Western medieval warfare, the death of a leader could unhinge an army, and it was important to reassure them if there was a rumour that he had fallen. There is a famous moment in the Battle of Hastings, which took place at the time Rodrigo was in the service of King Sancho, when the Normans believed that their leader, Duke William, had been killed, and began to retreat, whereupon the duke rushed forward and cried, 'Look at me! I live and I will conquer!' The depiction of the incident in the Bayeux Tapestry has an image of William removing his helmet to show his face and reassure his men that he is alive. It is exactly this urge that leads the Cid to arrange that he will ride out dead or alive. This is how we reach the end of the film with El Cid's dead body strapped to his horse riding out against the enemy, a tale from later Spanish legend. The voiceover which says, at the end of the film, 'And thus the Cid rode out of the gates of history and into legend,' is telling us no less than the truth.

The knight playing chess with Death on the seashore, in a famous early scene from *The Seventh Seal*.

6

PLAYING CHESS
WITH DEATH
The Seventh Seal
(1957)

Moving from *El Cid* to Ingmar Bergman's *The Seventh Seal*, which was released only four years earlier, is to step from Hollywood-style epic to art-house classic: from colour, wide-screen, a cast of thousands, a film six months in the shooting and lasting over three hours, to black-and-white, standard ratio, a cast of dozens, a film 35 days in the shooting and lasting an hour and a half. It is estimated that *El Cid* cost forty times as much to make as did *The Seventh Seal*. The characters and events of *The Seventh Seal* are all fictional but are placed in a specific historical context. With a little knowledge, we can work out that the film is set in mid-fourteenth-century Sweden. It is dominated by the visitation of the Black Death, the plague that killed about half the European population in the years 1347–50, and the film's portrayal of religious doubt, witchcraft, medieval drama and the flagellant movement can be compared to medieval realities. But we surely would not discuss the 'accuracy' of the film if meaning 'accuracy about historical events and personages'. None of the characters in the film is based on real people known from historical sources, and, apart from the overarching presence of the plague, there are no identifiable historical events. The interest of *The Seventh Seal* does not lie in that direction.

The title of the film comes from the final book of the Christian Bible, the Book of Revelation, also known as the Apocalypse (a word that, in its original use, means exactly the same as 'Revelation', but has come to be a term for any global cataclysm). What is 'revealed' in Revelation is the screenplay for the end of the world, as shown in the spirit to St John the Evangelist. He sees God on his heavenly throne, who holds in his right hand a book sealed with seven seals, which the Lamb of God then opens. As each of the first four seals is opened, John sees a rider ('the four horsemen of the Apocalypse'), after the fifth he sees the souls of the Christian martyrs and after the sixth there is a great earthquake, the heavens are rolled up and humanity hides from God's wrath. Then the seventh seal is opened, 'and when the Lamb opened the seventh seal, there was in heaven a silence which lasted about the space of half an hour. And the seven angels who had the seven trumpets prepared themselves to sound.' These are the words we hear in voiceover at the beginning of the film when we are viewing long shots of the cliffs and the stony shore before cutting to the knight and the squire, two of the main characters. The implication is that the action of the film takes place in that period, that 'space of half an hour', of suspended time. Symmetrically, this is also the passage from the Bible that the knight's wife reads at the end of the film, after most of the characters have assembled in her castle. She goes on reading, telling of the angels who blow their trumpets and the catastrophes that follow on the earth, until Death comes knocking at the door. The film is therefore just about as 'apocalyptic' as a film could be. The very first words we hear are from the opening of the Latin hymn *Dies irae, dies illa*, 'The day of wrath, that day', meaning Judgement Day.

Bergman (1918–2007), Sweden's most well-known director, was the son of a Lutheran minister and many of his films have a religious theme or, more usually, reflection on the loss of religious faith. His background was in theatre, which remained a passion throughout his life. *The Seventh Seal* grew out of a stage version and has a troupe of travelling actors as important characters. They are on their way to play at the All Saints festival at Helsingör (the Elsinore of Shakespeare's *Hamlet*, as Bergman, who directed performances of seven of Shakespeare's plays, would certainly know), which is on the Danish coast 3 kilometres (2 mi.) across from Scania, the southernmost part of modern Sweden (this is one of the few place names in the film). Bergman spoke warmly of the direct and concrete theatre of the medieval period and, just before shooting *The Seventh Seal*, had directed a radio broadcast of Hugo von Hofmannsthal's adaptation of the medieval morality play *Everyman*, which has Death as one of the characters. Indeed, looking back later on the years when he wrote and directed *The Seventh Seal*, Bergman said, 'I wrote stage plays for the screen in those days.'

The structure of the film is simple: a journey and incidents along the way. The knight and his squire have returned from the Crusades and are now travelling to his castle. As they do so, they encounter the travelling players, a church painter, a silent girl, a flagellant procession, a cuckolded husband, his wife and a witch about to be burned. Bergman acknowledged that the film was 'a road trip', a straightforward journey, in which the two figures we first see are gradually joined by others, like a rolling snowball.

The road trip is in fact a very medieval genre, which found its high point in the quest for the Holy Grail. In this tradition, *Monty Python and the Holy Grail* ties together its skits through the journeying of King Arthur and his squire and the accumulation of new characters on the way, just as in *The Seventh Seal*, a film of a rather different tone. In *The Seventh Seal*, the travelling players first enter the film as the knight and the squire ride past their covered waggon, tying them into the same frame of space and time. In the same way, in *Monty Python and the Holy Grail* the appearance of Arthur and his squire Patsy, seen from behind, entering frame and viewing Sir Bedivere, the witch and the peasant mob in the background, ties together the characters we know and the new characters. An episodic journey with interlaced stories is a form that has attracted narrators since the time of the *Odyssey*.

From the opening scenes a contrast is drawn between the serious, not to say solemn, knight and his avowedly cynical and flippant squire. This classic pairing of knight and squire, as seen also in *Don Quixote*, is part of a tradition going back to Shakespeare and beyond, of noble or upper-class people counterposed to their earthier servants. It is a contrast that is visible even from their postures as they lie on the beach, the knight reclining, facing the sky, his hand on his sword, the squire sleeping flat on his back with his legs spread, clutching an unsheathed dagger. After his encounter with the figure of Death, the knight wakes his squire with a prod of his foot, to be rewarded with a horrible grimace behind his back. There is no pretence of equality here, even though the two men have spent years together. In fact, one of the historically credible aspects of the film is the way it shows hierarchy and deference as taken for granted in the medieval world: the squire addresses the knight as 'sir'; Jof the actor stands and make a short bow on first meeting the knight; the witch's guards hesitate in dealing with the knight, evidently their social superior; the blacksmith urges his wife to courtesy to the 'noble lord', Death.

The knight, Antonius Block, is played by Max von Sydow (1929–2020), an actor of very distinctive features who came to international attention in this film and went on to have a long career, finding further fame in *The Exorcist* (1973), and carrying on working well into his eighties, appearing in the 2010 *Robin Hood*, a *Star Wars* film in 2015 and episodes of *Game of Thrones* in 2016. The knight seems to think that if there is no God then life has no meaning, but cannot find secure evidence ('knowledge') that there is a God. He prays but gets no answer; he never ceases asking questions, and his last words in the film are, 'In our darkness we call out to you Lord. Oh God, have mercy on us. For we are small, afraid and without knowledge . . . God, you that exist somewhere, that must exist somewhere, have mercy on us.' The squire, Jöns, is conceived of as a foil and opposite. He is not only worldly and cynical, but proud of his worldliness and cynicism. Yet he is shown with generous impulses: he spares the silent girl when she is at his mercy, and she is later shown riding pillion on his horse and resting on his shoulder during their evening break, clear signs of trust, and he saves Jof, one of the travelling players, from bullying in the tavern. We have no doubt that he is familiar with violence but he employs it, in the film at least, only in justifiable ways.

The exchange between the squire and the painter who is decorating the church with a painting of the Dance of Death reveals something more of the squire's outlook and also brings up for explicit discussion the relationship between art and religion, a big topic that mattered very much to Bergman. The Dance of Death is a motif from the late Middle Ages, in which people of all different stations in life, rich and poor, men and women, are shown in a long line, hand-in-hand with skeletons. It was meant to remind people of their mortality. Likewise, the story of the Three Living and the Three Dead, popular in the same period, told of three rich folk in the prime of life who encounter three skeletons, who warn them, 'As you are, so were we; as we are, so shall you be.' The Middle Ages, taken as a whole, was much possessed by death, but it does seem the case that the experience of the Black Death intensified the feeling. In the later fourteenth and fifteenth centuries we find alongside the Dance of Death the development of the cadaver tomb, in which the deceased is represented in effigy not only as in life but by a skeleton, or sometimes as a decomposing body, complete with worms. The church painter is quite clear what the purpose of his painting is – 'to remind people they will die.' 'That won't make them happier,' says the squire. 'Why always make them happy?' replies the painter, 'Why not frighten them a bit?' 'And they'll rush into the priest's embrace,' says the squire. 'Not my business,' responds the painter.

The view that religion is a response to human fear is held not only by sceptics and freethinkers but by some believers, like the blind monk Jorge in *The Name of the Rose*, who thought that 'without fear there can be no faith.' And the role of art, especially wall paintings in the public space of the church, in creating that fear and hence that need for 'the priest's embrace', emerges strongly from the debate between Andrei Rublev and Daniel in *Andrei Rublev*, in the scene when Andrei voices his unwillingness to paint a Last Judgement. In contrast to the indifference expressed by the painter in *The Seventh Seal*, Andrei says he does not want to scare people. Surviving wall paintings reinforce the idea that the purpose of such images was to instil fear: the fate of the damned and the horrors inflicted by the gleeful devils would be the background to every Sunday service. Bergman himself attested to the importance of medieval wall paintings in the genesis of *The Seventh Seal*. The play on which the film was based, he said, was suggested by late medieval Swedish wall paintings. Certainly, the film's depiction of Death cutting down the tree where the manager of the travelling players has taken refuge is similar to the image of death, as a skeleton, cutting down a tree with a man in it as depicted on the wall of Tensta Church in Uppland, and an even greater influence on the iconography of the film was a wall painting in Täby Church, also in Uppland, which contains a scene of a man playing chess with death, an image rarely found in surviving church paintings.

The conversation with the painter gives the squire a chance to display his carefully cultivated self-presentation as a worldly wise realist. He dismisses 'the ten wasted years' of his life, as he later calls them, in a facetious one-liner: 'our crusade was so stupid only an idealist could have invented it.' Some critics think it is an anachronism to have crusaders returning at this period, since the Crusades

Albertus Pictor, *Death Playing Chess*, 1480, mural painting in Täby Church, Sweden.

were over, but this is mistaken, since crusading continued in the Mediterranean and elsewhere throughout the later Middle Ages and a successful crusading expedition had captured Smyrna (Izmir) in 1344 just before the Black Death, although it is true that the knight and squire could not have spent 'ten years in the Holy Land', which was firmly under Muslim control at this time. The squire paints a caricature of himself with the painter's materials and then complements it with a self-portrait in words: 'He grins at Death, guffaws at the Lord, laughs at himself, smiles at the girls. His world is believable to no one but himself. Ridiculous to everyone, even himself. Meaningless in heaven and indifferent in hell.' There is also a serious and compassionate side to him, as we witness in the film, but here he paints himself, literally and metaphorically, as the opposite to his soul-searching, agonized master.

The painter has alerted both the squire and the viewer of the film to the horrors of the plague and to the existence of flagellants wandering the countryside and soon we encounter both, first the village that has been emptied by the disease (since 1950 an enormous amount of scholarly work has been devoted to the subject of these deserted medieval villages, many of which were never resettled) and second the flagellant procession that interrupts the player's comic performance. The entry of the flagellants is a great set piece of cinema – and, naturally, one parodied in *Monty Python and the Holy Grail*. Some in the procession are dressed as monks, some as ordinary lay people, some stripped to the waist; there are men and women; some are carrying a crucifix depicting the suffering Christ (identical to the one the knight has seen in church), others a reliquary with saint's relics, one is holding a skull; they are singing the *Dies irae*, whipping themselves and each other, smothered in a cloud of incense. This was indeed one response to the Black Death as described by contemporaries: processions headed by a cross, men and women singing hymns, throwing themselves upon the ground, whipping themselves. The chronicler Henry of Herford wrote, 'A man would need a heart of stone to watch this without tears,' and one of the onlookers in the film is indeed shown with tears running down her face. Flagellants did take it upon themselves to preach, as we see in the film. Their purpose was to do penance and thus appease God and persuade him to end the punishment he was inflicting on them in the form of the plague. The most famous Swedish playwright,

The flagellant procession, which the knight and his companions witness.

August Strindberg (1849–1912), whom Bergman revered, had also included flagellants fearful of the Last Judgement in his play *Saga of the Folkungs*, written in 1899 and set, like Bergman's film, in plague-ridden fourteenth-century Sweden. The Swedish literary scholar (and editor of Strindberg) John Landquist even accused Bergman of plagiarizing Strindberg's play.

The film, by purposeful cutting, carefully points out that, while the people of the town are moved and impressed by the flagellants, the main characters we have come to know, the knight, the squire and now also the silent girl from the deserted village, watch with stony faces. The players look on in bemusement and dismay from their improvised stage, which is now a backdrop to the sermon. After the procession moves on, the squire expresses his view in typical style, dismissing 'this bloody talk of doom' and going further than he has done so far: 'I've read, heard and experienced most stories we tell one another. Even the ghost story of God, Jesus Christ and the Holy Spirit I've absorbed without much emotion.'

The Middle Ages used to be conventionally labelled an Age of Faith and some have found even the knight's doubts, let alone the squire's scepticism, anachronistic. Yet this is a trick of perspective. In the medieval period literacy was not completely confined to monks and clergy, but it was predominantly their skill and hence it is mainly their viewpoint that has come down to us in writings from the period, and we easily overestimate the religious conformity of the time. Many people clearly did not think much about religion and others might have religious views quite different from those of the official Church. Around 1200 one London prior, Peter of Cornwall, wrote in his *Liber revelationum* in dismay, 'There are many people who do not believe that God exists and nor do they think that the human soul lives on after the death of the body.' And the existence

The knight and Mia, the female player, on the sunlit hill.

of heresy, as seen in *The Name of the Rose*, is well attested. If it was only an Age of Faith, why was there the Inquisition?

At exactly the mid-point of the film there occurs an idyllic sunlit scene, one of the few moments when the knight exhibits unclouded delight, and it is the innocence and warmth of a happy family that brings it out. He encounters Mia, the female member of the acting group, with her one-year-old son, and then the others (Jof, Mia's husband; Jöns, the squire; the silent girl) turn up and they sit on the grass together and feast on fresh milk and wild strawberries. *Wild Strawberries* was the title of the film that Bergman made immediately after *The Seventh Seal*, but with a very different setting, modern Sweden, and in this later film the wild strawberries stand for childhood recollections. In that film Bibi Andersson, who plays Mia in *The Seventh Seal*, has a role as a young hitchhiker, who finds her two male companions tiresome because they are always debating whether there is a God. This surely demonstrates that Bergman had either a magnificent sense of humour or none at all. Not everyone in *The Seventh Seal* is a doubter or cynic. Jof and Mia have no doubts and Jof is in fact a visionary, who is able to see things others cannot, like the apparition of the Virgin Mary teaching the baby Jesus to walk. He has the power to see the final arresting scene shown in the last shots of the film, the famous Dance of Death, in which the silhouetted figures of most of the main characters are led in a long line headed by Death with his scythe, 'in a solemn dance, away to the dark country' – while Mia continues to treat his visions with affectionate and half-doubting, half-believing amusement.

The comic subplot involving the blacksmith, the blacksmith's wife and Jonas, manager of the acting troupe, is a classic piece of broad farce, with a cuckolded husband, a flirtatious wife and an immoral seducer. It is fairly knockabout, with drunken stumbles, an insult contest and a fake suicide, and the squire's cynical analysis of the wife's womanly wiles as she seeks to regain her husband's favour may strike a jarring note with modern audiences ('she'll start crying in a minute . . . and now for his favourite dishes . . . God, why did you give us women?'). It is a curious fact that, in drama and literature from the past, tragedy survives better than comedy. Macbeth's soliloquy, 'Tomorrow, and tomorrow, and tomorrow,/ Creeps in this petty pace from day to day,/ To the last syllable of recorded time;/ And all our yesterdays have lighted fools/ The way to dusty death', remains a heart-stopping evocation of disillusionment, while the comic business with the porter in the same play, including his line, 'Faith, here's an English tailor come hither for stealing out of a French hose', now incomprehensible without a footnote, has not earned similar immortality.

The Seventh Seal was only made a lifetime ago, not six lifetimes ago, but there is a similar disparity between its serious, high-register scenes and its comic, low-register ones. Of course, this might have been intentional, since the travelling players do rely on slapstick and pantomime in their performance and so it might have been thought that the vain actor-manager should have an exaggerated style of acting and play farcical scenes in the 'real life' of the film, but, even so, comic portrayal of women by male authors of the past can now seem tired and stereotypical. It does, however, provide Bergman with the opportunity to introduce a number of in-jokes about actors. In the tavern scene the blacksmith tells Jof that people say his wife has run off with an actor, to which Jof replies, 'An actor? If she has such bad taste, let her go,' and after the blacksmith says he will kill the actor, Jof agrees, 'There are far too many of them. Even if he is blameless you should kill him.' It is at this point that the villainous Raval joins them and reveals that Jof too is an actor, whereupon the scene takes a chilling turn towards threat and violence, saved only by the arrival and intervention of Jöns the squire. The comic tone re-emerges later in the film, when Jonas, the actor who had indeed gone off with the blacksmith's wife, after faking his own suicide and praising his performance in that incident, is caught up a tree by Death. He pleads with Death, 'I've got a performance . . . Any special rules for actors?', but Death is uncompromising.

The sequences with the witch are some of the most memorable parts of the film. This is partly because she is not the traditional old woman but a young woman, almost a girl, with cropped hair and bare arms, whose sexuality is stressed, both by the fact that she has been accused of sexual relations with the Devil, and by her boast that the soldiers are 'afraid to touch me'. The knight and the squire first encounter her outside the church where Antonius Block confesses and Jöns the squire talks with the painter. She is in the stocks, her arms chained above her, guarded by soldiers, and is

The knight questions the witch about God and the Devil, shortly before she is burned. A guard listens suspiciously.

semi-conscious. The monk accompanying the guards explains that she is accused of bringing the plague. We next encounter her 42 minutes later – a very long time in a film – as the cavalcade of knight and squire, the silent girl, the travelling players Jof and Mia and their baby, the blacksmith and his wife, pause in a wood at night. They are apprehensive and nervous about the unnatural quiet. Thereupon, dramatically sinister music announces the arrival of a horse pulling a cart, on which the witch is bound, accompanied by the soldiers and a monk.

Travelling on together, they come to the place of execution, where the soldiers prepare the pyre to burn the young witch. Antonius Block is eager to talk to her – if she has had contact with the Devil, he can ask about that, for his 'highly personal reasons', as he puts it. The opening shot of this exchange is a wonder of composition, showing in the left foreground the face of one of the guards, increasingly disturbed by this unauthorized interrogation, in middle-ground right the knight seen from behind looking up at the tethered girl in the centre of the screen. He tells her he wants to meet the Devil to ask him about God – the knight never ceases to believe that there are secrets or hidden things to be revealed, despite, at one point in the film, being told by Death himself that he has no secrets. The girl, who seems to believe that she has indeed been in touch with the Devil ('he's with me everywhere'), tells Block to look into her eyes and he will see him, but Block says he sees only fear. When Block asks the guards why they have crushed the girl's hands, they tell him that the monk who is with them did it. Confronting the monk, Block asks him furiously, 'What have you done to that girl?', only to receive the reply, 'Do you never cease asking?', as the hooded figure reveals himself as Death. The knight and the squire do what they can for the girl, giving her water and some herb that will act to kill the pain, but they cannot resist the armed guards as they prepare to complete the execution, which is to take place by lowering the girl on a wooden ladder into the flames.

Since the 1970s a remarkably rich body of historical writing has been produced devoted to the analysis of European witchcraft, and its history is now much better known than previously. It is clear that, during the fifteenth century, a traditional fear of harmful magic, which had been legislated against for centuries, was strengthened and redirected by being associated with diabolism, the idea that witches made pacts with the Devil, attended sabbaths and so forth. The prosecutions and executions of the long period 1450–1750 are sometimes termed 'the great witch-hunt', when tens of thousands were put to death as witches. Statistics show that most of the accused were female and the majority were over fifty years of age, thus supporting the stereotype of witches as old women (fifty was old in this period). The scene in *The Seventh Seal* is thus not typical since it shows a young woman executed in the mid-fourteenth century, before the pace of prosecutions had really quickened. Moreover, it was not common to explain the outbreak of plague by the action of witches (unlike Jews, who were frequently blamed and killed during the outbreak of 1348). Thus, while the portrayal of the flagellant procession corresponds closely with contemporary sources, the witch is painted with a different palette, more general, more imaginary, conceivably influenced by the other young girl who went to the stake in film after film, Joan of Arc. But what it shows is certainly not impossible – witches were executed long before 'the great witch-hunt', and not all were old women. Moreover, there were cinematic precursors in Scandinavia that dealt with this subject. One of the most famous early films in Swedish cinema was *Häxen* (1922), a rather hallucinogenic semi-documentary history of witchcraft with re-enactments, which Bergman and the other film-makers would certainly have seen. It was titled *Witchcraft through the Ages* in English-language releases. Of even greater relevance is Carl Theodor Dreyer's *Day of Wrath* of 1943, set in seventeenth-century Denmark, which takes its very title from the *Dies irae*, and shows the witch being executed by being lowered on a wooden ladder into the flames, just as in Bergman's film.

There is one complete and unredeemed villain in *The Seventh Seal*, Raval. We are first introduced to him in a house in the deserted village where Jöns, the squire, has gone in search of water and has encountered the corpse of a woman lying flat on the floor. Jöns hears a sound in the loft above and hides himself behind a door. A figure then descends from the loft with a bag in his hands and begins to strip the corpse of its jewellery. He is interrupted by the arrival of a young woman. He tells her, 'Why do you look so surprised. I steal from the dead ... Each one of us saves his own skin. It's that simple.' He then comes up to her, and clearly plans to rape her – 'Don't try to scream. No one will hear you, neither God nor man.' But as he pushes her into the house, the squire is revealed standing behind the door. He fixes the thief with a steady, hostile stare and takes a step forward. 'I recognize you,' he says, 'even though it was long ago. You're Raval from the seminary in Roskilde. Doctor Mirabilis, Caelestis et Diabilis. Am I not right?' Roskilde is an important historical and ecclesiastical centre on the Danish island of Zealand, very close to Sweden, so the implication is that Raval was a teacher at the school for priests in that city. The first two Latin titles that Jöns gives him – Doctor Mirabilis, Doctor Caelestis – mean 'wonderful doctor or teacher' and 'heavenly doctor or teacher' and were actually applied to theologians of the Middle Ages. The third title – Doctor Diabilis – was not, since, although it is inaccurate Latin, it is clearly intended to mean 'diabolical doctor or teacher'. This is just the kind of irony we would expect from the squire. Jöns then goes on to identify Raval as the man who convinced the knight to go on crusade. He slams the door shut and asks Raval if he is afraid, then pushes him against the wall, saying, 'the Lord sent you to spit your heavenly venom and to poison the knight.' Raval pleads that this was done in good faith. The squire says that being a thief is a more suitable occupation for him, then forces him down and holds a knife to his throat. At this point the girl screams (the only sound she makes until the very end of the film, when she says, 'It is finished,' as Death approaches). The squire releases Raval, but threatens, if they meet again, to mark his face in the way criminals are marked.

They do meet again, at the village inn, a crowded place where men and women sit around eating and drinking, with the obligatory whole pig roasting on a spit. Raval is there, offering a stolen bracelet for sale to Jof, the actor, who happens to be sitting behind him. The blacksmith turns up, looking for the actor who has run off with his wife, and this is when Raval reveals to him that Jof is an actor. The atmosphere turns threatening. Raval has obviously seen the chance for a little sadistic fun. He threatens to mark Jof's face in the way criminals are marked, just as the squire has threatened him. The inn falls silent. Jof can see no sympathetic face and the blacksmith is stupidly convinced that he is the actor who has gone off with his wife. Eventually by thrusting a burning torch at his face, Raval forces Jof to climb on a table and dance like a bear. The entire company in the inn bursts out in hearty laughter, beating out the rhythm on the table with their mugs, in a frightening display of mob callousness. It is at the point when Raval is demanding that Jof, who is near collapse, should go on with his dance that Jöns the squire enters the inn. In a remarkably economical sequence – two shots totalling 20 seconds – Jöns grabs Raval, pushes him against the wall and slashes his face with a knife, saying simply 'Remember what I'd do to you if we met again? I'm a man of my word.' We then cut to the knight lying on a sunlit height above the sea.

Raval's final appearance is short but important, for it is the only moment in the film that we actually see someone die of the plague – we have seen corpses and an abandoned village, but not this. The knight and his party are in the woods at night, having recently witnessed the girl accused of witchcraft being prepared for her execution. Mia is singing to her baby, the blacksmith's wife is whimpering in distress, the silent girl reclines in the squire's arms. The atmosphere is ominous. Suddenly we hear a voice off-screen begging for water, and see the startled, alert faces of the company. On the far side of a giant uprooted tree, the bedraggled and terrified form of Raval appears. 'I've got the plague,' he gasps. The squire commands him to keep to the far side of the tree and he stumbles back and falls to the ground, crying, 'I'm scared of dying. I don't want to die, I don't want to!' He begs for help and the silent girl rises to bring him water, regardless of their previous encounter, but Jöns holds her back, saying, 'It doesn't help. It doesn't help.' Raval staggers and gasps. 'What's going to happen to me? Can't you even comfort me?' he asks. He screams and staggers. 'It's meaningless,' says the squire to the silent girl, 'It's completely meaningless.' Screaming and staggering, Raval finally collapses and dies.

Raval is always in scenes along with the squire, who defends his victims against him. Of all the characters in the film, the squire is the most insistent that idealism is idiocy and life is meaningless, yet he is the one shown protecting the girl when Raval threatens her with rape and protecting Jof when Raval is mercilessly tormenting him. Likewise, when observing the witch about to be burned, he is overcome: 'That little child! . . . I can't be bothered, I can't be bothered!' In contrast, Raval, the renegade clergyman, is explicit that 'each one of us saves his own skin'; he plunders the dead and indulges his own brutality and cruelty. And he is the one who dies alone in agony.

The knight, meanwhile, is working on his ambition: 'I want to use my respite for one meaningful act.' The act he finally achieves is to distract Death, so that Jof, Mia and their baby can escape, and they are thus not in the final group that arrives at the knight's castle for their final encounter with Death. They get away in their covered wagon, cower during the violent storm that night and emerge the next day to sunshine and birdsong. This is when Jof has his famous vision of the Dance of Death. Afterwards, Mia looks at him with loving but amused eyes and says, 'You and your dreams and visions!' They move on, Mia carrying the baby, Jof leading the horse with one hand and the other over Mia's shoulder, as disembodied heavenly voices sing 'Gloria'. For a film about plague and death, this is an upbeat ending.

The Seventh Seal was the classic art-house movie of the late 1950s and 1960s, that is, one revered by a small but vociferous section of society: intellectuals, bohemians, students (a far smaller proportion of the population then than now). It was deemed 'highbrow', was honoured at Cannes but never considered for an Academy Award and made only a modest amount of money. Nevertheless, it entered film legend and became something that could be referred to and parodied, from the mock-Swedish credits and self-battering monks of *Monty Python and the Holy Grail* to the scene in *De Düva* (The Dove) (1968) depicting a character playing badminton with Death, not to mention *Bill and Ted's Bogus Journey* and others. Terry Jones's book *The Saga of Erik the Viking* ends with Erik playing chess with Death (though this scene is not in the film based on the book). *The Seventh Seal* attracts parody because it either skirts or, according to one's view, embodies pretentiousness. Bergman was not afraid to have his characters say things like: 'Through my indifference to my fellow men, I have isolated myself from their company. Now I live in a world of phantoms. I am imprisoned in my dreams and fantasies', and 'Faith is a heavy burden.' It is thus his own fault that people discussed the meaning of the film. Some sought the key in existentialism, a French style of thought fashionable at the time the film was made, associated with the name of Jean-Paul Sartre. There is some plausibility to this. When Sartre attempted a simple description of existentialism (which was not his usual style), he listed a few of his core positions: that God does not exist, that there is no such thing as human nature, that human beings make themselves by their will, in a state of anguish, abandonment and despair. It is easy to see how all this could fit in with the knight's despairing spiritual quest. Other viewers and critics, however, took a different perspective, seeing the film as allegorical and the key being the threat of nuclear annihilation, something that Bergman himself casually alluded to in an interview, and indeed a topic that would be important in a later film of his, *Winter Light* (1963). This is one of the problems in talking about the meaning of a film. There is always the temptation to look at what one considers the Big Issues of the day, that is, the day the film was made, and then link the film and the issues. But if Bergman wanted to make a film about nuclear annihilation, why didn't he make a film about nuclear annihilation (as Tarkovsky did in his last film, *The Sacrifice*, which was, curiously enough, filmed in Sweden with one of Bergman's preferred cinematographers, Sven Nykvist)?

There is one quality of the film that has been identified both by those who praise it and those who do not. This is the fact that almost any frame could be printed out as a still photograph of great compositional power, a reflection of the talent of the cinematographer, Gunnar Fischer, as much as of Bergman. Although there is general agreement about this, some see it as a criticism, a sign of a static visual imagination, a failure to embrace the fact that motion pictures are *motion* pictures. This is perhaps linked to Bergman's experience of and commitment to the stage. A traditional theatre presents a framed tableau – individuals and objects in a visual rectangle before the eyes of the audience. Cinema offered the opportunity to transcend this, and some critics thought that Bergman had not seized that opportunity. This will naturally be a matter of opinion.

There are no directors who specialize in films about the Middle Ages, but Ingmar Bergman made two. His other film with a medieval setting, made a few years after *The Seventh Seal*, is *The Virgin Spring* (1960), which won an Academy Award for Best Foreign Language Film. The plot was inspired by a traditional Swedish ballad, though the film made several fundamental changes to the story. Bergman's film tells of a prosperous farmer, played by Max von Sydow, whose young and beautiful daughter, Karin, is raped and murdered by herdsmen while on her way to church. The herdsmen later stay at the farmer's house, not knowing who he is, and try to sell Karin's clothes. He kills them all. Also important in the plot is Karin's illegitimate half-sister, Ingeri, played by Gunnel Lindblom, who was the silent girl in *The Seventh Seal*. Her character in this later film is absolutely different: dark, malicious, unmarried but pregnant, a secret pagan; unlike the ladylike Karin, who rides side-saddle, Ingeri rides astride. She witnesses the rape and murder and reports where Karin's body can be found. The final scene of the film shows Max von Sydow and all the occupants of the farm by Karin's body. He has, unsurprisingly, a long speech to God, and, as he lifts up the body of his dead daughter, a spring miraculously wells up from the spot where she has been (the 'Virgin Spring' of the title). Ingeri washes her face in it; Karin's mother washes her child's face with water from it. The ending hints at some resolution, although the plot of the film to this point has been the rape and murder of a young girl and her father's savage revenge on the perpetrators.

The Virgin Spring was extremely unusual in actually depicting a rape, which it shows in all its sordid reality, made all the more distressing because of the way Karin has been presented to that point, as a spoiled young girl who likes pretty clothes and dancing. It is her extreme and innocent naivety that lets her fall into the power of the herdsmen. These scenes led to a great debate in the Swedish press and naturally created some problems with film censors in several countries. Like *The Seventh Seal*, *The Virgin Spring* is set in a generalized medieval Sweden with no identifiable historical characters or events. It also has the attention to realistic everyday detail of the earlier film, showing patterns of work and family tensions in a busy farm, with a credible depiction of the way religion fitted in with ordinary daily routines, and superb domestic interiors. Unlike *The Seventh Seal*, it has a unitary plot, limited to 24 hours and only two settings, the farm and the journey to the church.

After these two films with medieval settings, Bergman never made another. Most of his full-length films of the 1960s and '70s were set either in contemporary Sweden or the Sweden of the years around 1900, the time of his parents' childhood and youth. They are often marked by fragmented narratives, symbolism and surrealism, and became more sexually explicit. A common theme is the tortured artist. Bergman was in fact criticized for being apolitical at a time of increasing political activism, and for being fixated on a late Romantic obsession with the role of the artist. Bergman made his last feature film for the cinema in 1982, though he continued to work both in television and as a director of stage plays. *The Seventh Seal* and *The Virgin Spring*, released in 1957 and 1960, thus mark a short period when he was concerned with putting the Middle Ages on the screen. Given that Bergman directed seventy films (including shorts and TV films), two medieval films do not amount to much, but he clearly had a few years when he was thinking seriously about how to depict the era. He chose to show a world in which the highest social class represented is a (solitary) knight, Antonius Block in *The Seventh Seal*. There are no kings or aristocrats, so common in other films about the period, no heraldry or tournaments. In *The Virgin Spring*, there

The Dance of Death at the end of the film.

is no one of higher social status than a well-off farmer. In both films, it is a world that takes religion seriously but we see no monasteries or cathedrals, simply rural churches and the religious observances that could be undertaken at home, or, in the case of flagellants, a popular religious movement. The determinedly social democratic Sweden of the later twentieth century, with its egalitarian ethos, seems to have produced a kind of medieval mirror image in these films. But it is also a world of violence and danger. In *The Virgin Spring*, there are four killings. At the end of *The Seventh Seal*, almost all of the main characters are dead. With one very striking exception, the picture of the Middle Ages presented in *The Seventh Seal* is highly credible. That exception is, of course, the presence of personified Death. Otherwise, it is a model of realistic naturalism in clothes and buildings, and the dialogue contains no obvious anachronisms, as long as we are willing to believe that people in the Middle Ages might have religious doubts or express cynical scepticism. And, on consideration, even the recurrent presence of Death can be regarded as realistic.

Bergman later reminisced about the shooting of one of the last scenes in the film, the Dance of Death:

We had packed up for the day because of an approaching storm. Suddenly I caught sight of a strange cloud. Gunnar Fischer hastily set the camera back into place. Several of the actors had already returned to where we were staying, so a few grips and a couple of tourists danced in their place, having no idea what it was all about. The image that later became so famous was improvised in only a few minutes.

If this is true, it may explain why Death leads a different group of six in this dance from the six we have just seen encountering him in the knight's castle; the knight's wife and the silent girl are not here, but the actor-manager Jonas and the villain Raval, who both died earlier in the film, are. Perhaps there were not enough women available for this improvised shot. Be that as it may, the story is not without parallels, as told by other directors about other films. Director Anthony Mann recalled noticing the sun glinting on the armour of an extra coming out of the gates of Peñíscola (which was serving as Valencia) when shooting the last scenes of *El Cid* and immediately cried out, 'Look! That's what we want! We've got to get the sun!', and rushed his star, Charlton Heston, into position, so that the sunlight glinted on him as he emerged through the gateway to ride 'from history into legend'. Such anecdotes reflect more than the vanity of directors about their improvisational genius. They show something distinctive about the art form. In location filming, a passing feature of the sky and light can be seized on to make a striking, and lasting, image.

7

HEROIC LEADERSHIP
Alexander Nevsky
(1938)

The action of Sergei Eisenstein's *Alexander Nevsky* is set in 1242, when the Teutonic Knights based in Livonia (modern Estonia and Latvia) invaded Russia and were defeated at Lake Peipus (or Chud) by the forces of Novgorod under Prince Alexander Nevsky. The Teutonic Knights had been founded in the Holy Land to fight the Crusades against the Muslims but later were invited into Eastern Europe to fight local pagans as well. By the time of the Battle on the Ice, as Alexander Nevsky's victory is often termed, they had established their own state, which extended for hundreds of kilometres along the southern and eastern coast of the Baltic and had come into contact, and conflict, not only with pagans but with the Russians, who were Orthodox Christians. The clash was thus between not only two different groups of people, Russians and Germans (Teutonic Knights being recruited, as their name suggests, almost entirely from Germans), but two different kinds of Christianity – Eastern Orthodox and Latin Catholic. At the time of the battle, Russia had been Christian for 250 years, but it had received its Christianity from the Byzantine Empire, whose traditions and structures had come to differ from those of the Western or Latin Church, which recognized the pope as supreme. Eventually these differences sharpened to the point not only of mutual condemnations by the ecclesiastical authorities but of physical violence. In 1204 a Western crusading army, diverted from its original target, conquered and sacked Constantinople, capital of the Byzantine Empire. Warfare between Western crusaders and Orthodox Christians was nothing new at the time of the Battle on the Ice.

Russia in this period (as in the time of Andrei Rublev, discussed in an earlier chapter) was not a single unified state but was divided into several principalities (though their rulers were mostly from one extended family) and in the 1230s, just before the confrontation with the Teutonic Knights, most of these principalities had been conquered and made tributary by the Mongols under the leadership of Batu, grandson of Genghis Khan. Batu established his own, directly ruled, realm on the steppes east of Russia, which is known as the Khanate of the Golden Horde. The Russian princes, while not dispossessed, were expected to pay tribute, come 'to the Horde' when required and receive their authority from the Khan. One of the opening scenes of the film depicts a high Mongol official and his encounter with Alexander Nevsky. Alexander was given the nickname 'Nevsky' because, two years before the Battle on the Ice, he had won a victory against the Swedes in a battle on the river Neva (on which St Petersburg now stands). The hacking down of the enemy commander's tent, which is shown in Eisenstein's film during the Battle on the Ice, is actually recorded as taking place in this battle on the Neva. Alexander's victory over the Swedes is not depicted in the film but is mentioned repeatedly in its opening moments: the first words heard in the film, as Alexander's men are fishing, is a song about the battle they fought on the Neva; the Mongol official's first questions of him are 'Is it you they call Nevsky?' and 'Was it you who defeated the Swedes?' It is this military reputation that makes the citizens of Novgorod (or many of them) eager to summon him to repel the German advance.

Two things about Novgorod emerge from the film, both of them corresponding to historical fact: it was a trading city and the citizens of Novgorod had considerable autonomy, being able to choose and depose their prince – it has indeed been described as an elective principality (this explains its honorific title, 'Lord Novgorod'). Alexander had been expelled from the city not long before the time in which the film is set. That is why we find him fishing at the beginning of the film and why there is such a debate among the citizens about whether they should send for him. Novgorod was the only Russian principality to avoid direct subjugation to the Mongols, so its citizens retained the right to choose their prince. In the debate we see clearly the class divisions that may well reflect thirteenth-century reality but are also ideologically necessary for a film made in the Soviet Union under Stalin. The merchants are unpatriotic and, when urged to leave off trading for a while to confront the German threat, they argue that this would mean they would have unsold goods and suggest instead buying the safety of Novgorod. When Olga, the young love interest, asks them 'would you barter away the Russian land?', the jeering response is, 'Russian land? Is there any such thing?' (an alternative version of the subtitles has 'What Russia? Where have you seen it last?'), a cynical view which is backed up by a renegade Russian monk. An armourer, already presented as a sympathetic character, then kicks the monk to the ground and delivers a heartfelt criticism of the rich and urges the assembly to summon Alexander. The debate grows heated, with one strong young Russian, a model of Soviet youth, knocking aside those who do not wish to summon Alexander. The merchants offer the leadership to Domash, a local Novgorod notable, but he declines

Alexander Nevsky with Domash, who has declined to lead the forces of Novgorod and insisted that the citizens recall Alexander.

and says, 'We shall need a great man to lead us.' This is indeed one main message the film is intended to teach.

The director, Sergei Eisenstein (1898–1948), is regarded as one of the giants of Soviet film, important as a theorist of cinema as well as a practitioner. He is particularly associated with the idea of montage, the juxtaposition of various shots to create an overall impression on the viewer. A classic example occurs in his film *October* (1928) in a sequence which depicts the events of summer 1917, after the fall of the tsar, when the general commanding the army of the new provisional government attempted a coup and the head of government issued an appeal to defend the capital against him 'in the name of God and Country'. After these words are shown in the film, the next shot shows just the words 'in the name of God', after which Eisenstein cuts to images of the onion domes of Russian churches and carvings of Christ, then to Eastern idols and temples, to Buddha figures, to ritual masks and finally to primitive carved figures, perhaps from Africa or Polynesia. His point is simple: all religion is primitive superstition and, in invoking it, the provisional government shows that it is simply the old regime in new guise and due for replacement by the Bolsheviks. It should be pointed out, in fairness, that some sceptical critics regard montage as simply a fancy name for editing.

In addition to *Alexander Nevsky* and *October*, films by Eisenstein include *Battleship Potemkin* (1925), *Ivan the Terrible I* (1944) and *Ivan the Terrible II* (1946, released 1958). It is generally agreed that *Alexander Nevsky* is his least experimental film, perhaps because it was made at the height of Stalinist internal repression. Stalin's approval or the lack of it could mean life or death for artists in all

Eisenstein directing *Alexander Nevsky* in the summer of 1938.

media: the dictator's hostile reaction to Shostakovich's opera *Lady Macbeth of the Mtsensk District* in 1936 resulted in official denunciation of the composer, his temporary retreat from avant-garde music and the composition of what he called 'A Soviet Artist's Creative Response to Just Criticism' (his Fifth Symphony). He was more fortunate than many of his friends and colleagues who were executed. It is clear that *Alexander Nevsky* was made with the dictator breathing down the neck of the film-makers. One evening during the editing of the film a phone call came to the studio saying that Stalin wanted to see the film. According to one version of this story, in the rush to get the film to the Kremlin, one reel was left behind, so an unfinished and incomplete version of *Alexander Nevsky* was shown to Stalin, which won his approval, and hence the film was released as it was at that point. Another version says that the whole film was shown but that Stalin objected to one sequence, which was then removed. Whichever version is true, it is clear that Stalin took an interest in the film and that his personal approval was crucial. Eisenstein could see what was happening around him and took care to make a proclamation of his devotion and loyalty.

The film is 108 minutes long. Something like 30 minutes of this is devoted to the Battle on the Ice, not counting the preliminary skirmishes and the long scene among the dead and wounded on the field of battle after fighting has ended. It is hard to think of any other film in which more than a quarter of the total length is taken up with a single medieval battle. This is not because battle scenes are rare in cinema. The battle scene is in fact one of the most recurrent and often the most dramatic elements in historical film and has its own conventions.

The Chronicle of Novgorod gives the following account of the Battle on the Ice:

AD 1242. Prince Alexander with the men of Novgorod went in the winter in great strength against the land of the Estonians, against the Germans, that they might not boast, saying: 'We will humble the Slav race under us', for Pskov was already taken, and its administrators in prison. And Prince Alexander cleared Pskov, seized the Germans and Estonians, and having bound them in chains sent them to be imprisoned in Novgorod, and himself went against the Estonians. And Domash Tverdislavich and Kerbet were scouring the country and the Germans and Estonians met them by a bridge; and they fought there, and there they killed Domash, an honest man, and others with him. And the Prince turned back to the lake and the Germans and Estonians went after them. Seeing this, Prince Alexander and all the men of Novgorod drew up their forces by Lake Chud at Uzmen by the Raven's Rock; and the Germans and Estonians rode at them driving themselves like a wedge through their army; and there was a great slaughter of Germans and Estonians. And God and St Sophia and the Holy Martyrs Boris and Gleb, for whose sake the men of Novgorod shed their blood, by the great prayers of those saints, God helped Prince Alexander. And the Germans fell there and the Estonians gave shoulder (fled), and pursuing them fought with them on the ice, four or five miles short of the Subol shore. And there fell of the Estonians a countless number, and of the Germans 400, and fifty they took with their hands and brought to Novgorod. And they fought on April 5, on a Saturday, the Commemoration Day of the Holy Martyr Theodulus, to the glory of the Holy Mother of God.

Almost all of this appears in the film: the German conquest of Pskov, the killing of Domash in a skirmish, Raven's Rock, the German 'wedge', the battle on the ice. One of the most famous incidents of the film, the Germans falling through the ice and drowning in the chilly waters of the lake, does not. However, although it has been argued that this scene was the fruit of Eisenstein's own cinematic imagination, the account found in *The Nikonian Chronicle*, does say, 'Five hundred Germans were killed there . . . some others drowned in the water.' Since the battle was fought on the ice, they must have fallen through the ice to drown in the water.

Medieval battles were small-scale by modern standards, usually involving thousands or, at most, tens of thousands, rather than hundreds of thousands, and often lasting only a few hours. Since the range of missile weapons was limited, and they rarely determined the outcome on their own, combat needed to be at close quarters, and usually hand to hand. The opponents had to come closer and closer until they were within arm's reach. One convention of the medieval cinema battle, based, it seems very likely, on the historical reality, is the confrontation between the two armies, who can see each other but are not yet within fighting distance. The dramatic opportunity this presented was seized by Mel Gibson in *Braveheart*, even at the cost of losing the bridge in the Battle of Stirling Bridge, and it is brought to a height of cinematic tension by Eisenstein in *Alexander Nevsky*.

The battle sequence begins with a caption, '5 April 1242', an accurate date, unlike the approximation of *Braveheart*'s 'Scotland 1280 AD' or *Monty Python*'s random 'England 932 AD' We then see a dramatically cloudy sky with, in the far left-hand corner, a war banner and a standing figure, Alexander, looking out. Throughout these scenes Eisenstein is willing to give more of the screen to

Raven's Rock, where Alexander surveys the site of the coming battle.

featureless sky or ice than one would imagine a rational director would dare to do – 90 per cent of the screen in some takes (some earlier Soviet film-makers had also used this kind of framing). We then move to a closer view of another figure, standing on Raven's Rock. We see him looking out and then cut to the Russian troops below; they occupy the lower tenth of the screen, stretching in a dark horizontal line, with the sky taking up the other nine-tenths. At this distance we cannot make out any individuals, but we see spears and banners held upright. We cut back briefly to Alexander on Raven's Rock before focusing more closely on the Russian line, taken at a three-quarters angle and showing details of helmets, shield and spears. The first shot is taken from slightly in front of the line, the second from behind it, so we are now looking out with the Russian soldiers. This 'point-of-view' perspective is common in battle scenes and it places us firmly in one camp or the other. As yet, the Russian soldiers can see nothing in the distance and their bodies sway slightly from side to side as they try to peer out from their ranks.

We now cut to the first identifiable individuals in the Russian ranks, all of whom we have encountered before: Vasilisa, a young woman from Pskov who is determined to avenge her father; the brave and jocular armourer; the blonde youth. Each of them is looking out, off the screen, in apprehension and expectation. These are individuals we know. After another shot from behind the Russian troops, we cut to what they see – nothing. A flat icy surface (fake ice, the film was made in the Russian summer) and a big sky. All this time the images have been accompanied by slow, rhythmic, orchestral music but what we now hear is the theme music of the enemy, their echoing horns playing in unison. *Alexander Nevsky* was Eisenstein's first sound film to be released and he took the opportunity to collaborate with the Soviet Union's most famous composer, Sergei Prokofiev (1891–1953), to create a film in which music was completely integrated. Prokofiev had visited Hollywood and investigated the use of film music there (Eisenstein too was fascinated by Hollywood and was famously photographed with Mickey Mouse) and Eisenstein describes how he sometimes filmed sequences to fit in with music that Prokofiev had already composed, as well as the more familiar practice of showing the edited film to the composer and getting him to write music for it. Prokofiev was pleased enough with the result to recast the score for his *Alexander Nevsky* cantata.

At the horn motif, we see the reactions of the Russian army, listening and peering, and then cut to the enemy army, with a brief scene of the Catholic clergy blessing the Teutonic Knights. Unlike the Russians, who have helmets with open faces, the Germans, both cavalry and infantry, have closed helmets, which reveal nothing of their faces. Their eye-slits give only a grotesque simulacrum of a human face. So, the camerawork reveals people we know on the Russian side, a faceless enemy on the other side. The pace now quickens with throbbing, relentless music and the first appearance of the German battle line: a thirty-second shot from a fixed camera, the Knights occupying only the bottom tenth of the frame, slowly advancing towards us – the Russians, the camera, the viewer. Then a cut to a shot showing, for the first time, Germans and Russians in the same frame. The music increases in pace. We intercut between the waiting Russians and the advancing Knights, still at a distance. The horn motif recurs, we see the line of Knights from the side, now clearly in faster motion, then shots of the Knights from a low angle cantering forwards. Finally, as the music picks up even more pace, Eisenstein uses close-ups of the Knights in their enclosed helmets, their banners and cloaks marked with sign of the cross, their lances lowered for action. We cut back to the Russians looking outwards at the oncoming enemy (perhaps rather unnecessarily identified by the young warrior as 'The Germans!'). We see a full-screen image of Alexander ('the great man' Domash said they needed) looking out too.

At this point we see more and more detail of the Knights, especially their leaders with elaborate decorated helmets, as the music switches to chanted words, which are not translated in the subtitles and which have been the subject of some debate. It appears that the phrases we hear are a jumble from the Latin psalms, probably meaningless to the initial Soviet audience (as to many audiences since) but conveying a general sense of medieval Latin Christianity. The chanting continues as we cut to Alexander and his two chief commanders: 'It is time,' he says. The commanders, rivals in love as we know, embrace and take up their positions. The music switches back to its ominous orchestral rhythm and we have a high-angle crane shot surveying the ranks of Russian soldiers, dressed in dark colours, their faces visible beneath their helmets, their long spears held upright, waiting for action. Then shots from within the Russian ranks, looking out at the oncoming white line of Knights. The music speeds up, the knights draw closer and closer, the Russian spears go down into fighting position. At the very moment of impact between the two forces, the music stops.

The Battle on the Ice.

This whole sequence is a masterpiece of suspense. From the caption '5 April 1242' to the first clash is more than six minutes – a very long time in a film. Framing, camera angle, cutting and music are all in the service of showing apprehensive waiting and an impending conflict. The sudden stopping of the music at the moment of impact is a stroke of genius. Apart from a few commands from Alexander, we have heard virtually no diegetic sound – sound in the imagined world of the film, as distinct from Prokofiev's score – for six minutes; now suddenly we hear shouting and the clash of weapons, which will be all we hear for some time.

The year 1938 was not the only time that the Teutonic Knights suffered a major cinematic defeat in battle. Twenty-two years later they rode out again in Aleksander Ford's *Knights of the Teutonic Order* (*Krzyzacy*, also titled *Black Cross*) to face a Polish-Lithuanian army in 1410 (it shows the longevity of these crusading orders that they were still a major presence in the Baltic at that time). At the Battle of Grunwald, otherwise known as the Battle of Tannenberg, they were decisively defeated, and Ford's epic celebrates that event. The film, which was based on a novel by Henryk Sienkiewicz, has been called the greatest blockbuster in the history of Polish cinema. It premiered in Poland on the 550th anniversary of the battle, to the day, and the charge of the Knights might perhaps have brought to mind a similar armoured attack in 1939, the German invasion of Poland that began the Second World War. The film shows a famous incident before the battle, when the Grand Master of the Teutonic Knights sent two swords to the Polish king, Władysław II, with the message that this was to encourage him to stop skulking and come to battle, whereupon Władysław took the swords and proceeded to defeat the Knights. The swords then became part of the regalia of the Polish kings, and a giant statue of Władysław brandishing the two swords can now be seen in Central Park in New York. Just as the communist regime of the Soviet Union could summon up the Middle Ages to celebrate a national triumph over the Germans in 1938, so the communist Polish state could do the same in 1960.

The battle is the heart of Eisenstein's film, but other themes emerge too. As in *The Seventh Seal*, there is a comic-opera subplot involving a love triangle, although the one in *Alexander Nevsky* is different, since those involved in it are also heroic and not merely grotesque. Vasily Buslai and Gavrilo Oleksich both seek the hand in marriage of the lovely Olga. Vasily is bold, comical, slightly ridiculous, and dressed, when we first see him, in an outfit decorated with large roundels; Gavrilo is more serious and sober. They are aware of the contrast, Vasily offering himself as a 'laughter-loving man', compared to the 'sober, duller' Gavrilo. Gavrilo responds by telling Olga that she would be beaten if she married Vasily, but treated with reverence if she married him. She asks for more time to consider the matter but they are then interrupted by the bell summoning the citizens of Novgorod to a meeting to debate the emergency of the German advance. Some time later, we see them again, after Alexander's return to Novgorod and the decision to fight the Germans under his leadership, which delights all three of them. As the two men prepare to go off to battle, Olga says she will marry whichever of them shows greater valour.

We are now familiar with another two characters, whom we can follow through the chaos of the fighting. Both Vasily and Gavrilo are given important commands in the battle and show great courage, Vasily managing to combine this with some buffoonery. We pick up the thread of the love triangle when the scene moves from the fighting to the field of battle afterwards, littered with dead and dying, as the women come seeking their menfolk by torchlight.

Olga and her admirers, Vasily Buslai and Gavrilo Oleksich.

Vasily and Gavrilo lie among the wounded and hear Olga singing – 'Hear my voice, my heroes, answer me' – as she approaches. The tiny Olga manages to help the stricken pair of warriors off the field. We encounter them for one last time after the triumphant return of the Russian army. Olga, driving a sledge on which the two heroes lie (much to the amusement of the assembled crowd), asks Alexander to decide whom she is to marry but is pre-empted by the arrival of Vasily's mother – a truly broad-comedy figure – who cannot believe her son would ever be second in anything. Vasily has to beg her forgiveness, but reports that neither he nor Gavrilo was bravest in battle – this was the Amazonian Vasilisa from Pskov. So, Gavrilo marries Olga and Vasily marries Vasilisa, all this in the last few minutes of the film.

It is possible to have more than one opinion about this subplot. Its assumptions about men, women and marriage are unlikely to appeal to all members of a modern Western audience, but that is true of many things in films from earlier generations. This strand of the story is intended to provide some leaven to the otherwise heroic and tragic plot and it gives us these identifiable characters whose fortunes we follow throughout the film. It highlights the patriotism of the young Olga and the heroism of a female fighter, Vasilisa.

The figure of Alexander Nevsky offers neither love interest nor comedy. Although the historical prince had a family, it does not appear in the film. His stern patriotism is combined with a deep self-assurance about leadership. After his entry to Novgorod, Alexander says, 'I do not come to seek your love but to lead you in battle.' There are few humanizing touches. Even with his comrades-in-arms, he keeps an emotional distance. An example is provided by a scene the night before the battle. Prince Alexander is standing near a group of Russian soldiers who are being entertained by the armourer, whom we have already encountered as a patriot and a bit of a humourist. He is telling a story about a hare being chased by a vixen. The hare leads the vixen between two birch trees, where the vixen becomes trapped. The hare then deflowers her. This story was apparently funny in 1242. Alexander then turns towards them and asks, 'Trapped her between two branches, you say?' It is this story, it seems, that suggests to Alexander his tactics in the forthcoming battle, with the Russian vanguard holding still at the centre while two wings come in from either side. It has a strong parallel in the film *Braveheart*, when, in their woodland hideouts before the Battle of Stirling, Wallace and his followers are sitting on the ground, eating around their campfire and discussing the imminent threat of the English heavy cavalry and how to deal with them. The 'highland way' is to hit and run but Wallace is inspired by another thought. Looking up at the surrounding tall trees, he suggests making long spears. Then follows a bit of bawdy banter, but it is these long spears – actually sharpened stakes – that destroy the English cavalry charge in the battle. Now, in neither case is it likely that the leaders needed to be instructed in basic tactics. A pincer attack from either flank was a standard manoeuvre well before 1242 and long spears nothing new in 1297. What these scenes do is show the leader as a man among men, in a world of folksy badinage, but also always thinking one step ahead. But, as befits their difference in status, Wallace sits with the men, Alexander stands apart. Wallace is a participant in the male world of pre-combat camaraderie, Alexander adjacent to it.

Historical films of the Soviet era not only portrayed the threat from foreign foes but stressed the danger from enemies within, Russians willing to betray Russia, and, alongside the need for a great leader, *Alexander Nevsky* stresses the danger of turncoats, renegades and traitors. This comes out clearly in the way the prisoners are dealt with after the battle. The common soldiers in the army of the Teutonic Knights are sent away, because 'they were forced to fight'; the Knights are to be ransomed; but the Russian traitor Tverdilo is torn to pieces by the Russians, his compatriots whom he has betrayed. And Alexander tells the assembled people they should remember this moment of victory, when all had rallied to the cause of Russia: 'If you forget it – you will be as Judases all, traitors to the Russian land' ('Judas!' was the name that the keymaster of Vladimir Cathedral applied to the Russian prince who had allied with the Tartars in *Andrei Rublev*). Anyone failing to heed the call when needed, Nevsky adds, will be punished. This theme of 'enemies within' was a central feature of the Bolshevik regime from its beginning but became exceptionally heated during the dispute between Stalin and Trotsky (who was expelled from the Communist Party in 1927, exiled from the Soviet Union in 1929 and eventually murdered, on Stalin's orders, in 1940). The Moscow Show Trials of 1936–8, in which many old Bolsheviks were charged with treason and conspiring with Trotsky, and then convicted on the basis of fabricated evidence and forced confessions and imprisoned or executed, were taking place exactly at the time the film *Alexander Nevsky* was being made.

Eisenstein knew how perilous the situation was and how easily a public figure in the world of the arts, such as a director, might become the target of criticism and the victim of politically moti-vated charges, with the possibility of imprisonment or execution. He seized the chance to make bold and extravagant assertions of his loyalty and his devotion to Stalin. On 12 July 1938, during the making of the film, he published an article in *Izvestia*, the official Soviet newspaper, in which he described Russia as 'a country which has become a Socialist Motherland; a country which is being led to unprecedented victories by the greatest strategist in world history – Stalin'. A few months later Eisenstein marked the completion of the film by a piece called 'My Subject Is Patriotism' in which he pointed out the parallels between 1242 and 1938:

> In this picture we have approached the national and patriotic theme, which engages foremost minds not only in our country, but in the West as well. For the guardian of national dignity, of national pride, national independence and true patriotism throughout the world is first of all the Communist Party, is Communism. . . . We want our film not only to inspire those who are in the very thick of the fight against fascism, but to bring spirit, courage and confidence to those quarters of the world where fascism seems as invincible as the Order of Knights appeared in the thirteenth century . . . These feelings

are inspired and these forces led by the most splendid country in the world, which is experiencing the vigorous development of the great Stalinist epoch.

The contemporary propaganda message of the film scarcely needs any more underlining. We are in 1242: Russia is threatened by faceless Germans in the grip of sinister fanatical beliefs, but the common people of Russia will defend their land under the leadership of a stern but heroic figure. We are also of course in 1938: Russia is threatened by faceless Germans in the grip of sinister fanatical beliefs, but the common people of Russia will defend their land under the leadership of a stern but heroic figure. Stalin attended the premiere on 25 November 1938. Eisenstein was given the Order of Lenin early in 1939.

In August 1939 everything suddenly changed, with the signing of the Nazi–Soviet pact. This agreement, which led directly to the carve-up of Poland between her eastern and western neighbours, was a major political shock, as the two powers that had seemed to be the deepest enemies now collaborated in subjugating the Poles (David Low, cartoonist for the London *Evening Standard*, famously depicted the two dictators Hitler and Stalin greeting each other over a corpse). Western governments were confused, Western Communist parties dismayed or riven, as 'the Socialist Motherland' became friends with Hitler's Germany. Films inspired by bitter hostility to Germany, such as *Alexander Nevsky*, no longer suited state policy and it was withdrawn from distribution in the Soviet Union.

For two years Eisenstein had to reconcile himself with this new German–Soviet relationship, and was even given the task of directing Wagner's *Valkyrie* at the Bolshoi Theatre. But then abruptly, with the German invasion of the Soviet Union in June 1941, which took 'the greatest strategist in world history' by surprise, *Alexander Nevsky* was once again the right message and was re-released. Later that year the BBC, wishing to encourage sympathy for Britain's new ally, commissioned from Louis MacNeice a radio play in verse based on the film, which was broadcast on 8 December 1941, though delayed slightly by a news flash about the attack on Pearl Harbor a day earlier and the USA's declaration of war on Japan. In 1942 the Soviet Union instituted the Order of Alexander Nevsky for commanders in the Red Army who showed particular courage in combat, with a medal depicting the prince in helmet and armour (the Order still exists but is now mainly for long-serving civil servants and to the medal has been added the Russian imperial eagle). It is hard to think of a film that illustrates the impact of political events on the cinema more starkly and simply than *Alexander Nevsky*.

Any film made in the Soviet Union in 1938 had to negotiate its way carefully through dangerous ideological territory. It is not as if there were a simple and unchanging party line to adhere to. In the ninety years since the publication of *The Communist Manifesto*, Marxist thought had evolved, diversified and given rise to fierce internal controversies, made all the sharper and more dangerous once the Russian Revolution of 1917 had actually brought to power a government that espoused Communism and made it a defining feature of the state. *Alexander Nevsky* illustrates some of the complexities of film-making in the Soviet state, as shown by such features of the film as the place of religion, the role of the peasantry and the attitude towards nationalism.

There is religion in *Alexander Nevsky*, but of a curiously lop-sided kind. Prince Alexander Nevsky came to be regarded as a saint in the Orthodox church – that is, he was deemed an especially holy person who was to be honoured by religious veneration and who could be prayed to for supernatural help. A Life of Alexander, written perhaps in the later thirteenth century, already calls him 'the saintly Prince Alexander', while in 1547 the Council of Moscow sanctioned his universal cult as a saint and a liturgical office was composed, and in 1724 his remains were brought from Vladimir, where they had first been interred, to the new imperial capital of St Petersburg and were placed in the St Alexander Nevsky monastery there. There are today several Alexander Nevsky Cathedrals in Russia, and others in Paris (this is where Andrei Tarkovsky's funeral took place), in Sofia, Tallinn, Pittsburgh and Howell (New Jersey). There is no trace of this in the film. Alexander is a nationalist and a war leader, fighting for 'the Russian land'.

The Soviet Union was officially an atheist state. At the time of the Russian Revolution of 1917, the Russian Orthodox Church was deeply identified with the hated Tsarist regime and it supported the counter-revolutionary forces in the civil war. After the Bolshevik victory, repressive measures were taken against it. The campaign against religion was serious: priests were arrested and executed, legal restrictions of all kinds were imposed, churches were closed or demolished, notably the huge Cathedral of Christ the Saviour in Moscow, which was spectacularly dynamited in 1931 (it was rebuilt in the 1990s). A Soviet film-maker working in the 1930s could not present religion sympathetically, or even neutrally. The film does not alter history so dramatically as to exclude the presence of Orthodox churches and clergy completely (and cathedrals sometimes form a striking background to shots) but it gives them very little screen time, with the exception of the renegade monk. Naturally it ignores the claims of the medieval chroniclers that Alexander himself received saintly help in battle, from the Russian saints Boris and Gleb.

In his article of 12 July 1938 Eisenstein wrote, 'the only miracle in the battle on Lake Peipus was the genius of the Russian people, who for the first time began to sense their national, native power, their unity.' On the other hand, the Catholic Christianity of the Teutonic Knights is underlined in the film both visually and by the script. Hence the Catholics are much more Catholic than the Orthodox are Orthodox. This is reflected in the amount of time the film spends showing religious services: fairly extended for the Catholic Knights, almost non-existent for the Orthodox Russians (the clergy are present to welcome Alexander back from his victory, but quickly disappear).

Eisenstein and his collaborators did not have to exaggerate the intransigent religiosity of the medieval Knights and the clergy and monks who accompanied them. In the speech of the cardinal, sitting in the ruins of conquered Pskov, he asserts 'there is but one God in heaven and one deputy of God on earth . . . All who refuse to bow to Rome must be destroyed.' This is not a hostile caricature of the papal view. The papal bull *Unam sanctam*, issued by Pope Boniface VIII in 1302, declares 'there is one holy catholic and apostolic church, outside of which there is neither salvation nor the remission of sins . . . of this one and only church there is one body and one head: Christ and the vicar of Christ, St Peter, and the successor of St Peter . . . we declare that it is altogether necessary for every human creature to be subject to the bishop of Rome.' This is not a half-hearted assertion of papal claims. So it is not the portrayal of the fanatical side of the crusaders that is a misleading feature of the film but the omission of any religious consciousness or religious motivation on the part of the Orthodox Russians.

Just like religion, the portrayal of the peasantry had to be handled carefully, in order not to stray from the current party line. There is

The cardinal accompanying the Teutonic Knights seeing the battle not going well.

a large body of material discussing Marx's views of the peasantry, and it would be simplistic to say that in his long literary and political life he expressed only one unchanging attitude. It is clear, however, that, as an educated urban German Jew, he had little direct knowledge of peasant farmers and it is unquestionable that in *The Communist Manifesto* he describes the class as 'not revolutionary, but conservative' and speaks condescendingly of 'the idiocy of rural life'. Peasants have a role in the Marxist theory of historical development, which sees all societies as characterized by class struggle, between slaves and masters in the ancient world, between peasants and lords in the feudal period, between proletarian workers and capitalists in the modern industrial world, but that, of course, places peasants in the past. The current struggle puts the proletariat centre stage. It might therefore be surprising that the first successful

Communist revolution took place in Russia, a society with a huge peasant population. The ambiguous position of the peasantry was something that Bolshevik theorists addressed – Lenin spent pages analysing what the relationship between the peasantry and the proletariat should be. The task was complicated by the identification of a 'rich peasant' class (*kulaks*) as class enemies. In 1930 Stalin launched an all-out war against the *kulaks*, imprisoning and relocating hundreds of thousands of them; executions and extra-judicial violence were commonplace.

A Soviet film with a twentieth-century subject could not romanticize the peasantry without the danger of slipping into dangerous political positions. However, one set in the Middle Ages, like *Alexander Nevsky*, could treat the peasantry as an exploited class of the feudal period which might be animated and given leadership in time of crisis by a great man. This is how they make their appearance, presumably after long discussion between Eisenstein and his political minders. The film does not concentrate on the peasantry, but peasants are given a role in the national resistance. After the delegation from Novgorod has appealed to Alexander to lead them, he says they must 'rouse the peasants', before the scene changes to the mustering of the peasants, a self-contained section two and a half minutes long, against a background of the singing of a patriotic song:

> Arise, you Russian people! In a just battle to the death! Arise, people free and brave! Rise to defend our fair land! Our warriors will have honours, our fallen eternal glory. For the homes of our fathers, arise you Russian people! We shall not give up Russia, our enemies will be smitten! Russia has risen against the foe, to fight for Novgorod!

The peasants are dressed fairly uniformly in white smocks and conical hats, they carry crude weapons and many emerge from what look like subterranean dwellings. After a harangue by a mounted warrior, they march off in a great column, which Eisenstein films from behind, sometimes at foot level, and from above. They are seen in large numbers, crossing the rivers and marching up the hills, the mounted warrior at their head, always with Prokofiev's rousing tune in our ears. We do not see them being 'repressed', as happens to the peasant in *Monty Python and the Holy Grail*, and in fact we form no picture of the social world in which they live (unlike *Andrei Rublev*, where the brutality of the dominant boyar class is depicted). They are simply Russians responding to national need. When Alexander arrives in Novgorod, and the rich merchants oppose him, they are told to leave 'or the peasants will crush your bones'. It is these 'moneyed men' who are the clearest class enemies, not the feudal lords who are either absent or not identified in the film. Alexander Nevsky himself seems to derive his income from fishing. At a crucial point in the battle, the peasant levies are ordered into action and they rush forward with their crude weapons, some pulling knights from their horses with hooked staves. They are cheered on their return from the victory, still marching as a group. Some commentators on the film mistakenly characterize the Russian army as 'a peasant army'. It is not. What we know about it from the film is that it comprises the prince's retinue and the men of Novgorod, some of whom are artisans, as well as the peasant levy (and the single woman, Vasilisa). No peasant leaders are shown and we know none of them individually.

The film ends with the celebration of victory, the punishment of traitors and the resolution of the comic love triangle, but Eisenstein's original script had a quite different ending that was never filmed. This was intended to show Alexander's visit to the court of the

Khan of the Golden Horde and his subsequent death. He dies at a place called Kulikovo and he prophesies it will be the scene of a future Russian victory over the Mongols. As his body is carried across Russia, the scene fades to a Muscovite army about to fight the Mongols at Kulikovo under Dmitri Donskoi, Prince of Moscow, a descendant of Alexander Nevsky. The Russians defeat the Mongols, who flee. The Battle of Kulikovo, which took place in 1380, is often taken as a watershed in the rise of Moscow and the shift in power between Russians and Mongols (Tarkovsky had depicted it in the opening scene of the original screenplay of *Andrei Rublev*, though it was not filmed). This might seem like a tacked-on ending, but the Mongol threat has been left as a hanging presence in the film and so it could also be seen as tying up this loose end. In a similar fashion, *Braveheart* does not end with the execution of William Wallace but with the victory of Robert Bruce nine years later. This final sequence of Eisenstein's script, although not in the film, represents a reality about the actual Alexander Nevsky and the Horde that might be awkward for a Russian national hero – his subservience to the Golden Horde, the Mongol overlords.

The excision of this final scene makes the nationalistic tone of the film clearer and simpler. Though the opening sequence shows the Mongol presence, Alexander is explicit that the Germans must be dealt with first and the Mongols then disappear completely and the story becomes one of heroic defence of the Russian homeland against brutal German invaders. In the song that begins the film, celebrating the victory on the Neva, Alexander's men sing, 'we spilled our blood like water, all for the sake of our land, the great Mother Russia,' and in his final speech at the end of the film, he says 'he who comes to us with a sword, shall die by the sword. On this stands Russia, and on this she shall stand forever.' The good characters are dedicated to the motherland. When Alexander launches his decisive charge during the Battle on the Ice, he calls out 'For Russia!', exactly parallel to El Cid's 'For Spain!'

As mentioned in the chapter on *Braveheart*, some modern commentators believe that it is anachronistic to see nationalistic beliefs and motives in the medieval period, and this is actually a quite widely held assumption. But the evidence to the contrary is strong and it should be noticed in the passage from the *Chronicle of Novgorod*, cited above, that Alexander is described leading the men of Novgorod 'against the Germans, that they might not boast, saying: "We will humble the Slav race under us"', so clearly conceptualizing the struggle as a clash between Germans and Slavs. This is not a nineteenth-century interpretation of the battle but a medieval one. The idea that a deeply nationalistic film could be made in the Soviet Union in 1938 might have surprised (and dismayed) many old Communists. In its origin, the Communist movement was committed to internationalism. *The Communist Manifesto* of 1848 proclaimed that 'the working men have no country,' and its last line is 'workers of the world unite!' Since the foundation of the International Working Men's Association (or First International) in London in 1864, socialists and communists had seen their revolutionary task embodied in a genuinely international organization. However, the outbreak of the First World War in 1914 placed terrible pressure on socialist and communist parties in the opposing states, and most went along with their national governments and gave support to the war efforts of their own country. The Second International, created in 1889 as successor to that of 1864, collapsed.

The Bolshevik seizure of power in Russia in 1917 made the question a practical matter rather than a theoretical one. Though they anticipated a wave of revolutions in Western Europe, the Bolshevik leaders in fact soon realized their idea of world revolution was not coming to pass.

Just as the early Christians had to acknowledge that the end of the world was not imminent, as they had at first believed, so communists had to recognize that world revolution might take some time. As early as the summer of 1918 Lenin wrote, 'We are banking on the inevitability of the world revolution, but this does not mean that we are such fools as to bank on the revolution inevitably coming on a definite and early date.' Moreover, the Russian empire had been a multi-national state, and the new regime had to make decisions about its position on the various constituent peoples. Lenin accepted that they should have semi-autonomy within a federation, hence the creation the Union of Soviet Socialist Republics (USSR) in 1922. After Lenin's death in 1924, Stalin adopted an explicit policy of 'socialism in one country'. Since the largest ethnic group in the USSR was Russian, the 'country' involved could be seen by many as, simply, 'Russia'. It would now be possible for a state committed to Communism also to be nationalistic, as long as it was a secular nationalism and the ritual invocations of Russia as the 'Socialist Motherland' continued. Since the end of the Soviet Union in 1991, Russia has trod a path even more nationalistic than that adopted by Stalin, this time in alliance with the Orthodox Church rather than being opposed to it. In 2008 a Russian television contest to find 'the greatest Russian' placed Alexander Nevsky first, two places ahead of Stalin.

8

A SILENT EPIC
Die Nibelungen I: Siegfried
(1924)

With Fritz Lang's *Siegfried*, we reach silent film. Or, more precisely, we do not. Although the soundtrack had not yet been invented, and hence we cannot hear characters in the film speaking, no visit to a 'silent' movie would be silent. There was always music, either improvised by musicians on the spot or based on a printed score that had been issued along with the film and was keyed to its different scenes (this was the case with *Siegfried*). As a substitute for spoken dialogue there were intertitles, still shots of text conveying what the characters were saying (intertitles could also be used to identify locations and for other explanatory purposes). Both features, the live music and the textual intertitle, had as a consequence the chance of varying the experience of the film. Watching a scene of a silent film first with one piece of music, then with another, brings out very clearly the way sight and sound interact and shape each other; the experiences differ. And intertitles were highly important when films were exported to be shown in foreign countries, since the texts had to be translated into the language spoken there, and variant versions were possible – notably in the case of texts translated into English in Britain and in the USA.

The film is based on medieval Germanic legends. Such historical figures as can be dimly glimpsed in these legends (for example, the

Burgundian king Gunther, based at Worms, or, in the second part of the *Die Nibelungen, Kriemhild's Revenge*, Atli, or Attila, leader of the Huns) date to the first half of the fifth century but the written forms of the stories are much later than that. There are two main strands of the story in medieval literature. The *Nibelungenlied* is an anonymous verse epic in Middle High German, written down around 1200, which tells the story of Siegfried and the Burgundian royal house. The other body of material is in Old Norse and, though it draws on earlier legends, was written down in the thirteenth century in Iceland. It includes several poems in the so-called Older or Poetic Edda, but the main narrative is the *Volsunga saga*, which recounts the history of the Volsungs, including Sigurd the dragon-slayer (many characters have different names in the German and Norse versions). The film draws on both the German and the Norse versions. For instance, in the film, the character Brunhild is queen of Iceland and her dwelling is surrounded by a ring of magic fire. In the *Nibelungenlied*, Brunhild is queen of Iceland but there is no ring of fire. In the *Volsunga saga*, there is a ring of fire around her dwelling but she is not queen of Iceland.

It was the late eighteenth and early nineteenth centuries that saw the renewal of interest in medieval epics in several languages, including the *Nibelungenlied*, which was 're-discovered' in 1755 and given publicity by the Swiss literary and historical scholar Johann Jakob Bodmer who called it 'a kind of *Iliad*'. The first complete printed edition came out in 1782. Three years earlier the medieval Spanish *Song of the Cid* had appeared in print for the first time. An English translation of this was published by the Romantic poet Robert Southey in 1808. The first edition of the Old English epic poem *Beowulf* was published by the Icelandic scholar Thorkelin in Copenhagen in 1815, with the first complete edition to be published in England in 1833, followed by a translation into modern English in 1837. The first edition of the Old French *Song of Roland*, edited by Francisque Michel, appeared in 1837. Thus, within less than six decades, European culture had been enriched with the publication of the great early epics of medieval Spanish, German, English and French literature. This efflorescence was both inspired by the Romantic movement and an inspiration to it, for these poems fitted in with the re-evaluation of the Middle Ages that was an essential feature of Romanticism and they were also the vehicle for the nationalism that was a cousin or sibling of Romanticism. This nationalist aspect is very apparent in the case of the *Nibelungenlied*. In 1815 a modern German version of the poem was issued to German soldiers fighting Napoleon; it was a special 'edition for the field and the camp'. The later nineteenth-century Romantics continued to be attracted to the legend. Friedrich Hebbel's *Die Nibelungen*, published in 1862, was a drama in three parts, consisting of a short preface, followed by *Siegfried's Death* and *Kriemhild's Revenge*, each in five acts – Lang's film has the same overall title, *Die Nibelungen*, and is in two parts, *Siegfried* and *Kriemhild's Revenge*. One of the most famous incarnations of the story is Wagner's Ring cycle (1848–76), which draws more on the Norse than the German traditions, while the poet and socialist William Morris produced an English translation of the *Volsunga saga* version.

All this Romantic and nationalist past is significant in understanding the film version by Fritz Lang, which was dedicated 'to the German people'. Lang (1890–1976) was an important filmmaker both in Weimar Germany (the German republic of 1919–33), where *Siegfried* was made, and later, after his flight from Germany, in Hollywood. His other films from the Weimar period include *Dr Mabuse the Gambler* (1922), *Metropolis* (1927), the music for which was composed by Gottfried Huppertz, who also composed the music for *Die Nibelungen*, and *M* (1931). In these films his wife, Thea von Harbou, was an important collaborator, especially as screenwriter. The couple divorced in 1933 and, while Lang made his way to France and then America, Thea von Harbou remained in Germany throughout the Nazi period and was seemingly untroubled by the Nazi regime – after the war she was detained and interrogated by the British for several months. There is a famous debate about Lang and the Nazis. Lang himself repeatedly told the story that, after the Nazis came to power, he was summoned to see Goebbels, the Minister of Propaganda. He went, very nervously, because his last film had been criticized by the Nazis. Goebbels, however, was not interested in that. He wanted Lang to head the regime's film industry (Goebbels, like Hitler, was a film fanatic). Lang decided he had better be frank, and told Goebbels that his mother was of Jewish descent. Goebbels laughed, and replied, 'Herr Lang, *we* decide who is Jewish.' Lang asked for time to consider and went and booked a train to Paris. However, Lang's account has been much debated. Is it factual reportage? Fantasy? Or somewhere in between, a dressed-up version of a real encounter? Whatever the answers to those questions, it is certainly the case that Lang moved to Paris in 1933 and then to the USA in the following year. He continued to make films in these new homes (he made more than forty in total).

Siegfried is divided into seven episodes, each numbered and termed '*Gesang*' in the German intertitles, which means 'song', 'poem' or 'canto', this last term being used in English translations for release in Britain and the USA. The basic subdivision of the medieval poem is the *Aventiure*; there are 38 in total, including both the story of Siegfried (18) and Kriemhild's revenge (20). The *Gesang* or Canto in the film thus does not correspond exactly with an *Aventiure* in the poem, but the choice of this word evokes the origin of the story in oral performance and recitation. The film opens in the primeval forest, with semi-naked dwarf figures in animal skins. Among them Siegfried stands out as an Aryan hero, tall, strong, blond and bare-chested. He is forging a sword under the watchful eyes of the dwarf Mime. This is very much how Wagner's opera *Siegfried* opens. This version of Siegfried, who is dressed in animal skins, lives deep in the primeval forest with dwarfs and rides without saddle or stirrups, is drawn far more from Old Norse sources than from the *Nibelungenlied*. In that poem Siegfried is introduced as a king's son who has been raised as befitted his status, always rides with an escort and is dressed in 'magnificent clothes'. More than sixty lines are dedicated to his knighting and the festivities that celebrated it. He

Paul Richter as Siegfried forging his sword.

is situated at the heart of courtly society, not in the barbarian Iron Age of the opening of the film.

Siegfried is famous as a dragon-slayer, but in the *Nibelungenlied*, unlike in the *Volsunga saga*, the dragon-slaying episode is referred to only briefly, as one of the mighty deeds for which Siegfried is renowned. However, no film director would miss the chance to show a dragon, so Lang devotes some time to the encounter of the hero and the dragon. The dragon looks comic to modern audiences but could have been impressive at the time, as it was 18 metres (60 ft) long (so 3 m/10 feet longer than the dragon in *Beowulf*) and breathes fire. An impartial observer of this scene would have to say that the dragon only fights Siegfried in self-defence. The first *Gesang* or Canto ends with Siegfried bathing in the dragon's blood, which gives him invulnerability and enables him to understand

Siegfried bathing in the dragon's blood, which will make him invulnerable, after he has killed it.

the language of the birds. The second *Gesang* transfers us at once to the courtly and ceremonious world of Worms, where the court minstrel is seen entertaining the royal family of Burgundy with the song of Siegfried's exploits. Just as Siegfried first hears of the beautiful Burgundian princess Kriemhild from the talk of the primitive forest dwellers around Mime's forge and immediately says he will woo her, in true medieval fashion falling in love with someone he has never seen, or at least in the fashion of medieval romance literature, so Kriemhild first hears of Siegfried from the song of the minstrel, who recounts Siegfried's defeat of the dwarf king Alberich and his acquisition of the Nibelung treasure and the cap of invisibility. So in the film's world, as in that of the poem, these are past events, shown as flashbacks. An alternative approach would have been to film these events in their actual place in the narrative, as a feat of the young Siegfried, but Lang and Thea von Harbou retained the recounted nature of the deed. This choice has the effect of diminishing the episodic nature of the story of Siegfried, since instead of one scene after another – sword-forging, dragon-slaying, seizure of the Nibelung treasure, arrival at Worms – we cut from the dragon scene to Worms, hence highlighting the unity of a drama centred on the Burgundian court and leading step by step to a tragic conclusion. This use of reported action can be found elsewhere in European epic, notably in the *Odyssey*, a large part of which consists of Odysseus' account of his past adventures.

Once Siegfried arrives at the Burgundian court, no long a barechested bareback rider but a courtly knight with an escort of kings, most of the components of the plot have been assembled: Siegfried, the hero; Kriemhild, his love; the weak and vacillating King Gunther; the ominous figure of Hagen, with a loyalty above all to the Burgundian state. The film now moves on to the main driving force of the plot, the subjugation of Brunhild, whom Gunther – again having heard of her but never having seen her – wishes to have as his wife. As mentioned, in the film, just as in the *Nibelungenlied*, she is the queen of Iceland. In the film, but not in the *Nibelungenlied*, her court is composed, it seems, entirely of young women. Unlike the refined ladies of the Burgundian court, these women wear their long hair loose, they dress in knee-length skirts and boots of animal skin and they gather and move in groups, rather like inmates of a barbarian girls' school.

Brunhild will only accept a husband on condition that he defeats her in three trials of strength, casting a weight, undertaking a long jump and throwing a spear, failure being punished by death – the shattered weapons of those who have failed decorate her hall. Brunhild presumes that the hero coming to challenge her is Siegfried and is almost scornful when she is told it is in fact Gunther who seeks her hand. Before the contest, Siegfried leaves on a pretext, puts on his cap of invisibility and then returns to give Gunther invisible help in the three tests. The last of these requires the contestants to hurl a spear at their opponent, who is protected by their shield. Gunther's spear, really thrown by Siegfried, splits Brunhild's shield in two and casts her to the ground. The end of the scene has her on her hands and knees, her helmet fallen from her head, in despair and defeat.

Before this humiliating defeat, Brunhild is portrayed as a warrior woman, strong, defiant, clad in armour and a magnificent winged helmet. On the journey to the Burgundian court, she is dressed in long ceremonious robes but is clearly not reconciled to her fate and when Gunther approaches her, she knocks him down, and asks if he really is the man who beat her in the three contests. Upon her arrival at court, supposed to be a grand and joyous reception, Brunhild's

Hanna Ralph as Brunhild, queen of Iceland.

expression and demeanour show her discontent and unwillingness to accept her new situation. Siegfried has once more to use his magic cap, which allows him to change shape as well as become invisible, assume Gunther's appearance and break Brunhild's will by force before Gunther can have sex with her. After he does, she loses her great strength, and, in the words of the *Nibelungenlied*, 'henceforth she was no stronger than any other woman.'

The shape-changing sequence, just like the earlier invisibility scenes, is one thing that the newish technology of cinema could present before the viewers' eyes in a way previously impossible. Lang already had experience of such wonders of cinema in *Destiny* (*Der müde Tod*), a film he made three years before *Siegfried* and which shows people walking through walls, people turning into other people, a magic carpet flying through the air and a paper scroll unrolling itself without the touch of human hand. It is significant that one of the early pioneers of the moving picture, Georges Méliès, was a professional magician and, long before CGI, cinema could show the magical, without any of the complicated business that was required in the theatre to present such illusions.

The Burgundian court is not a happy place. Brunhild is suspicious and worries away at the enigma of the marriage of Siegfried and Kriemhild. In this strand of the story, sex and questions of social hierarchy are mixed. Brunhild expresses outrage when she sees that Kriemhild, a princess, is being given in marriage to Siegfried, who, she believes, is a vassal of the king. This is because in Iceland he had pretended to be Gunther's vassal (*man* or *eigen* in the *Nibelungenlied*). On his first arrival at the Burgundian court, in the film version, Siegfried had already proudly announced, 'I never was a king's vassal [*Vassal*, the same word in German] and never will be!' This aristocratic disdain for the status of vassal is reflected in a medieval anecdote about a ninth-century nobleman, Welf, who is said to have disowned his son when he learnt he had become the emperor's vassal (*man*). Brunhild is highly conscious of status, but perhaps her brooding is also meant to convey her unconscious feeling that Siegfried was really the hero destined for her. In the *Volsunga saga* version of the story it is quite explicit that she sees Siegfried's wife as her sexual rival: she tells her 'I cannot bear that you enjoy him.'

Sex and status come crashing together in the climactic scene of the dispute on the steps of the cathedral. The quarrel is over who is to enter the building first, Brunhild or Kriemhild, a matter of universal and deep concern in the hierarchical, visual and public world of the Middle Ages. This is when Kriemhild, who has been told the secret by Siegfried, reveals that it was he, not Gunther, who tamed Brunhild before the marriage was consummated. In both the *Nibelungenlied* and the film, after Siegfried subdues Brunhild, he then leaves Gunther to actually take her virginity, but there are Old Norse versions in which Siegfried really does take Brunhild's virginity – and this is what Kriemhild says in the *Nibelungenlied*, whether through ignorance or malice is not clear. She calls Brunhild a 'concubine' and says that 'Siegfried was the first to enjoy your body.' It is a delicate question as to which is creepier, to have someone take your bride's virginity on your behalf or to have them simply crush her physically so you can do it yourself. But if you are a party to such a sordid agreement between men, then it is obviously vital that you both keep eternal silence about it, which Siegfried fails to do. One cannot help agreeing with Hagen's words to Siegfried in the film: 'Your babbling (*Schwatzen*), hero, was worse than murder!' (In Hebbel's drama *Die Nibelungen* of 1862 Hagen uses a form of the same word: *Er hat geschwatzt!* – He has babbled!)

In the film, Kriemhild tells Brunhild that it was Siegfried, not Gunther, who rode through the flames and defeated her in the three tests. This is enough for Brunhild to try to kill herself. Hagen stops her. 'Kill Siegfried!' she tells him. Already, whether she suspects that it was also Siegfried in Gunther's form who tamed her in the bedroom or not, her goal is not the destruction of Kriemhild, who has humiliated her, or Gunther, who has deceived her, but Siegfried, who has done both. In the film, as part of her plot to have Siegfried killed, she tells Gunther (falsely of course in terms of the plot of the film) that he took her virginity. Putting aside the distracting thought that this suggests Gunther could not tell whether he was sleeping with a virgin or not, her claim is a perfect tactic to motivate the irresolute king. He had been willing to win Brunhild on false pretences but the thought that he had himself been deceived and cuckolded makes him willing to be a party to the treacherous killing of his brother-in-law. And Brunhild's revenge is sweetened when, after Siegfried has been killed, she tells Gunther that he did not actually have sex with her.

Although the dragon's blood has made Siegfried invulnerable, there is one weak spot on his body: a place where a leaf fell unnoticed on his back while bathing in the blood. It seems to be a (brilliant) innovation of the film-makers that it was a last swish of the dragon's tail that dislodged this leaf, thus ensuring posthumous revenge. Siegfried is treacherously killed during a hunt. Readers of, or listeners to, the *Nibelungenlied* would not be surprised by the incident, since the poet announces it well ahead of time, in the first *Aventiure* of the poem, and reminds the audience again at the beginning of *Aventiure* 16, when the hunting party sets out: 'they took his life by a cool spring.' Suspense is often the main effect aimed at by modern thriller-writers and makers of action films, but the older

Siegfried's death in the forest, at the hands of Hagen.

Germanic literature seems never to have encountered the concept. Instead, there are premonitions, ominous asides – 'many men were to die because of that' – or even, as here, an exact statement about a future major event in the narrative. After this opening of *Aventiure* 16, there are then 150 lines describing the hunt, including a comic interlude when Siegfried catches a bear. Is this an aesthetic mistake, an indulgent deviation from the tragic story, or is it a calculated delay to increase the tension, even though we know what is coming? Or is it simply giving the aristocratic audience what it wants – a description of a hunting scene? Since the European upper class has always had an obsession with hunting, this is quite plausible – in *King Solomon's Mines*, the Europeans heading deep into central Africa in search of Sir Henry Curtis's missing brother encounter a herd of elephants and immediately forget about their quest, at Sir Henry's proposal: 'I vote we stop here a day or two, and have a go at them.' They kill nine. So perhaps, when the medieval poet reached this point in the story, he was like those Italian and German composers in the nineteenth century who wanted to stage their operas in Paris but found that opera-goers there demanded a 'ballet' in their opera and had to shoe-horn one in. On the fourth hand, since he devotes line after line to elaborate descriptions of courtly dress, knighting ceremonies and tournaments, perhaps the poet was at one with his aristocratic audience in his tastes. In the film, no actual hunting is shown. It cuts from the departure of the hunting party to a scene later in the day, when a rich booty of dead animals is being carried to the hunters' woodland encampment. Siegfried ends his life, as he began it in the film, deep in the woods.

Is Siegfried a hero? The title of the film is simply his name, usually an indication that this is the hero (as in *Braveheart*, *El Cid*, *Robin Hood* or *Joan of Arc*). Moreover, Siegfried is referred to as a hero (*Held*) by other characters in the film. However, if we look closely at who does this and when, some curious patterns emerge. The first person to address Siegfried as 'hero' – he does so twice – is Alberich, who has failed in his own attack on him and now pleads for his life. Brunhild greets Siegfried, thinking it is he who has come to win her, with the words, 'Welcome, hero!' She intends, of course, to defeat him in a trial of strength. The person who uses the word most frequently is Hagen (four times), both in referring to Siegfried and in addressing him directly. Not all these can be read as simple expressions of respect: 'Your babbling, hero, was worse than murder!' can only be savage irony. It seems to be Siegfried's enemies and opponents who use the word most. The only exception is King Gunther, who calls Siegfried 'hero' when giving him Kriemhild's hand, but perhaps he cancels this out by the only other occasion he addresses him in this way, just before he goes to his death, through treachery to which Gunther is a party. So, although the word 'hero' is attached to Siegfried in the film, it arises in supplication, challenge and irony, rather than in straightforward celebration or admiration.

Moreover, are his actions presented as consistently heroic? He is quick to violence, assaulting Mime's neighbours in the woods when they laugh at his proposal to seek out Kriemhild and attacking the dragon on no provocation; within three minutes of his welcome in Worms, he and his men are on the point of fighting the Burgundians. He kills a dragon and a dwarf and is strong enough to overcome the Amazonian woman Brunhild, but we never see him in combat with other men. In fact, the only humans killed in the film are Siegfried himself and Brunhild, who takes her own life as she sits beside his corpse (as if to compensate for this low body-count, the second part of *Die Nibelungen*, *Kriemhild's Revenge*, culminates in a fifty-minute bloodbath). In contrast to the Siegfried of the film, the Siegfried of the medieval poem, the *Nibelungenlied*, is more of a traditional warrior-hero, who leads an army against the Saxons and Danes who are threatening to invade the land of the Burgundians, captures their kings and slays many. This is also the style of many other heroes of medieval film: both William Wallace and El Cid are constantly seen fighting other men, in single combat and in battle, and very often outnumbered. The heart of Siegfried's hero-status in the film is the taming of a warrior woman. Gunther knows only 'the strongest hero' can win Brunhild. The Icelandic soothsayer tells Brunhild that the ship brings 'foreign heroes', and, as just mentioned, she challenges him using just this word. But his success against her involves a deep, and repeated, deceit.

If there is doubt about Siegfried's status as 'hero', there is also room for discussion about whether the film can be classified as

Expressionist, as it often is. This is a label frequently applied to the cinema of early Weimar Germany and it may be worth discussing the nature of such a term and whether it can be usefully applied to *Siegfried*. Labels for artistic styles and movements are of three types. Some are the inventions of people who were not themselves participants in those styles and movements and lived long afterwards – no one in the Middle Ages called their architectural style 'Gothic'. So modern art historians and others can, if they wish, discuss what was and was not Gothic but they cannot invoke the words of medieval builders and masons using that term to back up their arguments. In contrast, the names of other artistic movements were coined at the time, very self-consciously, by those involved, as in the case of Futurism, whose founder Filippo Marinetti published a Manifesto of Futurism in 1909. The Impressionists are a curious case, since they were certainly a self-conscious group, organizing their own exhibition in 1874, but they then adopted the name 'Impressionists' given to them in derision by a critic of this exhibition. 'Expressionism' is a label of a third type, neither a purely retrospective term, like Gothic, nor one explicitly embraced by a self-conscious group, like Futurism. When the word appears in English, German and French in the first decade of the twentieth century, usually in connection with painting, it is used by critics to characterize the art they are talking about, an art that gave priority to the expression of feeling over a naturalistic representation of factual reality. The term spread internationally and was also applied to many different art forms, including cinema. It even appears in one of Lang's films, when a character asks Dr Mabuse what he thinks of *Expressionismus*, to which the arch-criminal Mabuse replies that it is *Spielerei*, meaning 'fun, sport, jesting'. Clearly, the labels that were adopted consciously by contemporaries, like Futurism, need to be discussed seriously as self-designations, but when it comes to those invented retrospectively or devised by critics, there is room for disagreement about their usefulness. They are clearly helpful as a way of shelving books in a library ('shelved under E for Expressionism'), but there are those who are sceptical about whether they have explanatory power and do not find attempts to define them a fruitful intellectual exercise.

In the case of *Siegfried* and German Expressionism, one might investigate whether the term is appropriate by considering, on the one hand, the acting, and, on the other, the whole overall visual effect (setting, lighting, costumes, decor). The acting style in silent film was a matter discussed at the time. In 1913 D. W. Griffith, the famous pioneer of American cinema and director of the racist classic *The Birth of a Nation* (1915), listed some of the innovations he claimed to have introduced to the art of film, including a less mannered style of acting – 'restraint of expression', as he put it. If this was so, the news does not appear to have reached Lang. Many viewers in the twenty-first century would regard the heavy make-up, extreme gestures and intense facial expressions of the actors in *Siegfried* as unnaturalistic or exaggerated, though it is important to remember that what we call 'naturalistic' depends on what we think is natural and what we call 'exaggerated' depends on what we think is normal and neither 'natural' nor 'normal' are simple to define. It is also perfectly clear that a highly stylized, non-naturalistic acting style can convey emotion and tell a story just as well as more naturalistic techniques, as in Japanese Noh Theatre. But some features of the acting style in *Siegfried* can be seen, not as 'expressionist' in any specific sense but simply as one response to the demands of acting in silent film.

In Germany in the 1920s most film actors began as stage actors, and often continued to perform in theatre productions throughout their career. Compared with traditional acting on the stage, silent film, which was the dominant form of cinema for over thirty years, changed the nature of acting in two completely opposite ways, presenting actors with both new opportunities and new challenges. First, film abolished the distance between actors and audience. The close-up allowed the human face to be viewed on a giant scale, something previously possible only for pharaohs, emperors and other such powerful individuals in monumental sculpture. The creation of the end-product of the film through editing and multiple takes meant that the audience's attention could be directed to exactly the person the film-makers wanted to focus on (as well as allowing mistakes of any kind to be remedied by repeated takes, something impossible in a live stage performance). In theory, this shift from stage acting, where the distance between actor and audience made strong expression and action desirable in order to be visible, could have resulted in a more understated style of acting in film, since there was now no need to bridge the physical distance from the viewer. But this was balanced by the second big difference from traditional theatre. The new medium was *silent* film. The audience would not hear the actors speaking. They had gained the close-up but lost the voice. Hence, as Agnes Platt put it in *Practical Hints on Acting for the Cinema*, which was published in 1921, three years before *Siegfried* was released, 'the whole effect of the drama depends on facial play and gesture, unaided by word.' This might well lead to strong expression and gesture, which can strike modern viewers as melodramatic, even comical. She also noted, interestingly, the way that actors in silent film usually did speak their lines, even though they would not be heard, and she recommended that they use brief and relevant wording that carried the plot forward, both to give their facial movement authenticity and in case there were viewers who could read lips, as many deaf people can.

Ironically, for a silent film, *Siegfried*'s ultimate sources, both the *Nibelungenlied* and the *Volsunga saga*, are rich in memorable dialogue. For example, in the saga, when Sigurd (the Siegfried figure) approaches Brynhild in the form of Gunnar (the Gunther figure), proposing marriage, she replies (in Jesse Byock's translation), 'Do not speak of such things to me, unless you surpass every other man and you will kill those who have asked for me in marriage, if you have the courage to do so. I was in battle with the king of Gardariki [Russia] and our weapons were stained with the blood of men, and this I still desire.' This is pretty uncompromising. It would also take a long time to read on an intertitle. The technical conditions of silent film thus had aesthetic consequences. Any film is thin on dialogue in comparison with a novel, but in silent film this is extreme. It does not mean that the script of a silent film cannot be good, but it does mean it has to be lean.

It also means much has to be done by gesture. We have already mentioned that *The Name of the Rose* had the distinguished medievalist Jean-Claude Schmitt as 'comportment adviser', and the film-makers of *Siegfried* had also done their homework. An example would be Kriemhild bringing the bowl of drink to Siegfried on his first arrival in Worms, when he and his men and the Burgundians are on the point of coming to blows. Her very appearance brings peace. She then advances slowly, the bowl held in both hands, towards Siegfried, who is casting eyes upon her for the first time. It is ninety seconds between her first arrival, quelling the fighters, and Siegfried taking the first sip, and ninety seconds is a long time in a film, especially when it is not only a silent film but one in which this scene is meant to take place in total silence in the Burgundian court. The noble lady with the cup offering the strong drink is thus the focus of the film at this point and one who changes the whole dynamic of the action. This is not the film-makers' invention but corresponds to actual practice in the Middle Ages and to descriptions in medieval literature. Here, for example, is a passage from the medieval best-seller *History of the Kings of Britain* by Geoffrey of Monmouth, describing the visit of the British king Vortigern to the Saxon warrior Hengist, whose daughter is famous for her beauty:

> As he was being entertained with a royal banquet, the girl came out of an inner room, carrying a golden goblet, full of wine. Approaching the king, she curtseyed and said 'Wassail, Lord King!' He, seeing the girl's face, marvelled at her great beauty and became inflamed . . . Vortigern ordered the girl to drink, then took the goblet from her hand, kissed her, and drank.

Faster than Siegfried, Vortigern wastes no time and marries the girl that same night. It does not work out well (then again, the story of Siegfried and Kriemhild does not work out well), but it indicates that the formal offering of drink was one way in which well-born ladies could appear in the public space of the court and have direct interaction with men; this was entirely honourable, because semi-ritual. It may well be that Lang's depiction of this slow, public, ritual process struck viewers as non-naturalistic because they were unfamiliar with it as a medieval reality. So there are limits to the value of labelling the acting in the film 'expressionist', or, even more so, 'Expressionist'.

Turning to the overall visual effect of the film, it is immediately apparent that its style is particularly stunning. The choreography of the set pieces is unforgettable: when Siegfried is being told of the Burgundian court for the first time, the screen shows a vision of the court, in which the foreground is occupied by the huge figures of four knights, facing away from us and wearing tunics with distinctive zig-zag patterns, while the royal family and their retinue progress slowly beyond them from right to left; when Brunhild arrives at Worms, she leaves the ship on a bridge made of shields held up by two rows of soldiers, up to their waists in water; the confrontation between Kriemhild and Brunhild opens with a long shot of the cathedral steps, wide and empty, the doorway at the top at dead centre, and then from the bottom left corner the figure of Kriemhild, all in white, begins a diagonal ascent of the steps followed by her handmaidens, also in white, before there is a cut to a closer shot of Brunhild, in dark clothing, seen from behind, climbing the steps followed by her handmaidens, then a shot showing her clearly noticing Kriemhild off-screen, culminating in a long shot again, of the white procession on the stairs being confronted with the black procession. Virtually any still from the film will show a wonder of composition, yet without the narrative ever losing forward direction.

The set and costumes in film have a very distinctive visual aesthetic. Lang had studied architecture and painting and it shows. Geometrical patterns, such as zig-zags, arrows, lozenges and roundels, abound, on clothes, on walls, on ceilings. The costumes were designed by Paul Gerd Guderian, whose older brother was to be a famous tank commander in the Second World War, and who died aged only 28 during the making of the film. Perhaps he was influenced by the illustrations in a simplified version of the *Nibelungenlied*, published in 1908 as *Die Nibelungen dem Deutschen Volke wiedererzählt* (The Story of the Nibelungs Retold for the German People), which has exactly the same aesthetic as Lang's Burgundian court. Whether or not we choose to use the label 'Expressionist', it is clear

Carl Otto Czeschka: illustration from Franz Keim, *Die Nibelungen dem Deutschen Volke wiedererzählt* (1909).

that *Siegfried* is characterized by stylized gesture, choreographic action, bold and large-scale geometric designs and grand symmetries.

This distinctive aesthetic was subject to a celebrated political critique. In his book *From Caligari to Hitler: A Psychological History of the German Film*, published in 1947, Siegfried Kracauer (1889–1966) traced a direct line from the aesthetic of *Die Nibelungen* to the Nuremberg rallies of the Nazis:

> Absolute authority asserts itself by arranging people under its domination in pleasing designs. This can also be seen in the Nazi regime, which manifested strong ornamental inclinations in organizing masses ... *Triumph of the Will*, the official Nazi film of the Nuremberg Party Convention in 1934, proves that in shaping their mass-ornaments the Nazi decorators drew inspiration from *Nibelungen*.

Kracauer, who was Jewish, left Germany in 1933 when the Nazis came to power and was eventually able to seek refuge in the United States, where *From Caligari to Hitler* was written. He hoped the book would help 'in the planning of films which will effectively implement the cultural aims of the United Nations'. Kracauer singles out the figure of Hagen in Lang's *Siegfried* as foreshadowing 'a well-known type of Nazi leader'. It is not clear how much hindsight there is in this statement, because the actor who played Hagen, Hans Adalbert Schlettow, indeed became an enthusiastic Nazi and died during the fighting in Berlin in spring 1945. Perhaps Kracauer was aware of this, perhaps not. The bifurcation of Schlettow's and Kracauer's fortunes in mid-twentieth-century Germany is given added poignancy by knowing that they were both born in Frankfurt am Main within twelve months of each other.

The 'Caligari' in the title of his book refers to the film *The Cabinet of Dr Caligari*, released in 1920, highly praised at the time, and one to which Kracauer devoted many pages. The plot involves the mysterious and sinister Dr Caligari, who has a fairground display featuring a somnambulist (played by Conrad Veidt – many years later memorably shot dead by Humphrey Bogart in *Casablanca*) who can predict the future but also, as we see, is a serial killer, his mind controlled by Caligari. Caligari, it turns out, is the director of a local lunatic asylum and, when finally unmasked, is put in a straitjacket in his own asylum. Then we have a framing device which shows us that this whole tale is being told by an inmate of that asylum, who, after he attacks the director of the asylum, himself ends up in a straitjacket. The film makes no attempt at realism in its sets, where we encounter triangular doors, dark corridors and fantastic ornamentation, and the acting style is of the exaggerated type we find in *Siegfried*.

Kracauer called *The Cabinet of Dr Caligari* the 'archetype of all forthcoming postwar films', that is, the films of the Weimar period, when Germany was facing the consequences of defeat in the Great War, including loss of territory and population, and when many believed that the war had been lost not on the battlefield but by betrayal, a stab in the back. Writing in exile in the 1940s, Kracauer knew what the end result was: a Nazi dictatorship, another World War and the attempted annihilation of the Jews. Having seen his world destroyed, Kracauer naturally wanted an explanation. Seeking it, at least in part, in the cinema of the time might seem odd, but Kracauer considered that 'the technique, the story content, and the evolution of the films of a nation are fully understandable only in relation to the actual psychological pattern of this nation.' So he thought that the cinema was a key to the 'inner life of the nation', shaped by the psychology, perhaps unconscious, of that nation: 'films are forced to answer to mass desires.' In his hypnotic power over the somnambulist, Caligari exercises 'a technique foreshadowing, in content and purpose, that manipulation of the soul which Hitler was the first to practice on a gigantic scale'. The film, 'like the Nazi world', is full of 'sinister portents, acts of terror and outbursts of panic'; it is characterized by 'a strong sadism and an appetite for destruction', traits which have 'prominence in the German collective soul'.

Whatever we think of concepts like 'the German collective soul', or of the equation in Kracauer's title of an innovative horror film of 1920 and the Nazi dictator, it is worth considering Lang's *Siegfried* in its time and place, Germany in 1924, and asking what one tells us about the other. Some points are more important than others. Kracauer's suggestion that 'arranging people in pleasing designs' is an expression of power has some interest. Getting human beings

The Burgundian court on the cathedral steps.

to form geometrical shapes, which is not their usual behaviour, is indeed a common expression of power, not only in mass rallies but in the army, as seen in ceremonial marches, fighting squares and parade-ground ranks. In *Siegfried*, it is associated with the Burgundian court, and is an expression not only of power but of a refined, courtly, artificial way of life. The court at Worms very rarely looks as if it is fun but it does look stately. And yet to draw a direct line to the Nuremberg rallies is to ignore the fact that symmetry, precision and grand scale are simply part of the nature of spectacular public ritual. They could be used just as easily in a ceremony celebrating world peace or opening the Olympic Games. And in the world of the film, the geometric certainties of Worms also contrast with the total unpredictable fluidity of the Icelandic court, where the members of this all-girl society whirl around like leaves in a gusty wind.

It is hard to deny (though it has been denied) that the film's portrayal of Alberich, the dwarf king who possesses the Nibelung treasure, including the magical cap so vital to the plot, is a hostile antisemitic stereotype. He is short, bearded and has an extravagantly hooked nose. He attacks Siegfried treacherously not once but twice. He is extremely rich and tries to buy his way out of the situation. Yet we should not rush to draw a direct connection between the antisemitism in the films of Weimar Germany and the Nazi 'Final Solution'. In the 1920s antisemitism was widely diffused in Europe and the USA. This does not mean that it is forgivable, but it does mean that it is not an unusual, individually thought-out position, nor is it specific to Germany. It may be that we see it differently because we know what happened to the Jews in Germany and Eastern Europe under the Nazis, but the sinister interpretation of the art of the Weimar period, as a kind of foreshadowing of the nightmare that was to come, is reading history backwards. Then there is the question of how it affects our viewing of the film. It is not actually a very important feature of *Siegfried*. The portrayal of the Huns in the second part of *Die Nibelungen, Kriemhild's Revenge*, is a much more sustained and developed racial caricature, in this case of the 'oriental', although mingled with American Indians and cavemen: the Huns are bare-chested, often with braided hair, great horsemen, great archers, quick to attack and quick to run away, childlike in their admiration for the beautiful Kriemhild. Yet, of course, this depiction of the Huns had no close contemporary relevance, as a portrayal of the Jews did. Lang was, as mentioned, of partly Jewish descent himself, so what should the viewer's reaction be to this antisemitic moment in the film? Should the film be banned? How far should artists' unpalatable opinions affect our judgement of their work? Should we refuse to read Lang's contemporary, Virginia Woolf, because of her notorious antisemitism (despite the fact that she married a Jew)? Should the willingness of Robert Burns to accept a job on a Jamaican slave plantation, despite writing 'The Slave's Lament', mean Burns Night should be abolished?

At the heart of the film, rather than intimations of the Third Reich, lies a dramatic pentangle: Siegfried and Kriemhild, Gunther and Brunhild, and Hagen. The double wedding of the two couples that takes place at the halfway point in the film, around one hour and a quarter in, sets the scene for the remaining half, which ends with Siegfried's body lying in state in the cathedral. Between the two weddings and the funeral, we have the quarrel between Kriemhild and Brunhild, Kriemhild's disastrous revelation about the deceit practised on Brunhild, the plot against Siegfried by Hagen with Gunther's connivance, and the murder. The film diverges fundamentally from the medieval epic in the way it portrays the confrontation between Kriemhild and Brunhild. In the *Nibelungenlied* Siegfried offers to swear a solemn oath that it is not true that he has told Kriemhild that he was the first to sleep with Brunhild (which, in the poem, is what she has claimed). Gunther publicly accepts Siegfried's innocence. The two of them exchange an understanding look, and Siegfried says that women should be brought up to avoid mindless gossip. Later, in private, he beats Kriemhild up. Meanwhile, Hagen, struck by Brunhild's distress, has begun to plan Siegfried's murder. 'Shall we raise cuckoos?', he asks, implying both that Siegfried has laid his eggs in another's nest, and that he would grow to destroy his hosts. The film radically simplifies this by showing both Gunther and Siegfried unable to deny what Kriemhild has said, that it was Siegfried in disguise who tamed (rather than slept with) Brunhild. This is when Brunhild attempts to kill herself before insisting that Siegfried must be killed, later saying she will not eat or drink until Siegfried is dead (something drawn from Hebbel's drama). So in the film the deceit practised upon Brunhild has been publicly revealed. Yet Hagen, who was a party to the deception, is now Brunhild's avenger. His commitment to the Burgundian dynasty demands that Siegfried, the disruptive babbler, be removed. Part Two of the *Nibelungen*, *Kriemhild's Revenge*, shows that this loyalty is reciprocal, as one by one the Burgundians are slaughtered at Kriemhild's command, yet refuse to give up Hagen. Kriemhild had been deceived into giving away to Hagen the secret of Siegfried's vulnerable spot, just as Brunhild has been deceived by Gunther and Siegfried. Now she takes her revenge. Summing up the plot of this tragic and bloody story, the anonymous author of the *Nibelungenlied* wrote, 'Many warriors were destroyed by the quarrel of two women.' Not by the treacherous deceits of men?

WRAPPING UP

The eight films discussed in this book are certainly not a scientific sample, but they enable a few general points to be made. It is clear that, when making films about the Middle Ages, the film-makers virtually never begin with a careful investigation of the original contemporary sources. This does not mean that films do not draw on original sources, but they always mix them with later legendary and literary elaborations, the film-makers often not knowing the distinction, as well as free inventions, of course. *Braveheart* and *El Cid* are perfect examples of this process, both of them bringing in a tale of love and revenge from these later stories, the love of 'Murron' inspiring Wallace's revenge, Rodrigo's killing of Chimène's father requiring, impossibly, her revenge. While there is no doubt that Wallace did kill the sheriff of Lanark (this was a charge in his final indictment in 1305), the idea that he did so because the sheriff had executed his lover occurs for the first time in the chronicle of Andrew Wyntoun, written in the period 1390–1420, so at least 85 years and perhaps a century or more later. It would have been possible to portray the killing of the sheriff as inspired by purely political and patriotic motives, but it was natural for the film-makers to prefer the more personal and romantic interpretation. Similarly, the film-makers of *El Cid* focused instinctively on the tangled emotions stirred up by Rodrigo's dilemma – his sense of honour requires him to fight the father of the woman he loves – and Chimène's, that she is duty-bound to revenge her father's death on the man she loves. Otherwise, in fact, there would be virtually nothing to say about their relationship, since the strictly contemporary evidence for Rodrigo's wife does not extend much further than her name.

There is one type of film with a medieval setting that is informed not accidentally but fundamentally by its reliance on later literary and legendary elaboration, namely films of Shakespeare's medieval plays: Olivier's *Henry V*, Welles's or Polanski's *Macbeth*, and so on. Here the raw historical material has already been transformed not only by generations, or even centuries, of storytelling, anecdote and invention, but by the fire of literary genius: this is Shakespeare's Middle Ages. After the initial decision that the film-makers have to make – how much of Shakespeare's dialogue to cut – they then must make another. It concerns costume and set. There are three basic options: Elizabethan/Jacobean, that is, the period when the plays were written, thus harmonizing with the style of the language; modern, of various types to make various points, usually political; or from the period in which the historical figures actually lived. So, in *Macbeth*, the actors could be wearing twentieth-century clothes and uniforms or could be in ruffs and wear rapiers or could be in whatever costume the designers imagine was the style in eleventh-century Scotland. Olivier's *Henry V* ingeniously combines a Tudor framing scene set in the Globe Theatre with the main action clearly attempting (and largely achieving) fifteenth-century authenticity (despite the ludicrous depiction of knights being raised onto their horses by the use of small cranes). By the time we reach the Battle of Agincourt we are out in open fields and have quite forgotten that we are watching a play, until the last four minutes of the film, which return us to the Globe Theatre. But if one of Shakespeare's history plays set in the Middle Ages is filmed with the characters in modern dress, there is really nothing 'medieval' about it at all, except the names of the characters.

It is sometimes surprising what kind of original medieval source material survives the fiction-making machine. An episode from *The Thirteenth Warrior* (1999) provides a good example. This film, despite being based on a book by Michael Crichton, author of the very successful *Jurassic Park*, and directed by John McTiernan, director of the very successful *Die Hard*, was not well received by critics and did not make a profit. It tells the story of a tenth-century Muslim, Ibn Fadhlan, played by Antonio Banderas, who joins a group of Vikings and eventually participates in their bloody fight against marauding cannibal monsters (the original book was titled *Eaters of the Dead*). An early scene shows a Viking funeral. The body of the dead king is placed on a boat, surrounded by his possessions, and the men raise and lower a young woman, who recites 'Lo, there do I see my father. Lo, there do I see my mother, my sisters and my brothers. Lo, there do I see the line of my people back to the beginning. Lo, they do call to me. They bid me take my place among them . . .' The corpse is then incinerated, along with the girl. This scene is neither the product of Michael Crichton's imagination nor a result of the film-makers' desire for a sensational piece of cinema (though the scene would not have been in the film without that imagination and that desire) but is actually reported by Ibn Fadhlan, who was a real person, in the account he wrote of his journey in central Asia in the year 921. Among many other events and observations that he recorded was an encounter with Scandinavian traders (the Rus, who gave their name to Russia) and what he says is extremely important evidence for Viking customs and beliefs. He describes their clothes and weapons, the women's jewellery, their deplorable bodily hygiene, the slave girls they abuse, their wooden idols and a funeral, which is the model for that in the film and involves a boat, the men raising and lowering a slave girl while she recites 'there I see my father and my mother' and so forth, and final incineration. Crichton knew this account, which formed the basis for the early part of his novel, before his book veered off into complete fiction and fantasy. So, here is a fragment from a tenth-century Arabic text embodied in a film produced by a branch of Walt Disney Studios in the penultimate year of the twentieth century.

Incidentally, one thing that *The Thirteenth Warrior* does well, which is a great rarity in historical film, is to address the fact that different people spoke different languages. Usually all the characters speak the language of the film-makers, so that the Teutonic Knights in *Alexander Nevsky* speak Russian and both Spaniards and North Africans in *El Cid* speak English, and so forth. In *Braveheart*, there is some use of Latin and French, so that William Wallace, whose linguistic skills his enemies underrate, can understand the Latin that the princess's hostile English adviser speaks, on the assumption that Wallace will not know what he is saying to her, and Wallace can charm her by a few words of French (the use of authentic languages is obviously something that fascinated Gibson, who has his characters speaking Aramaic in *The Passion of the Christ* and Mayan in *Apocalypto*). *The Thirteenth Warrior* takes this much further. In the opening part of the film, Ibn Fadhlan cannot understand the Nordic language spoken by the Vikings and relies on his older guide (played by Omar Sharif) as translator. Bridge languages are necessary, so that during the funeral scene there is a Viking who knows Latin translating what the girl is saying in Nordic into Latin to the Omar

Sharif character who then translates the Latin for Ibn Fadhlan. He translates it of course into English, for the viewers of the film as well as for Ibn Fadhlan. So, in this part of the film, when English is spoken it corresponds to the Arabic that was the common language of Ibn Fadhlan and his mentor. As the film progresses, Ibn Fadhlan travels with the Vikings but no longer with his mentor. When the Vikings chat around the campfire in their own Nordic language, he (along with the viewer) cannot understand them. But we see him, night after night, observing what they say, watching their lips, noticing repetitions. Gradually, by an inspired piece of the film-makers' creative thinking, the Vikings begin to use the odd English phrase among their Nordic – Ibn Fadhlan is learning their language, and English now corresponds to Nordic. Eventually, his grasp of their language is so good that he understands everything, and one evening he hears one of them make an unflattering remark about his, Ibn Fadhlan's, mother. He responds at once in their own language (Nordic to them, English to us): 'My mother was . . . a pure woman from . . . a noble family. And I . . . at least . . . know who my father is . . . you pig-eating son of a whore!' The Vikings have been listening in astonishment and, when they have prevented their insulted comrade from killing Ibn Fadhlan, they ask him, 'Where did you learn our language?' Perhaps with a touch of contempt, he replies, 'I listened.' There can be no better depiction of language learning in the history of cinema.

The medieval and early modern storytellers who elaborated the legends of great men and events of the past and the twentieth-century film-makers were motivated by exactly the same impulse – to create a good story. The film-makers' choices thus tell us something about what they thought counted as a good story, something that will vary from period to period and place to place. One force at work is simplification. For example, *El Cid* depicts the conflict between Sancho and Alfonso, the sons of King Ferdinand, but, in reality, there was a third brother, Garcia. His removal from the story is an example of the kind of silent simplification that is absolutely defensible in historical film. In *Braveheart*, there is a cut straight from Wallace's death in 1305 to the Battle of Bannockburn in 1314. It would indeed have been complex and confusing to try to portray the tangled story of the intervening years – Bruce's inauguration as king of Scots in 1306, his uphill struggle against the English, the campaign of 1314, in which the English army was led by Edward II (who of course only appears in the film as the effeminate prince) – but this understandable simplification is combined with a completely false picture, that in 1314 the Scots under Bruce had come to submit to the English army. The motivation for that change is unclear. Simplification is also necessary when adapting a film script from written works, either medieval, such as the *Nibelungenlied*, or modern, such as *The Name of the Rose*. In the former case, an example would be Siegfried's military campaigns on behalf of the Burgundians, which were cut entirely, and the hunting scene, which was pruned to minimum, while in the latter the young Adso is turned from a Benedictine to a Franciscan, to simplify why he is travelling with the Franciscan William of Baskerville. All these changes make the narrative simpler and clearer.

And film-makers are naturally drawn to any story or motif that produces strong visual images, like the dead body of El Cid riding out strapped to his horse, a piece of thirteenth-century legendary material that would immediately have caught the eye of a screenwriter. Lang wanted to depict a fight with a dragon, not have it reported, while Tarkovsky filmed the torture of the keymaster at Vladimir using the medieval chronicle account as his script. This desire to present the viewer with something memorable is rarely restrained by fear of anachronism. Drastic examples can be found in *Braveheart*, where the woad warpaint and bagpipes are striking visual symbols of Scotland even though they are drawn, respectively, from a period far earlier and a period far later than the setting of the story around 1300, and the mild anachronisms of the tournament in *El Cid* have been discussed in the chapter on that film, adopted presumably because they made the scene more colourful. *Andrei Rublev*'s scene showing a medieval Russian attempting to invent the hot-air balloon is slightly different, in that it may have happened, since the attempt fails and therefore would have left no trace in the historical record. The scene demonstrates imagination not anachronism (it was actually a scene Tarkovsky was willing to drop when asked by the U.S. distributor of the film to shorten its running time).

Another imperative for storytellers is the need for a love interest, virtually without exception heterosexual. And here was a (limited) place for women in cinema. In the twentieth century the vast majority of producers, scriptwriters, directors and film crew were men. There were, naturally, exceptions, such as the scriptwriters Thea von Harbou, wife of Fritz Lang, and Marguerite Roberts, who worked on more than thirty films, including *Ivanhoe* (1952), though for that she was initially uncredited since she was blacklisted for her political opinions. And there was the energetic Gemma Bellincioni, who wrote, directed and starred in *Joanna I of Anjou, Queen of Naples* (1920). But, in general, it was only in casting that the focus was as much on women – 'actresses' as they were known – as men.

The big roles for women are as the object and sometimes the subject of romantic love. In film as in life, love takes different forms. In *El Cid* there is dignified romantic love, with the potential for tragedy; in *Alexander Nevsky*, romantic love with a comic opera twist; in *Siegfried*, tragic romantic love. Women play a big role in *Siegfried*. The plot turns around the pursuit of two women, Kriemhild and Brunhild, the wrongs done to them and the revenge they seek. The story continues in Part Two of the *Nibelungen*, *Kriemhild's Revenge*, when the demure love interest of part one becomes a fanatical avenger. In *Braveheart*, the situation is the reverse, as William Wallace's path to national champion is sparked by his desire to avenge his lost love. The most idyllic picture of a woman is Bibi Andersson in *The Seventh Seal* – serene, beautiful, a mother, a loving if sometimes sceptical wife.

There are, however, other roles for female characters in twentieth-century films about the Middle Ages. Some medieval films do concentrate on mothers. *The Lion in Winter* (1968) is a good example, where the sons of Eleanor of Aquitaine (played by Katharine Hepburn) are fixated upon her, a matriarch with a wryly modern sensibility. Many of the films discussed in this book also have secondary female characters keen on sex. In *Braveheart* it is the princess's pert French lady-in-waiting, who sleeps with one of the guards, thinks that Englishmen do not know what tongues are for and exchanges flirtatious looks with the strong but somewhat bashful Hamish, a semi-comic parallel to the noble love of Wallace and the princess. In *The Name of the Rose* there is the peasant girl willing to sleep with Adso on first sight, and in *Monty Python and the Holy Grail* the young blondes keen on oral sex. *Andrei Rublev* portrays the promiscuity of the pagans. In *The Seventh Seal*, Lisa, the blacksmith's wife, is active in sexual pursuit, in a kind of farcical exaggerated style.

Then there are films about Joan of Arc, the peasant girl who turned around the fortunes of France in the Hundred Years War before being captured, tried and burned at the stake in 1431. They form a large category and one of the rare cases where a film is actually titled after a female protagonist. Also, curiously enough, the female protagonist is a virgin who dresses as a man, an astonishing mixed message since the official ideology of the medieval Church idealized virginity but regarded cross-dressing as (in the words of the Bible) 'an abomination'. And films about Joan of Arc exhibit yet another unique feature, since Joan's amazing story is very well documented. Particularly important are the records of her trial, in which her own views and answers are recorded, in the face of hostile inquisition. And because much of what is known about Joan comes from trial proceedings, in which her direct speech and that of her judges is recorded in large amounts, it is possible to make a film about her based entirely on strictly contemporary source material. This is the case in Carl Theodor Dreyer's *The Passion of Joan of Arc* of 1928, with Maria Falconetti as Joan, the script of which is in large part drawn from these detailed trial records. The conversion of trial records into a screenplay can be done with minimal changes as they consist primarily of dialogue. Dreyer's film actually begins with short shots of a (modern) hand turning the pages of the record of Joan's trial in the archives. Robert Bresson's 1962 film was titled simply *The Trial of Joan of Arc*, recognizing the fact that our intimate knowledge of Joan derives from that inquisitorial process. But Joan is exceptional. Most female characters, in film as in life, are not cross-dressing virgin warriors. However, in one respect, Joan's life and fate do share a feature with those of other women. She was accused by her enemies of sorcery and witchcraft, and this association of women with magic crops up in several of the films discussed in this book. Female witches appear in *The Name of the Rose*, *Monty Python and the Holy Grail* and *The Seventh Seal*, in each case as the subject of trial and condemnation, and in *Andrei Rublev* and

Siegfried there are pagan women who engage in non-Christian rituals, fertility rites in the first, fortune-telling in the second.

The other great serial protagonist in medieval films, apart from Joan of Arc, is Robin Hood, the royalist outlaw. Robin and Joan are opposites. Robin is entirely fictional, a legendary creation of the later Middle Ages and the following centuries, while Joan is the medieval person we know most intimately. Robin has been incarnated in many different forms over time, from the classic versions of Douglas Fairbanks in 1922 and Errol Flynn in 1938, to the cartoon version of 1973 and the spoof version *Men in Tights* of 1993, and he has responded to social and cultural changes, for instance becoming more sensitive to women's issues in 1976, when Maid Marian (played by Audrey Hepburn) is promoted to equal billing in *Robin and Marian*, and acquiring a black sidekick in 1991 in Kevin Costner's version. There are some standard features of the story, with the archery, the greenwood, the Merrie Men, and villains like the Sheriff of Nottingham and Prince John – 'Prince' was not a contemporary title but one applied to John much later and then popularized, like so much of our picture of the Middle Ages, by Walter Scott. And in these films England is always suffering injustice and the danger of usurpation as John plots against his absent brother, Richard the Lionheart. Things are not resolved and justice restored until the return of Good King Richard.

Richard's absence from England (he was, in fact, in the kingdom for only six months of his ten-year reign) is explained partly because of his wars in France and partly because of his absence on crusade. Twentieth-century cinema generally treated Richard as a heroic figure and the crusades as a sandy medieval equivalent of a 'Cowboys and Indians' story, in which the Indians/Muslims might well have good and honourable qualities but there was no doubt about who was 'us'. The figure of Saladin, the Muslim leader who fought King Richard during the Third Crusade of 1189–92, could be presented favourably rather than as a pure jihadist villain (such as Ben Yusuf in *El Cid*), and in Warner Brothers' *King Richard and the Crusaders* of 1954, which is based (loosely) on Walter Scott's novel *The Talisman*, the Muslim leader Ilderim (who is later revealed to be Saladin in disguise) is brave, generous and chivalrous. This is in the tradition of *The Talisman*, where Scott wrote, 'the distinctions of religions, nay, the fanatical zeal which animated the followers of the Cross and the Crescent against each other, was much softened by a feeling so natural to generous combatants, and especially cherished by the spirit of chivalry.' In this film the unusual casting of George Sanders, best remembered for his suave cads and villains, as King Richard is overshadowed by the curious choice of Rex Harrison in brownface as Ilderim/Saladin. The film is also notable for the Lady Edith's immortal line, speaking to the king: 'War! War! That's all you think of, Dick Plantagenet!', although this is not, in fact, the first use of this remarkable form of address, for 'Dick Plantagenet' crops up as early as 1840 in George Darley's play *Thomas à Becket* (it is not in Scott). An alternative vision of the Third Crusade can be found in the great Egyptian director Youssef Chahine's *Saladin* of 1963, with Hamdy Gheith as King Richard (not in whiteface).

There are very few morally ambiguous figures in the films discussed in this book. Villains and heroes are clearly demarcated. Atrocities early in the film, such as the mass hanging of the Scots nobles in *Braveheart* or the Teutonic Knights throwing babies onto bonfires in *Alexander Nevsky*, make it obvious who the bad guys are and hence which side we, the viewers, are meant to be on. Some of the bad guys are religious bigots and may be given a fair amount of screen time to make their bad opinions clear: Jorge de Burgos and Bernard Gui, in their different ways, in *The Name of the Rose*; Ben Yusuf in *El Cid*; the Catholic clergy in *Alexander Nevsky*. All of them die. Others are less eloquent but still undertake the repressive business of pursuing and persecuting others for their beliefs: the soldiers and monks in both *Andrei Rublev* and *The Seventh Seal*, the peasants so keen on a witch-burning in *Monty Python and the Holy Grail*. But the most common bad guys are national enemies, just as the most common heroes are national heroes.

The concept of the Middle Ages was invented in Europe, and its purpose was to give a label to European history between the fall of the Roman Empire and the Renaissance, that is, in the period approximately AD 500–1500. There is reasonable, and sometimes unreasonable, discussion about whether it can be applied to other parts of the world. The term 'Medieval Baghdad' does not sound too outlandish, though clearly the history of the Islamic world cannot be defined by the fall of Rome and the Renaissance; 'Medieval India' is sometimes used but often meets objections; 'Medieval China' might well be viewed as a term that is as incongruous as 'Tang Europe' or 'Ming Europe'. The same question can be asked about historical films made in countries like China, Japan or India. For example, can Akira Kurosawa's *Seven Samurai* (1954), *Throne of Blood* (1957) or *Kagemusha* (1980) be labelled 'medieval' (the last of these depicts an actual historical battle of 1575)? There is a Japanese term for the genre of historical film (*jidai-geki*) and, while most films of this type are set in the post-medieval period, as defined by European criteria, they do show a warrior class, castles and swordfights, things associated with the Middle Ages in the popular imagination of Western filmgoers. The great French medievalist Marc Bloch included in his celebrated work *Feudal Society* (1939–40) a brief discussion of whether that label 'feudal' could be applied to Japan, concluding, 'like Europe Japan went through this phase.' Not a few scholars who write about medieval cinema are happy to include in their discussion non-European films with a setting in the pre-industrial past. The boundaries of the subject are not always clear-cut.

No such doubt arises in the case of Europe, and it is not hard to understand why the film industry of a European country would make films about the Middle Ages which are set in the country they were filmed in: *The Seventh Seal* was filmed in Sweden, set in Sweden, and has a Swedish director and cast; *Andrei Rublev* and *Alexander Nevsky* were filmed in Russia, set in Russia, and have a Russian director and cast. They refer to the 'national past'. But what of that behemoth of twentieth-century film, Hollywood? Of course, many Americans are of European descent, but this rarely manifests itself in historical films aimed at particular ethnic groups. Having no Middle Ages, the USA could adopt different attitudes to the European Middle Ages: ignore it, romanticize it, demonize it, use it as a stage-set for American concerns, and so forth. The American film industry definitely wanted to use it and hence, despite America not having its own Middle Ages, American films have been a powerful generator of images of that period of European history. Of the films discussed in this book (all of which were filmed in Europe), the two with the strongest American imprint are *Braveheart* and *El Cid*, which had American directors, screenwriters and leading actors.

In most European countries there was a strong tradition of viewing national feeling positively. It was deemed noble to fight for one's country. People might talk proudly of 'national character'. The new art form of cinema had strong roots in the culture of the nineteenth century, which already had its national traditions in fields like classical music, as in the case of the strongly nationalistic Verdi and

Wagner, and literature, for example the historical novels of Scott, Manzoni and Victor Hugo, and the moving picture too could be used to express this devotion to the nation, as is obvious in the case of several of the films discussed here. It is, in particular, defensive nationalism that can be idealized, whether it is Scottish as in *Braveheart*, Spanish as in *El Cid*, or Russian as in *Alexander Nevsky*. In each of these films, nationalism is stirred into violent life by a threat, a threat from outside that seeks to crush and destroy the nation, and a national leader emerges to head the resistance. His task is complicated by divisions, and even betrayal, among his own people, but he transcends them to achieve national unity, even if it happens after his death, as in *Braveheart* and, in a sense, *El Cid*. These men are heroes: the films are named after them, the titles consisting of the nickname that they won by their exploits: 'Braveheart', a soubriquet invented for the film; 'El Cid', the admiring title given to this Christian knight by a Muslim; 'Nevsky', commemorating Alexander's victory over Swedish invaders on the river Neva. Although American films about the Middle Ages are not about the history of one's own country, they can still present nationalism as heroic, and hence we find American stars like Charlton Heston and Mel Gibson playing Scottish or Spanish national heroes and Americans writing and directing the films they appear in. In *El Cid*, the story of 'Spain's greatest hero' is told without a single one of the major actors being Spanish.

If these films usually present 'the nation' unambiguously as a good thing, their portrayal of religion is more complicated. In the Middle Ages, it is generally agreed, the power and wealth of the Church were greater than in any other period. In most parts of medieval Europe, it was necessary to be a baptised Christian in order to be a full member of society and, even when Jews and Muslims were tolerated, they were liable to various forms of legal discrimination. Some of this intolerance is represented in the films, such as the activities of the inquisitor Bernard Gui and the hunting down of pagans in *Andrei Rublev*. It is rare that there is anything in these films that could be called positive religious motivation. In *Braveheart*, we see a priest at the burial of Wallace's father and brother, and another gives a blessing before the Battle of Stirling, but what motivates the main character is love of a woman and love of a nation, two things that get tangled up in his mind. In *Alexander Nevsky* it is the bad characters who are motivated by religious fervour, the heroes by nationalist fervour, their own religious life virtually invisible. *The Name of the Rose* is the film that presents the full-time religious life of a Benedictine community most systematically, yet, once more, religious commitment and passion is a feature of the bad characters. The hero, Willam of Baskerville, is tolerant and sceptical by inclination, perhaps like his creator, the secular and non-religious Umberto Eco. The closest thing to a Christian hero is El Cid, who carries on his shoulder a large crucifix from the burning church after the Muslim raid at the beginning of the film, and later gives water to a mysterious leper named Lazarus standing beneath three crosses, the central one bearing the crucified Christ, but these moments are few and serve primarily to show Rodrigo's dutifulness and compassion, and occur in a film dedicated to the proposition that Muslims and Christians can live together, and only bigots and fanatics think they cannot or should not. In *Siegfried*, the rituals of the Church appear as the conventional duty of the court but religion seems to motivate no one (in Part Two of the *Nibelungen*, *Kriemhild's Revenge*, neither religion nor the Church appear at all).

While the institutional Church is rarely a significant presence, two of the films considered here do concentrate on the inner spiritual life, *Andrei Rublev* and *The Seventh Seal*. What they are interested in, however, is their subjects' doubts and their problems with belief. The knight is constantly questioning but seems to find no answers. His most definite religious commitment, the decision to go on crusade, has involved him in something 'so stupid only an idealist could have invented it'. Andrei Rublev is also a troubled soul, worrying about the purpose of religious art, disturbed by physical love, eventually taking a vow of silence. Both Bergman and Tarkovsky thought faith and belief very important questions, but ones that they conceived of in an individualist sense: Bergman reacting against the institutional religion he had grown up in (Lutheranism), Tarkovsky growing up in an officially atheist state.

One can find examples of films that present medieval Christianity in a wholeheartedly positive way. A perfect illustration is Roberto Rossellini's *The Flowers of St Francis* (1950), depicting the beginning of the Franciscan Order and based on stories collected after Francis's death (so, like many of the films discussed in this book, representing medieval legend as much as medieval fact). The film's original Italian title, *Francesco, giullare di Dio* (Francis, God's Jester) conveys the spirit of the film very well. It uses mainly non-professional actors, is shot with extreme simplicity and presents a number of vignettes, little episodes with no real continuity, showing the inspired literalism of the early friars: Jesus had said to his disciples, 'provide no shoes for your journey', so the early friars went barefoot. In the film a big role is given to Fra' Ginepro (Brother Juniper), whose qualities as a Holy Fool inspire Francis's affection (and amusement) and give him a kind of invincibility in tribulation. The final scene shows Francis sending out his brethren into the world to preach peace. If we have seen *The Name of the Rose*, we are aware of what a sad future conflict awaited the Order.

All the films discussed in this book, like most films, have music as part of their fabric, even the 'silent' *Siegfried*, which had a score composed specifically for it (although, of course, that might not have been available everywhere it was screened). The English premiere of the film took place in the Royal Albert Hall with music provided by the London Symphony Orchestra. Music can create a mood, introduce a new character or scene, suggest which country we are in, follow the action closely or less closely. Some musicians are contemptuous of the idea that we should have pictures in our heads when listening to music, considering that this dilutes a purely aural and intellectual experience, but 'programme music', designed to be illustrative or evocative of a defined and detailed set of images or even a narrative, has a long history. There is an example in Vivaldi's *Four Seasons*, published in 1725, which had programme notes in the form of sonnets by the composer, and headings – 'Languor caused by the heat – the Cuckoo – the Turtledove – the Goldfinch – Gentle Zephyrs – Various winds – the North-Wind – Young Countryman's Lament', but the great age of music that summoned up images or told a story was the programmatic music of nineteenth-century Romanticism, such as Berlioz's *Symphonie fantastique* or Smetana's *Vltava*. The composers and musicians of the first generation of cinema, paradoxically the 'silent era', would be familiar with late Romantic programme music. In that sense, film music pre-dated the invention of film. As early as 1908 a composer with as great a reputation as Camille Saint-Saëns was recruited to write the score for the fifteen-minute French film *The Assassination of the Duc de Guise* (dir. André Calmettes and Charles Le Bargy). With the transition to sound in the late 1920s, image and music could be bound together indissolubly, and it became standard practice for a film to have a composer. A formative and influential figure was Erich Wolfgang

Korngold (1897–1957), an Austrian Jew who fled to America in the Nazi period. He composed music for more than twenty Hollywood films, but began as, and continued to be, a serious classical composer. His music for *The Adventures of Robin Hood* (1938), which won him an Academy Award, has been compared to German Romantic tone poems. These roots explain why music in films about the Middle Ages is more frequently lush and symphonic than an attempted recreation of the sound of medieval music, though the latter may be tried for specific moments – a fanfare for the entry of a king, chant in a church, or country dance music for a rustic wedding.

Several of the composers who worked on the eight films in this book had a reputation as film composers. James Horner, who composed the music for *Braveheart* and *The Name of the Rose*, won an Academy Award and Golden Globe for *Titanic* (1997); Vyacheslav Ovchinnikov, composer for *Andrei Rublev*, also did the music for *Ivan's Childhood*, Tarkovsky's first feature film, and more than thirty other films; Miklós Rózsa, composer for *El Cid*, was a triple Academy Award winner, and composer of music for 95 films from 1937 to 1989, including *Ivanhoe* (1952); Erik Nordgren, composer of the ominous music for *The Seventh Seal*, wrote the music for 47 films, including most of Bergman's early films. Probably the most famous collaboration is that of Prokofiev and Eisenstein on *Alexander Nevsky* and they worked together again on *Ivan the Terrible, Part One* (1944). Gottfried Huppertz, composer for *Siegfried*, also composed the music for Lang's *Metropolis*. *Monty Python and the Holy Grail*, with a very small budget, used a large amount of stock music from a music library, but the troupe's regular collaborator, Neil Innes, also composed some pieces, notably the Camelot song. Film music can have a life of its own. The album of the music for *Braveheart*, which was performed, like the music for the *Siegfried* premiere, by the London Symphony Orchestra, and conducted by the composer, James Horner, sold millions worldwide. The tracks each have a thematic title, such 'Wallace Courts Murron' or 'For the Love of a Princess'. In this way the mood of the film could be recaptured while doing the ironing.

Our visual picture of the Middle Ages is shaped not only by films about medieval Europe but by films set in imaginary worlds that their creators have modelled on medieval Europe. The Middle Ages produced its own fantasies – stories of Arthur, legends such as the *Nibelungenlied* – but there is plenty of modern medievalizing fantasy too. The Middle Earth of J.R.R. Tolkien and the Narnia of C. S. Lewis are notable examples, both of which have been adapted for the screen, the former more successfully than the latter. The worldwide and enduring success of the fantasy worlds of Tolkien and Lewis is, on the surface, surprising, not because they were white males, since this was true of almost half the population of the United Kingdom of their generation, but because they were Christian dons. 'Dons' here means 'fellows of Oxford or Cambridge colleges', and both Tolkien and Lewis spent most of their working lives as members of these distinctive institutions: all male, the original gated communities, guarded by 'porters' who were often ex-military men, and offering the dons a simulacrum of country-house living, with servants, silver on the table and archaic dining rituals. But, regardless of the arcane world in which they lived, both authors were deeply learned scholars of the Middle Ages and hence they could bring realism and depth to their worlds, Tolkien even giving Middle Earth its own range of languages. When C. S. Lewis explained to his presumed child audience that people in Narnia wore bright and comfortable clothing in comparison with the stiff and starchy 'best' of today, he could draw on his knowledge of medieval costume, when both men and women of the propertied classes had flowing and colourful garments for display. Lewis and Tolkien were also great walkers, which makes their descriptions of journeying in a world without mechanical transport so convincing when they describe distances, rates of progress, getting lost and so forth, and they had both fought in a war, so their battle scenes have a particular authority.

Tolkien's *Lord of the Rings* trilogy and Lewis's seven Narnia books appeared at the same time, in the early 1950s, and both have been going strong ever since. A curious feature that they share is that the fully epic medieval world in the books is not the only one, but is observed by anachronistic others – in Tolkien it is the Hobbits of the Shire, with their tea and coffee, pubs, and pipe-smoking (always a good sign for Tolkien as for Lewis, who, in *Prince Caspian*, notes that the treacherous dwarf 'was not a smoker'), while in the Narnia books it is the children from 'our world'. This means that the values and habits of the epic world can be depicted with an explicitness and emphasis that would otherwise be gratingly heavy-handed, since they can be seen through the eyes of middle-class English children (as in Narnia) or surrogates for middle-class English children (as in *The Hobbit* and *The Lord of the Rings*), who notice the differences of this medieval setting they find themselves in. And, since both Tolkien and Lewis were experts on medieval literature (as distinct from history), they could draw effortlessly on stories from the Middle Ages in constructing their own dragons, who guard treasure, dwarfs, who mine underground, swords that must be reforged, and so forth. Both authors were educated during the Edwardian period, when late Romanticism was booming, and it is hard not to see the influence of Wagner on *The Lord of the Rings*, though this is something that Tolkien vigorously denied. He wrote his own version of the *Volsunga saga* and was perhaps touchy at the suggestion that his inspiration was mediated rather than direct from the medieval source. The international and continuing success of the fantasy of Tolkien and Lewis is, in some ways, as improbable as the fortunes of Monty Python. It is not obvious why these two products of the British middle class, in one case Edwardian Romantic medievalism, in the other schoolboy and undergraduate humour of the 1950s and '60s, should have had such long-lasting influence in shaping pictures and stereotypes of the medieval. And, of course, medievalizing fantasy worlds continue to multiply, some inspired by Middle Earth.

No directors specialize in medieval films. In fact, few have even made more than one: Bergman made two, Robert Bresson two – *The Trial of Joan of Arc* (1962) and *Lancelot du Lac* (1974). So directors approaching a film with a medieval setting are not like directors who specialize in westerns or romantic comedies, who have a ready-made set of conventions and tropes that they have employed in several films already. They usually come to a medieval film without much prior knowledge of the period, or even a particular desire to say something about the Middle Ages, but as a film-maker, concerned with story, casting, location and all the technical issues of filming (as well as, of course, with making money). They may have people in set design and costume who are committed to historical accuracy, but they may not. Film-makers are not sitting a history exam; they want to make a successful film. In pursuit of this goal, they are prepared to be eclectic, to take material from wherever they wish. This is why the plot of the first part of *El Cid*, an eleventh-century Spanish knight, is largely based on the work of a seventeenth-centry French dramatist. Film-makers can also be ruthless with the material they are working with. Umberto Eco's novel *The Name of the Rose* is coloured throughout by its author's deep knowledge of the intellectual culture of medieval Europe but virtually all of this was discarded by the film-makers when they constructed their 'medieval mystery story'. In this case, the omission was most probably an aesthetic decision, jettisoning material that would bog the story down and confuse or bore viewers, but omissions can be more politically inspired. Alexander Nevsky is not shown submitting to the Mongols, as he did, and as Eisenstein originally intended, because it would confuse the tale of a national hero, which the film represented. El Cid is not shown burning alive one of the Muslim officials in Valencia, which he did, because he is to be made a champion of honour and a pioneer of tolerance.

Four of the eight films discussed in this book are titled after an actual historical figure and depict events that can be precisely dated and located; two others, *The Name of the Rose* and *The Seventh Seal*, have settings where date and place can be inferred; only *Monty Python and the Holy Grail* and *Siegfried*, in their very different ways, have purely imaginary settings (the city of Worms in *Siegfried* is hardly an exception). So although it is certainly not the sole purpose of this book to get to the 'historical reality' behind the films, for most of them questions of accuracy, authenticity, fidelity – the same question in different words – arise very naturally. It would be wrong to place such questions at centre stage on all occasions but it would also be wrong to dismiss them as irrelevant to analysis of a film, by arguing that 'a film is a film' and needs to be judged on its own terms. As explored in the chapter on *Braveheart*, questions of 'accuracy' can mean different things and they may matter more in one film than another. But if a film presents a man called William Wallace who fought the English in the cause of Scotland's independence, and there was indeed really such a man, it is entirely natural for the audience to wonder if the other personages and events that the film presents are also real, a question that does not arise with King Arthur, Guinevere and Lancelot any more than with Luke Skywalker, Princess Leia and Han Solo. In analysing the films, I have attempted to address those questions.

When we watch a film about the Middle Ages, there are many different times encoded in the experience – not only the medieval subject and the present screen and viewer, but the long centuries of elaboration that the subject has undergone in legend and story, the formative force of romanticism and nationalism in the nineteenth century and finally the world in which the film was made. The focus here is on films made in the twentieth century, so while this book has been about the Middle Ages, it is also about the twentieth century. In order to understand the eight films discussed here, one needs to know about knights and castles, monks and peasants, but also about Nazism and Communism, the British class system and American politics. As is clear from the case studies in this book, films are shaped by the attitudes, beliefs and politics of the time and place where they were made, and that will affect our viewing experience. Putting history on the screen gives us a vivid way of imagining the past, but it is also always about the present.

FURTHER READING

This list includes only items in English, although mention has to be made of the 1,200-page volume of François Amy de La Bretèque, *L'Imaginaire médiéval dans le cinéma occidental* (Paris, 2004). Many of the items listed under 'General' contain detailed discussions of the individual films analysed in this book. In this list I have made an attempt to include writers with varied perspectives and viewpoints, some of them quite different from my own.

GENERAL

Aberth, John, *A Knight at the Movies: Medieval History on Film* (New York and London, 2003)

Airlie, Stuart, 'Strange Eventful Histories: The Middle Ages in the Cinema', in *The Medieval World*, ed. Peter Linehan and Janet L. Nelson, 2nd edn (Abingdon, 2018), pp. 195–219

Aronstein, Susan, *Hollywood Knights: Arthurian Cinema and the Politics of Nostalgia* (Basingstoke and New York, 2005)

Bernau, Anke, and Bettina Bildhauer, eds, *Medieval Film* (Manchester, 2009)

Bildhauer, Bettina, *Filming the Middle Ages* (London, 2011)

— , 'Medievalism and Cinema', in *The Cambridge Companion to Medievalism*, ed. Louise D'Arcens (Cambridge, 2016), pp. 45–59

Burt, Richard, *Medieval and Early Modern Film and Media* (New York, 2008)

Driver, Martha W., and Sid F. Ray, eds, *The Medieval Hero on Screen: Representations from Beowulf to Buffy* (Jefferson, NC, 2004)

Elliott, Andrew B. R., *Remaking the Middle Ages: The Methods of Cinema and History in Portraying the Medieval World* (Jefferson, NC, 2011)

Finke, Laurie A., and Martin B. Shichtman, *Cinematic Illuminations: The Middle Ages on Film* (Baltimore, MD, 2009)

Haines, John, *Music in Films on the Middle Ages: Authenticity vs. Fantasy* (New York, 2014)

Harty, Kevin J., *The Reel Middle Ages . . . Films about Medieval Europe* (Jefferson, NC, 1999)

— , ed., *King Arthur on Film: New Essays on Arthurian Cinema* (Jefferson, NC, 1999)

— , ed., *Cinema Arthuriana*, revd edn (Jefferson, NC, 2002)

— , ed., *The Vikings on Film: Essays on Depictions of the Nordic Middle Age*s (Jefferson, NC, 2011)

Haydock, Nickolas, *Movie Medievalism: The Imaginary Middle Ages* (Jefferson, NC, 2008)

Haydock, Nickolas, and E. L. Risden, eds, *Hollywood in the Holy Land: Essays on Film Depictions of the Crusades and Christian–Muslim Clashes* (Jefferson, NC, 2009)

Johnston, Andrew James, Margitta Rouse and Philipp Hinz, eds, *The Medieval Motion Picture: The Politics of Adaptation* (New York, 2014)

Lindley, Arthur, 'The Ahistoricism of Medieval Film', *Screening the Past*, www.screeningthepast.com, 1998

Medieval Women in Film, Medieval Feminist Newsletter, Subsidia, I (2000)

Movie Medievalism, Exemplaria, XIX/2 (2007)

Ramey, Lynn T., and Tison Pugh, eds, *Race, Class, and Gender in 'Medieval' Cinema* (Basingstoke and New York, 2007)

BRAVEHEART

Barrow, Geoffrey, *Robert Bruce and the Community of the Realm of Scotland*, 4th edn (Edinburgh, 2005)

Bartlett, Robert, '*Braveheart* and Sexual Revenge', in *Emotion, Violence, Vengeance and Law in the Middle Ages: Essays in Honour of William Ian Miller*, ed. Kate Gilbert and Stephen D. White (Leiden, 2018), pp. 255–70

Blind Harry's Wallace, ed. William Hamilton of Gilbertfield (Edinburgh, 1998)

Boureau, Alain, *The Lord's First Night: The Myth of the droit de cuissage*, trans. Lydia G. Cochrane (Chicago, IL, 1998)

Cowan, Edward J., ed., *The Wallace Book* (Edinburgh, 2007)

Fisher, Andrew, *William Wallace*, 2nd edn (Edinburgh, 2002)

Hague, Euan, 'Scotland on Film: Attitudes and Opinions about *Braveheart*', *Etudes écossaises*, VI (1999/2000), pp. 75–89

Keller, James S., 'Masculinity and Marginality in *Rob Roy* and *Braveheart*', *Journal of Popular Film and Television*, XXIV/4 (1997), pp. 146–51
McArthur, Colin, *Brigadoon, 'Braveheart', and the Scots: Distortions of Scotland in Hollywood Cinema* (London and New York, 2003)
Morton, Graeme, *William Wallace: Man and Myth* (Stroud, 2001)
Sharp, Michael D., 'Remaking Medieval Heroism: Nationalism and Sexuality in *Braveheart*', *Florilegium*, XV (1998), pp. 251–66

THE NAME OF THE ROSE

Burr, David, *The Spiritual Franciscans: From Protest to Persecution in the Century after Saint Francis* (University Park, PA, 2001)
Cartmell, Deborah, and Imelda Whelehan, eds, *Adaptations: From Text to Screen, Screen to Text* (London and New York, 1999)
Eco, Umberto, *The Name of the Rose*, trans. William Weaver (London and New York, 1983)
— , *Reflections on 'The Name of the Rose'*, trans. William Weaver (London, 1994)
Haft, Adele J., Jane G. White, and Robert J. White, *The Key to 'The Name of the Rose'*, new edn (Ann Arbor, MI, 1999)
Hill, Derek, *Inquisition in the Fourteenth Century: The Manuals of Bernard Gui and Nicholas Eymerich* (Woodbridge, 2019)
Manzoni, Alessandro, *On the Historical Novel*, trans. Sandra Bermann (Lincoln, NE, 1984)

MONTY PYTHON AND THE HOLY GRAIL

Burde, Mark, 'Monty Python's Medieval Masterpiece', *Arthurian Yearbook*, III (1993), pp. 3–20
Jones, Terry, *Chaucer's Knight: The Portrait of a Medieval Mercenary* (London, 1980)
— , and Alan Ereira, *Crusades* (London, 1994)
Neufeld, Christine M., '"Lovely Filth": Monty Python and the Matter of the Holy Grail', in *The Holy Grail on Film : Essays on the Cinematic Quest*, ed. Kevin J. Harty (Jefferson, NC, 2015), pp. 81–97
Pearsall, Derek, *Arthurian Romance: A Short Introduction* (Oxford, 2003)
Pugh, Tison, 'Queer Medievalisms: A Case Study of *Monty Python and the Holy Grail*', in *The Cambridge Companion to Medievalism*, ed. Louise D'Arcens (Cambridge, 2016), pp. 210–23

The Pythons' Autobiography by the Pythons [Graham Chapman, John Cleese, Terry Gilliam, Eric Idle, Terry Jones and Michael Palin], ed. Bob McCabe (London, 2003)

Twain, Mark, *A Connecticut Yankee in King Arthur's Court* [1889] (London, 1986)

Yeager, R. F., and Toshiyuki Takamiya, eds, *The Medieval Python: The Purposive and Provocative Work of Terry Jones* (New York, 2012)

ANDREI RUBLEV

Alexander-Garrett, Layla, *Andrei Tarkovsky: The Collector of Dreams*, trans. Maria Amadei Ashot (London, 2012)

Bird, Robert, *Andrei Rublev* (London, 2004)

Hughes, Lindsey, 'Art and Liturgy in Russia: Rublev and His Successors', in *Cambridge History of Christianity*, vol. V: *Eastern Christianity*, ed. Michael Angold (Cambridge, 2006), pp. 276–301

Lazarev, Viktor Nikitich, *The Russian Icon from Its Origins to the Sixteenth Century*, ed. G. I. Vzdornov and Nancy McDarby, trans. Colette Joly Dees (Collegeville, MN, 1997)

Martin, Sean, *Andrei Tarkovsky* (Harpenden, 2005)

The Nikonian Chronicle, trans. Serge A. Zenkovsky, 5 vols (Princeton, NJ, 1984–9), vol. IV, pp. 182–4

Tarkovsky, Andrei, *Andrei Rublev* (London, 1992) (original screenplay in novella form)

Tarkovsky, Andrey [*sic*], *Sculpting in Time: Reflections on Cinema*, trans. Kitty Hunter-Blair, revd edn (London, 1989)

Turovskaya, Maya, *Tarkovsky: Cinema as Poetry*, ed. Ian Christie, trans. Natasha Ward (London, 1989), esp. chapters One and Four

Youngblood, Denis J., '*Andrei Rublev*: The Medieval Epic as Post-Utopian History', in *The Persistence of History: Cinema, Television and the Modern Event*, ed. Vivian Sobchack (New York, 1996), pp. 127–43

EL CID

Barzman, Norma, *The Red and the Blacklist: The Intimate Memoir of a Hollywood Expatriate* (New York, 2003), pp. 306–34

Corneille, Pierre, *Le Cid*, trans. John Cairncross (London, 1975)

Fletcher, Richard, *The Quest for El Cid* (London, 1989)

Freeman, Thomas S., 'Filming a Legend: Anthony Mann's *El Cid* (1961)',

in *Biography and History in Film*, ed. Thomas S. Freeman and David
L. Smith (London, 2019), pp. 43–75

Heston, Charlton, *In the Arena: The Autobiography* (New York and
London, 1995)

Historia Roderici, trans. Richard Fletcher, in *The World of El Cid: Chronicles
of the Spanish Reconquest*, ed. Simon Barton and Richard Fletcher
(Manchester, 2000), pp. 90–147

Jancovich, Mark, '"The Purest Knight of All": Nation, History and
Representation in *El Cid*', *Cinema Journal*, XL (2000), pp. 79–103

Las mocedades de Rodrigo: The Youthful Deeds of Rodrigo, the Cid, ed. and
trans. Matthew Bailey (Toronto, 2007)

The Poem of the Cid: A Dual-Language Edition with Parallel Text, trans.
Burton Raffel (London, 2009)

Rosendorf, Neal M., 'Hollywood in Madrid: American Film Producers
and the Franco Regime, 1950–70', *Historical Journal of Film, Radio
and Television*, XXVII/1 (March 2007), pp. 77–109

Trow, M. J., *El Cid: The Making of a Legend* (Stroud, 2007)

Weiss, Julian, '"El Cid" (Rodrigo Díaz de Vivar)', in *The Cambridge
Companion to the Literature of the Crusades*, ed. Anthony Bale
(Cambridge, 2019), pp. 184–99

Winkler, Martin M., 'Mythic and Cinematic Traditions in Anthony Mann's
El Cid', *Mosaic*, XXVI (1993), pp. 89–111

THE SEVENTH SEAL

Bragg, Melvyn, *The Seventh Seal* (London, 1993)

Cowie, Peter, *Ingmar Bergman*, revd edn (London, 1992)

Lagerås, Per, ed., *Environment, Society and the Black Death: An
Interdisciplinary Approach to the Late-Medieval Crisis in Sweden*
(Oxford, 2015)

Paden, William D., 'Reconstructing the Middle Ages: The Monk's Sermon
in *The Seventh Seal*', in *Medievalism in the Modern World: Essays in
Honour of Leslie J. Workman*, ed. Richard Utz and Thomas A. Shippey
(Turnhout, 1998), pp. 287–305

Schubert, Linda, 'Plainchant in Motion Pictures: The "Dies irae" in Film
Scores', *Florilegium*, XV (1998), pp. 207–29

Steene, Birgitta, *Ingmar Bergman: A Reference Guide* (Amsterdam, 2005),
pp. 222–8

— , ed., *Focus on 'The Seventh Seal'* (Englewood Cliffs, NJ, 1972)

ALEXANDER NEVSKY

Barna, Yon, *Eisenstein*, trans. Lise Hunter (London, 1973)

Bartig, Kevin, *Composing for the Red Screen: Prokofiev and Soviet Film* (New York, 2013)

Bergan, Ronald, *Sergei Eisenstein: A Life in Conflict* (London, 1997)

Bordwell, David, *The Cinema of Eisenstein* (Cambridge, MA, and London, 1993)

Christiansen, Eric, *The Northern Crusades* (London, 1980)

The Chronicle of Novgorod, 1016–1471, trans. Robert Michell and Nevill Forbes (London, 1914)

Egorova, Tatiana, *Soviet Film Music: An Historical Survey*, trans. Tatiana A. Ganf and Natalia A. Egunova (Amsterdam, 1997), pp. 59–68

Eisenstein, Sergei, *Selected Works*, vol. III: *Writings 1934–47*, ed. Richard Taylor, trans. William Powell (London, 1996)

Franklin, Simon, 'Rus', in *The New Cambridge Medieval History*, vol. V: *c. 1198–c. 1300*, ed. David Abulafia (Cambridge, 1999), pp. 796–808

Gallez, David, 'The Prokofiev–Eisenstein Collaboration: *Nevsky* and *Ivan* Revisited', *Cinema Journal*, XVII (1978), pp. 13–35

Goodwin, James, *Eisenstein, Cinema, and History* (Champaign, IL, 1993)

Isoaho, Mari, *The Image of Aleksandr Nevskiy in Medieval Russia: Warrior and Saint* (Leiden, 2006)

Merritt, Russell, 'Recharging *Alexander Nevsky*: Tracking the Eisenstein/Prokoviev War Horse', *Film Quarterly*, XLVIII/2 (1995), pp. 34–47

Mowitt, John, *Text: The Genealogy of an Antidisciplinary Object* (Durham, NC, 1992), pp. 187–213

Ostrowski, Donald, 'Alexander Nevskii's "Battle on the Ice": The Creation of a Legend', *Russian History*, XXXIII/2/4 (2006), pp. 289–312

Roberts, Philip D., 'Prokofiev's Score and Cantata for Eisenstein's *Alexander Nevsky*', *Semiotica*, XXI (1977), pp. 151–66

DIE NIBELUNGEN I: SIEGFRIED

Gunning, Tom, *The Films of Fritz Lang: Allegories of Vision and Modernity* (London, 2000)

Hake, Sabine, 'Architectural Hi/stories: Fritz Lang and *The Nibelungs*', *Wide Angle*, XII/3 (July 1990), pp. 38–57

Hauer, Stanley R., 'The Sources of Fritz Lang's *Die Nibelungen*', *Literature/Film Quarterly*, XVIII/2 (1990), pp. 103–10

Kaes, Anton, *Shell Shock Cinema: Weimar Culture and the Wounds of War* (Princeton, NJ, 2009)

McGilligan, Patrick, *Fritz Lang: The Nature of the Beast* (London, 1997)

Mueller, Adeline, 'Listening for Wagner in Fritz Lang's *Die Nibelungen*', in *Wagner and Cinema*, ed. Jeongwon Joe and Sander L. Gilman (Bloomington, IN, 2010), pp. 85–107

The Nibelungenlied, trans. A. T. Hatto (London, 1965)

The Saga of the Volsungs, trans. Jesse L. Byock (Berkeley, CA, 1990; London, 1999)

Stiles, Victoria M., 'Fritz Lang's Definitive *Siegfried* and Its Versions', *Literature/Film Quarterly*, XIII/4 (1985), pp. 258–74

PHOTO ACKNOWLEDGEMENTS

The author and publishers wish to express their thanks to the below sources of illustrative material and/or permission to reproduce it. Some locations of artworks are also given below, in the interest of brevity:

Everett Collection Inc/Alamy Stock Photo: p. 153; photo Imagno/Getty Images: p. 236; Library of Congress, Prints and Photographs Division, Washington, DC: p. 239; Musée de la Tapisserie de Bayeux, photo Myrabella (public domain): p. 158; The State Tretyakov Gallery, Moscow: p. 128; Täby kyrka, Uppland: p. 167; TCD/Prod.DB/Alamy Stock Photo: p. 219.

INDEX

Page in *italics* indicates illustrations

287